Schooling and Language Minority Students: A Theoretico-Practical Framework

Third Edition

Edited by
Charles F. Leyba, Ph.D.

Published by
LBD Publishers

Originally developed in cooperation with
California State Department of Education
Sacramento, California

ISBN: 1-933408-02-2

This publication was funded in whole or in part by a contract (G007902844) between
the California State Department of Education and the United States Education
Department. The opinions expressed herein do not, however, necessarily reflect the
positions or policy of the United States Education Department; no official endorse-
ment by the United States Education Department should be inferred.

Published by
LBD Publishers
4247 Whiteside Street
Los Angeles, CA 90063
Phone: (323) 526-7110
Fax: (323) 526-7112
www.legalbooksdistributing.com

Developed in cooperation with
California State Department of Education
Sacramento, California

Earlier editions published by
Evaluation, Dissemination and Assessment Center

First edition published 1981
Second edition published 1994
Second printing 1996
Third printing 1997
Fourth printing 1999
Third edition 2005

Printed in the U.S.

Acknowledgments

Sincere appreciation, in the first instance, must be extended to three pioneering authors whose work appeared in the first edition and appears in this third edition as well: James Cummins, Stephen Krashen, and Eleanor Thonis.

We welcome and extend equally sincere appreciation to two authors, Marguerite Ann Snow and Alan Crawford, whose excellent contributions to the second edition replace those of Dorothy Legarreta-Marcaida and Tracy Terrell who have passed away since publication of the first edition.

Dr. Dolson, Project Team Leader in developing the first edition, has contributed a revised Appendix for the second edition. This Appendix has been retained in its original since its design, structure, and recommendations are universal in value and of historic, archival significance.

The authors singly and in combination represent the most scholarly and universally recognized authorities as can be found in a single volume. Indeed, the Director of the Latino Teacher Project of the University of Southern California identified this text as one of the two finest on the planet for the preparation of teachers of English Language learners.

In short, the high quality found in the current edition is due to, and fully merited by, the persons mentioned.

Charles F. Leyba, Ph.D.
Director
Evaluation, Dissemination and Assessment Center

Biographical Sketches

ALAN N. CRAWFORD is Emeritus Professor of Education at California State University, Los Angeles. During the United Nations-sponsored International Literacy Year, 1990, he served as Senior Literacy Specialist at UNESCO in Paris. In 1996–1997, he was a Fulbright senior scholar in Ecuador. In 2000, he was Professional-in-Residence at the American embassy in Baku, Azerbaijan. He has consulted on language and literacy issues for UNESCO, the World Bank, UNDP, and ministries of education in Peru, Bolivia, Guatemala, the Dominican Republic, Belize, Panama, Ecuador, Latvia, Mongolia, Kyrgyzstan, Tanzania, Kenya, and many other countries. He is the author/co-author of many books and articles on second language acquisition and literacy for second language learners, as well as reading/language arts programs in both English and Spanish.

JIM CUMMINS teaches in the Department of Curriculum, Teaching and Learning of the Ontario Institute for Studies in Education of the University of Toronto. His research has focused on the nature of language proficiency and second language acquisition with particular emphasis on the social and educational barriers that limit academic success for culturally diverse students. His publications include *Language, Power, and Pedagogy: Bilingual Children in the Crossfire* (Multilingual Matters, 2000) and *Negotiating Identities: Education for Empowerment in a Diverse Society* (California Association for Bilingual Education, 2001).

DAVID P. DOLSON has a B.S. from the University of Califormia, an M.S. from the University of Southern California, and an Ed.D. from the University of San Francisco. In 2005, Dr. Dolson will complete 30 years of service with the California Department of Education. For most of that period, he worked in the area of evaluation and research on programs for language minority students. His most recent assignment is as an Education Programs Consultant for the Language Policy and Leadership Office. In addition to this volume, Dr. Dolson was editor of *Studies in Immersion Education: A Collection for U.S. Educators* (California Department of Education, 1984) and author of "Longitudinal Study of Three Program Models for Language Minority Students: A Critical Examination of Report Findings" (*Bilingual Research Quarterly*, 16:1, Winter 1991) and "World Class Education for Children in California: A

Comparison of the Two-Way Bilingual Immersion and European School Model" in *Multilingualism for All* (Swets and Zeitinger, Amsterdam, 1995). In 1995, Dr. Dolson was invited by the first indigenous Vice President of Bolivia, Victor Hugo Cárdenas Conde, to participate on an international panel for multilingual and pluricultural educational reform. In 2004, Dr. Dolson published "Foreign Aide: A Language Lesson from Bolivia" (*Language Magazine*, 3:11, July 2004).

STEPHEN KRASHEN is a Professor of Linguistics at the University of Southern California. He has published extensively on second language acquisition theory, second language teaching, and neurolinguistics. He is the author of *Second Language Acquisition and Second Language Learning* (Pergamon Press, 1981), co-author of *The Human Brain* (Prentice-Hall, 1977), and co-editor of *Research in Second Language Acquisition* (Newbury House, 1980).

MARGUERITE ANN SNOW (Ph.D. in Applied Linguistics, UCLA, 1985) is Professor in the Charter College of Education at California State University, Los Angeles, where she teaches in the TESOL M.A. program. She is co-author of *Content-Based Second Language Instruction* (1989, 2003), and co-editor of *The Multicultural Classroom: Readings for Content-Area Teachers* (1992) and *The Content-Based Classroom: Perspectives on Integrating Language and Content* (1997). She is also editor of *Implementing the ESL Standards for Pre-12-Students in Teacher Education* (2000) and co-editor of *Academic Success: Strategies for K-12 Mainstream Teachers* (2005). She has published in *TESOL Quarterly, Applied Linguistics,* and *The Modern Language Journal.* She had a Fulbright fellowship in Hong Kong and received, along with her co-authors, the Pimsleur Award from ACTFL for the best research study in foreign language education. In addition to working closely with ESL and mainstream public school teachers in the U.S., she has trained EFL teachers worldwide.

ELEANOR WALL THONIS was the district psychologist for Wheatland Elementary School District; a part-time instructor, University of California, Berkeley; and the consultant for bilingual education in the Marysville Unified School District. She has served as the director of the area Reading Center and is the author of several publications on reading for language minority students.

Introduction

The purpose of the first edition of the *Theoretical Framework* was to collect, organize, and present to educators a comprehensive and understandable review of research on language minority education. It was thought that such information would improve the ability of educators to predict individual and group outcomes for specific types of students, given certain types of instructional treatments, under different types of background conditions. The articles contained in the first volume were viewed as an initial step in the promotion of effective programs and practices for schooling language minority students. The status of the volume was described in the following manner:

> This publication is a progress report, not a collection of proven answers. The theoretical framework implied in this volume is, however, based on the best information that science can provide at this time. The research herein reported does not lead to perfect programs with perfect outcomes, nor does it answer all the questions regarding language development, language acquisition, and cognitive/academic development in bilingual contexts. But, taken collectively, these articles form the beginning of a research-based theoretical framework for planning and improving bilingual education programs. (p. ii)

This new edition represents a third progress report. Those involved in this revision have reviewed their papers making up the 1994 volume and attempted to (1) refine and clarify basic concepts, (2) update the supporting evidence for the primary hypotheses and postulates, and (3) identify and further explain the major implications of the research. Most importantly, the authors have expanded upon the original research base and added new and increasingly important information on various cultural, social, and political ramifications of language minority education. What has not been changed in this edition is the persistent focus on the potential practical applications of the research—a feature that makes this publication particularly useful to educators.

When the first edition of the *Theoretical Framework* was published in 1981, California's schools had an enrollment of 810,000 language minority students, 375,000 of whom were classified, on the basis of objective assessment, as students of limited English proficiency (LEP). By 1993, these numbers had nearly doubled, with schools reporting enrollments of 1,700,000 language minority and 1,200,000 LEP students, respectively. At present, California has more than half of all the language minority students enrolled in kindergarten through grade 12 in the United States. These demographic trends suggest that racial and ethnic minorities, including language minority students, have become the new numerical majority in the state. From a demographic perspective, the issue of language minority education is more important than ever.

The contributions to the first volume clearly promoted the establishment of rigorous language and academic programs in which participants would become successful students and proficient bilinguals. Many educators, succumbing to fierce social, political, and economic opposition to bilingual education, decided instead to implement early-exit transitional bilingual programs in which the primary language of the language minority students was more likely to be used to support structured English immersion (a.k.a. sheltered, specially designed academic instruction in English—SDAIE) instruction rather than as a vehicle to develop high levels of literacy and provide full access to the core curriculum. These educators speculated that such programs would be sufficient to provide language minority students with equal educational opportunities. Recent studies have provided clear evidence that most early-exit bilingual and structured immersion programs fail to close the academic gap between language minority and native speakers of English. This finding has sparked renewed interest in developing comprehensive bilingual program designs that elude the inherent flaws of compensatory models. The articles in this volume address the theoretical underpinnings, the programmatic structures, and the essential instructional elements associated with these more effective and powerful approaches.

The underlying theme of the first edition of the *Theoretical Framework* was that educators of language minority students must become knowledgeable of a myriad of linguistic, academic, and sociocultural factors in order to be thoroughly competent providers of formal schooling for this at-risk group of children and youth. Now, in addition, we realize that the provision of adequate educational programs for non-English-background students is a very significant part of the much larger struggle for social justice for minority groups. Under this scenario, educators must decide on the role they will play in challenging those aspects of our educational system that work against rather than facilitate the establishment of authentic bilingual and crosscultural programs that empower minority groups and enlighten the majority group. As formidable as this sounds, our success in advocating for these fundamental changes in our educational system may well determine the degree to which future generations of Americans from all racial, ethnic, and language groups are able to live together in harmony.

David P. Dolson
Project Team Leader
Bilingual Education Office
Currently Consultant, Office of Program Policy and Coordination
California Department of Education

Contents

Part One: Theoretical Foundations

Part Two: Strategies for Implementation

Part One
Theoretical Foundations

Teaching the Language of Academic Success: A Framework for School-Based Language Policies

Jim Cummins

Introduction

In June 1998, California voters reversed almost 25 years of educational policy in that state by passing Proposition 227 by a margin of 61% to 39%. Proposition 227 was aimed at eliminating the use of bilingual children's first language (L1) for instructional purposes except in very exceptional circumstances. The origins of this controversy go back 25 years to the 1974 ruling of the Supreme Court in the *Lau v. Nichols* case. According to the Court judgment, the civil rights of non-English-speaking students were violated when the school took no steps to help them acquire the language of instruction:

> . . . there is no equality of treatment merely by providing students with the same facilities, textbooks, teachers, and curriculum; for students who do not understand English are effectively foreclosed from any meaningful education. Basic English skills are at the very core of what these public schools teach. Imposition of a requirement that, before a child can effectively participate in the educational program, he must already have acquired those basic skills is to make a mockery of public education. We know that those who do not understand English are certain to find their classroom experiences wholly incomprehensible and in no way meaningful. (cited in Crawford, 1992, p. 253)

The Court did not mandate bilingual education; rather it mandated that schools take effective measures to overcome the educational disadvantages resulting from a home-school language mismatch. The Office of Civil Rights, however, interpreted the Supreme Court's decision as effectively mandating transitional bilingual education unless a school district could prove that another approach would be equally or more effective. The Office of Civil Rights' interpretation of the Supreme Court decision sparked outrage among media commentators and educators in school districts which, for the most part, were totally unprepared to offer any form of bilingual instruction. The controversy has raged unabated since that time.

The debate leading up to the Proposition 227 referendum in California crystallized all of the arguments that had been advanced for and against bilingual education in the previous quarter century. Both sides claimed "equity" as their central guiding principle. Opponents of bilingual programs argued that limited English proficient students were being denied access to both English and academic advancement as a result of being instructed for part of the day through their L1. Exposure to English was being diluted and, as a result, it was not surprising that bilingual students continued to experience difficulty in academic aspects of English. Only maximum exposure to English (frequently termed "time-on-task") could remediate children's linguistic difficulties in that language on entry to school. Early in 1998, former Speaker of the House, Newt Gingrich, expressed the views of many conservative policy-makers: "When we allow children to stay trapped in bilingual programs where they do not learn English, we are destroying their economic future" (Hornblower, 1998, p. 44). According to Hornblower, "He and other Republicans call for a return to the traditional expectation that immigrants will quickly learn English as the price of admission to America" (p. 44).

Proponents of bilingual education argued that L1 instruction in the early grades was necessary to ensure that students understood academic content and experienced a successful start to their schooling. Reading and writing skills acquired initially through the L1 provided a foundation upon which strong English language development could be built. The research literature on bilingual development provided consistent evidence for transfer of academic skills and knowledge across languages. Thus, L1 proficiency could be promoted at no cost to children's academic development in English. Furthermore, the fact that teachers spoke the language of parents increased the likelihood of parental involvement and support for their children's learning. This, together with the reinforcement of children's sense of self as a result of the incorporation of their language and culture in the school program, contributed to long-term academic growth.

In the context of Proposition 227, bilingual advocates argued that bilingual education itself could not logically be regarded as a cause of continued high levels of academic failure among bilingual students since only 30% of limited English proficient students in California were in any form of bilingual education. Gándara (1999) points out that in 1996 "more than one-third of teachers in bilingual classrooms were not fully credentialed, and while little is actually known about these teachers, the likelihood is that many were relying heavily on one of the 29,000 bilingual paraprofessionals employed in California's schools" (1999, p. 2). Thus, even before Proposition 227, 70% of California's English learners (EL) were either in an all-English program or not receiving any services at all. Advocates of bilingual education could thus logically argue that the academic difficulties of EL students were more appropriately attributed to the *absence* of effective bilingual programs than to bilingual education in some absolute sense.

The educational arguments on both sides of the issue represent, to a considerable extent, a surface structure for more deeply rooted ideological divisions. Opponents of bilingual education frequently characterized the use of languages other than English in schools as "un-American" and many also expressed concerns about the number of immigrants entering the United States and the consequent growth of cultural and linguistic diversity (Crawford, 1992b). To them, the institutionalization of bilingual education by federal and state governments threatened to fragment the nation. This ideological opposition to bilingual education frequently resulted either in lukewarm implementation of bilingual education or outright attempts to sabotage the program (Wong Fillmore, 1992).

Underlying the educational arguments of many bilingual education advocates was the conviction that a history of oppressive power relations was a significant contributing factor to bilingual students' underachievement. For many generations, bilingual students had been punished for any use of their L1 in the school context and were discriminated against in virtually all areas of education, from segregated schools to biased curriculum and assessment practices. Schools traditionally had communicated a sense of shame in regard to children's language and cultural background rather than a sense of affirmation and pride. Thus, some degree of genuine recognition or institutionalization of children's language and culture in the schools was a prerequisite to reversing this legacy of coercive power relations.

This orientation was linked to the perceived desirability of adopting a pluralist rather than an assimilationist social policy in which the value of different cultures and groups was recognized and their contributions to American society respected (Banks, 1996; Ovando & McLaren, 1999; Nieto, 1999). Implementation of multicultural education in schools was the logical expression of this pluralist orientation to social policy. In the case of bilingual students, promotion of pride in students' language and culture through bilingual programs was frequently regarded as an integral component of a broader philosophy of multicultural education (Nieto, 1999).

This chapter attempts to provide a framework for understanding how the interactions that bilingual students experience in schools create the conditions for academic success or failure. The initial sections focus on linguistic and cognitive aspects of students' development while the subsequent sections attempt to place students' linguistic and cognitive development into a broader sociopolitical context.

Among the relevant linguistic and cognitive issues are the nature of language proficiency and its relationship to the development of reading abilities beyond the early grades, the effects of bilingualism on children's cognitive and educational development, and the relationship between students' first and second languages (L1 and L2). Research focused on these issues can answer questions such as how long it typically takes EL students to catch up academically in English as compared to gaining fluency in conversational English. The research can also address questions about the relationship between bilingual students' L1 and L2 and the outcomes of different kinds of bilingual programs. However, linguistic and psychological research provides few answers to questions regarding why some culturally diverse groups tend to experience persistent long-term under-achievement, nor does it give us clear directions regarding the kinds of educational interventions that will be effective in reversing this underachievement.

For answers to these issues we need to shift to a sociological and sociopolitical orientation. We need to ask questions such as: Why is it that underachievement tends to be concentrated among social groups that have experienced long-term devaluation of their identities in the broader society much more than social groups that have immigrated to the host country more recently? How are patterns of discrimination in the wider society reflected (or challenged) in the school context? To what extent do structures that have been set up in the school, such as the content of the curriculum, assessment practices, and the language of instruction, contribute to perpetuating discrimination and underachievement among certain groups of students? How can subtle and more obvious manifestations of bias be challenged by educators and communities working together? To what extent can we see our classroom instruction as "neutral" with respect to relations of status and power in the wider society? For example, what messages are being communicated to students when we set out to do our jobs by "just teaching the curriculum" as compared to teaching the curriculum in such a way that bilingual/EL students' cultural and linguistic identities are affirmed?

The Psycholinguistic Knowledge Base

In discussing the psycholinguistic knowledge base that exists to guide instructional policies for EL students, I consider first the nature of language proficiency and its relationship to the phenomenon of the *Fourth Grade Slump* (Chall, Jacobs, & Baldwin, 1990). I then summarize what research suggests are central conditions for the development of academic language proficiency and reading comprehension. Then data relating to the effects of bilingualism on children's development are summarized. Finally, the issue of the relationship between the development of academic abilities in L1 and L2 is examined.

The Nature of Language Proficiency

In order to understand patterns of academic development among EL students, we must distinguish between three very different aspects of proficiency in a language: (a) conversational fluency, (b) discrete language skills, and (c) academic language proficiency. The rationale for making these distinctions is that each dimension of proficiency follows very different developmental paths among both EL and non-EL students and each responds differently to particular kinds of instructional practices in school.

Conversational fluency. This dimension of language proficiency represents the ability to carry on a conversation in familiar face-to-face situations. The vast majority of native speakers of English have developed conversational fluency when they enter school at age 5. This fluency involves use of high frequency words and simple grammatical constructions. EL students generally develop fluency in conversational aspects of English within a year or two of intensive exposure to the language either in school or in the environment.

Discrete language skills. These skills reflect specific phonological, literacy and grammatical knowledge that students can acquire in two ways: (a) through direct instruction; (b) through immersion in a literacy- and language-rich environment either in home or school. Students exposed to a literacy-rich environment in the home generally acquire initial literacy-related skills, such as phonemic awareness and letter-sound correspondences, with minimal difficulty in the early grades of schooling.

Some of these discrete language skills are acquired early in schooling and some continue to be acquired throughout schooling (e.g., spelling). The discrete language skills acquired early include knowledge of the letters of the alphabet, the sounds represented by individual letters and combinations of letters, and the ability to decode written words into appropriate sounds. Some of these skills such as phonemic awareness and knowledge of the letters of the alphabet show consistently moderate relationships with the acquisition of word decoding skills (Snow, Burns, & Griffin, 1998; National Reading Panel, 2000).

EL students can learn these specific language skills concurrently with their development of basic vocabulary and conversational fluency. However, little direct transference is observed to other aspects of oral language proficiency such as linguistic concepts, vocabulary, sentence memory, and word memory (Geva, 2000; Kwan & Willows, 1998). Similar findings are reported by Verhoeven (2000) for minority language students in the Dutch context and by Lambert and Tucker (1972) for English-speaking students in French immersion programs.

Academic language proficiency. This dimension of proficiency includes knowledge of the less frequent vocabulary of English as well as the ability to interpret and produce increasingly complex written language. As students progress through the grades, they encounter far more low frequency words (primarily from Greek and Latin sources), complex syntax (e.g., passives), and abstract expressions that are virtually never heard in everyday conversation. Students are required to understand linguistically and conceptually demanding texts in the content areas (e.g., literature, social studies, science, mathematics) and to use this language in an accurate and coherent way in their own writing.

Acquiring academic language is challenging for all students. For example, schools spend at least 12 years trying to extend the conversational language that native-speaking children bring to school into these more complex academic language spheres. It is hardly surprising, therefore, that research has repeatedly shown that EL students, on average, require *at least* 5 years of exposure to academic English to catch up to native-speaker norms (Cummins, 1981a; Hakuta, Butler, & Witt, 2000; Klesmer, 1994; Thomas & Collier, 2002).

In addition to the complexity of the academic language they are attempting to acquire, EL students must catch up to a moving target.

Every year, native-speakers are making large gains in their reading and writing abilities and in their knowledge of vocabulary. In order to catch up to grade norms within 6 years, EL students must make 15 months gain in every 10-month school year. By contrast, the typical native-speaking student is expected to make 10 months gain in a 10-month school year (Collier & Thomas, 1999).

All three aspects of language proficiency are important. However, policy-makers and the media frequently confuse them. Many EL students who have acquired conversational fluency and decoding skills in English are still a long way from grade-level performance in academic language proficiency (Cummins, 2001; Krashen, 2001). Students who can "read" English fluently may have only a very limited understanding of the words they can decode. As documented in the following sections, direct instruction approaches that can be effective in developing decoding skills are of very limited utility in promoting reading comprehension and academic language proficiency more generally.

The Fourth Grade Slump Phenomenon

The differences between academic language proficiency and both conversational fluency and discrete language skills are highlighted by what is commonly termed the *fourth grade slump* (Chall, Jacobs & Baldwin, 1990; Rand Reading Study Group, 2002). The fourth grade slump refers to the phenomenon whereby low-income students who demonstrate grade level reading performance in the primary grades (1-3) begin to fall significantly behind grade norms starting at grade 4, with the discrepancy growing larger with each succeeding grade. Chall and her colleagues reported that grades 2 and 3 low-income students were on grade level on tests of word recognition, oral reading, spelling, and word meaning. However, between grades 4 and 11, the extent of deceleration in reading performance was "overwhelming" (1990, p. 43). Chall et al. attribute these trends to low-income students' weakness in academic vocabularies. They point out that at grade 4 and beyond, "the reading materials become more complex, technical and abstract and are beyond the everyday experiences of most children" (1990, p. 45). In the primary grades where students were on grade level in word meaning, most of the words students were asked to define were common, familiar and concrete words. Chall et al. note:

> Whereas the major hurdles prior to grade 4 are learning to recognize in print the thousands of words whose meanings are already known and reading these fluently in connected

texts with comprehension, the hurdle of grade 4 and beyond
is coping with increasingly complex language and thought.
(1990, p. 45)

Numerous other studies have documented either significant gaps
between decoding and comprehension performance or actual declines in
reading comprehension among low-income students in the later grades
of elementary school (Becker, 1977; Becker & Gersten, 1982; Venezky,
1998). These trends characterize direct instruction and scripted programs that place much more emphasis on the development of phonics
and phonemic awareness in the early grades than on the expansion of
vocabulary and reading comprehension abilities through extensive
engagement with authentic texts. For example, Becker & Gersten
(1982), in discussing students' performance on the DISTAR direct
instruction program used between Kindergarten and grade 3, document
significant declines in three school districts between grade 3 and grade
6 in Total Reading percentiles of the Metropolitan Achievement Test. In
these districts, students' performance fell from the 31st to the 16th percentile, the 52nd to the 26th percentile and the 28th to the 17th percentile respectively. In a fourth district, there was a decline between grade
3 and grade 5 from the 40th to the 20th percentile.

A similar gap between word level decoding and reading comprehension skills has been noted by Venezky (1998) in reviewing data from
the *Success for All* program. According to the Rand Reading Study
Group, "the reading comprehension scores of disadvantaged children
who were graduates of this program were substantially below national
normative standards despite the fact that their scores on measures of
word-level skills (word recognition, letter-sound decoding) were comparable to national standards" (2002, p. 93).

In short, the fourth grade slump reflects the fact that neither "language proficiency" nor "reading ability" are unitary constructs. Reading
comprehension does not develop automatically on the basis of decoding
skills; similarly, academic language proficiency is largely unrelated to
students' conversational fluency in English or their knowledge of discrete language skills. A core component of academic language proficiency is vocabulary knowledge and the vocabulary load in the
curriculum increases dramatically after the primary grades. The development of academic language proficiency, for both EL and non-EL students, requires that students *gain access to academic language* by
means of extensive reading and also that they are supported in *harvest-
ing the language* they encounter in literature and content area texts.

Teaching the Language of Academic Success

Fielding and Pearson (1994, p. 62) highlight four instructional components that research suggests are strongly related to reading comprehension outcomes:

- Large amounts of time for actual text reading;

- Teacher-directed instruction in comprehension strategies;

- Opportunities for peer and collaborative learning; and

- Occasions for students to talk to a teacher and one another about their responses to reading.

Extensive reading is crucial for academic language development because less frequent vocabulary, most of which derives from Greek and Latin sources, is found primarily in written text. According to Corson:

> Printed texts provided much more exposure to [Graeco-Latin] words than oral ones. For example, even children's books contained 50% more rare words than either adult prime-time television or the conversations of university graduates; popular magazines had three times as many rare words as television and informal conversation. (1997, p. 677)

The research is unequivocal is showing strong relationships for both L1 and L2 learners between opportunities to read and development of vocabulary and reading comprehension abilities (e.g., Elley, 1991; Krashen, 1993; Postlethwaite & Ross, 1992; Tizard, Schofield & Hewison, 1982). Research also supports the importance of explicit instruction in comprehension strategies and explanation of word meanings (Biemiller, 1998; Rand Reading Study Group, 2002).

By contrast, the teaching of phonics is largely *unrelated* to reading comprehension among normally-achieving and low-achieving readers after kindergarten and grade 1 (Ehri, Nunes, Stahl & Willows, 2001). This pattern is illustrated in the Postlethwaite and Ross (1992) study of reading achievement in 32 systems of education around the world. More than 50 variables were ranked in order of importance for reading comprehension at grades 4 and 8 levels. The significance of reading frequency in promoting reading development (at the grade 4 level) is evident from the high rankings of variables such as *Amount of free voluntary reading* (#2), *Reading in class* (#3), *Amount of reading materials in the school* (#8), *Having a classroom library* (#11), and *Frequency of borrowing books from a library* (#12). With respect to teaching methods, a focus on *Comprehension instruction* was ranked #9 and *Emphasis on literature* was ranked #17, both considerably higher than whether or not the school engaged in explicit *Phonics teaching* (#41).

In short, immersion in a rich literacy environment where students have ample encouragement and opportunity to read (and write) extensively is crucial for the development of reading comprehension and academic language proficiency. This is true for all students but it is particularly significant for EL students who are attempting to catch up to native-speakers in academic language proficiency.

The Positive Effects of Additive Bilingualism

There are close to 150 empirical studies carried out during the past 30 or so years that have reported a positive association between additive bilingualism and students' linguistic, cognitive, or academic growth. The most consistent findings among these research studies are that bilinguals show more developed awareness of language (metalinguistic abilities) and that they have advantages in learning additional languages. The term "additive bilingualism" refers to the form of bilingualism that results when students add a second language to their intellectual tool-kit while continuing to develop conceptually and academically in their first language.

This pattern of findings suggests that the proficiency attained by bilingual students in their two languages may exert important influences on their academic and intellectual development. Specifically, I suggested in 1976 that there may be threshold levels of proficiency in both languages that students must attain in order to maximize the cognitive, academic, and linguistic stimulation they extract from social and academic interactions with their environment (Cummins, 1976, 1979, 1981a). Continued development of both languages into literate domains (additive bilingualism) is a precondition for enhanced cognitive, linguistic, and academic growth. By contrast, when bilingual students develop low or minimal literacy in L1 and L2 as a result of inadequate instructional support (e.g., in submersion programs), their ability to understand increasingly complex instruction (in L2) and benefit from their schooling will decline. The causal factors here are instructional and sociopolitical, but students' L1 and L2 academic proficiency acts as a mediating or intervening variable that influences the quality and quantity of their classroom participation, and hence academic growth.

Although supported by research (e.g., Lasagabaster, 1998; Ricciardelli, 1992), the threshold hypothesis remains speculative. The central and well-supported finding is that the continued development of bilingual students' two languages during elementary school entails the potential of positive academic, linguistic and cognitive consequences.

The linguistic and academic benefits of additive bilingualism provide an additional reason to support bilingual students in maintaining their L1 while they are acquiring English. Not only does maintenance of L1 help students to communicate with parents and grandparents in their families, and increase the collective linguistic competence of the entire society, it enhances the intellectual and academic resources of individual bilingual students. At an instructional level, we should be asking how we can build on this potential advantage in the classroom by focusing students' attention on language and helping them become more adept at manipulating language in abstract academic situations. It is particularly important in English-medium classrooms to communicate positive messages to students and parents about the value of the home language and to encourage its development (see Schecter & Cummins, 2003, for examples). In the absence of L1 instruction in school, students frequently lose their L1 fluency resulting in communication gaps in the home.

Interdependence of First and Second Languages

The interdependence principle has been stated as follows (Cummins, 1981a):

> To the extent that instruction in Lx is effective in promoting proficiency in Lx, transfer of this proficiency to Ly will occur provided there is adequate exposure to Ly (either in school or environment) and adequate motivation to learn Ly. (p. 29)

The term *common underlying proficiency* (CUP) has also been used to refer to the cognitive/academic proficiency that underlies academic performance in both languages.

Consider the following research data that support this principle:

- In virtually every bilingual program that has ever been evaluated, whether intended for linguistic majority or minority students, spending instructional time teaching through the minority language entails no academic costs for students' academic development in the majority language (Baker, 1996; Cummins & Corson, 1997).

- An impressive number of research studies have documented a moderately strong correlation between bilingual students' L1 and L2 literacy skills in situations where students have the opportunity to develop literacy in both languages. It is worth noting that these findings also apply to the relationships among very dissimilar languages in addition to languages that are more closely related, although the strength of relationship is often reduced (e.g., Arabic-French, Dutch-Turkish, Japanese-English, Chinese-English, Basque-Spanish) (Cummins, 1991; Cummins et al., 1984; Genesee, 1979; Sierra & Olaziregi, 1991; Verhoeven & Aarts, 1998; Wagner, 1998).

A comprehensive review of U.S. research on cognitive reading processes among EL students concluded that this research consistently supported the common underlying proficiency model:

> . . . considerable evidence emerged to support the CUP model. United States ESL readers used knowledge of their native language as they read in English. This supports a prominent current view that native-language development can enhance ESL reading. (Fitzgerald, 1995, p.181)

In short, the research data show clearly that within a bilingual program, instructional time can be focused on developing students' literacy skills in their primary language without adverse effects on the development of their literacy skills in English. Furthermore, the relationship between first and second language literacy skills suggests that effective development of primary language literacy skills can provide a conceptual foundation for long-term growth in English literacy skills. This does not imply, however, that transfer of literacy and academic language knowledge will happen automatically; there is usually also a need for formal instruction in the target language to realize the benefits of cross-linguistic transfer.

Summary

This sketch of psycholinguistic data regarding bilingual academic development shows that a substantial research and theoretical basis for policy decisions regarding EL students' education does exist. In other words, policy-makers can predict with considerable confidence the probable effects of bilingual programs for majority and minority students implemented in very different sociopolitical contexts.

First, they can be confident that if the program is effective in continuing to develop students' academic skills in both languages, no cognitive confusion or handicap will result; in fact, students may benefit in subtle ways from access to two linguistic systems.

Second, they can predict that bilingual/EL students will take considerably longer to develop grade-appropriate levels of L2 academic knowledge (e.g., literacy skills) in comparison to how long it takes to acquire peer-appropriate levels of L2 conversational skills, at least in situations where there is access to the L2 in the environment.

Third, they should be aware that although EL students may pick up reasonably fluent decoding skills in English, this does not imply that reading comprehension abilities will develop to a similar level. Instruction for reading comprehension development must place a strong emphasis on extensive reading of text in a variety of genres and discussion of these texts in a way that goes beyond simple literal understanding.

Fourth, policy-makers can be confident that for both majority and minority students, spending instructional time partly through the minority language will not result in lower levels of academic performance in the majority language, provided of course the instructional program is effective in developing academic skills in the minority language. This is because at deeper levels of conceptual and academic functioning, there is considerable overlap or interdependence across languages. Conceptual knowledge developed in one language helps to make input in the other language comprehensible.

These psycholinguistic principles by themselves provide a reliable basis for the prediction of program outcomes in situations that are not characterized by unequal power relations between dominant and subordinated groups (e.g., L2 immersion programs for students from dominant language backgrounds). However, they do not explain the considerable variation in academic achievement among culturally and linguistically diverse groups nor do they tell us why some groups have experienced persistent school failure over generations. The next section addresses these issues and elaborates a framework that combines a causal analysis of educational failure with an intervention framework for reversing this pattern of failure. The focus is on how unequal power relations are played out and can be challenged in the interactions between educators and students in the school context.

A Framework for Reversing School Failure

The starting point for understanding why students choose to engage academically or, alternatively, withdraw from academic effort is to acknowledge that *human relationships are at the heart of schooling*. All of us intuitively know this from our own schooling experiences. If we felt that a teacher believed in us and cared for us then we put forth much more effort than if we felt that she or he did not like us or considered us not very capable. A major study carried out in southern California in the early 1990s documented this "common-sense" phenomenon:

> Relationships dominated all participant discussions about issues of schooling in the U.S. No group inside the schools felt adequately respected, connected or affirmed. Students, over and over again, raised the issue of care. What they liked best about school was when people, particularly teachers, cared about them or did special things for them. Dominating their complaints were being ignored, not being cared for and receiving negative treatment. (Poplin & Weeres, 1992, p. 19)

Teachers in these schools reported that their best experiences were when they connected with students and were able to help them in some way. However, they also reported that they did not always understand students who were culturally different from themselves. They also felt isolated and unappreciated inside schools by students, administrators, and parents as well as within the larger society.

What determines the kinds of relationships that educators establish with culturally diverse students? To answer this question we need to look at the relationships that exist between dominant and subordinated communities in the wider society and how these relationships (henceforth *macro-interactions*) influence both the structures that are set up in schools and the way educators define their roles within the school context.

When patterns of school success and failure among culturally diverse students are examined within an international perspective, it becomes evident that power and status relations between dominant and subordinated groups exert a major influence. Subordinated groups that fail academically have generally been discriminated against over many generations. They react to this discrimination along a continuum ranging from internalization of a sense of ambivalence or insecurity about their identities to rejection of, and active resistance to, dominant group values. At both extremes, alienation from schooling and mental withdrawal from academic effort have been a frequent consequence. These trends can be examined in relation to John Ogbu's theoretical framework.

Ogbu's Theoretical Framework

Ogbu (1978, 1992) illustrates the influence of societal power relations on educational achievement with reference to the situation of Burakumin in Japan. Burakumin perform poorly in Japanese schools as a result of their low social status but perform well after immigration to the United States because educators are unaware of their low social status in their home country. Thus, educators tend to have the same high academic expectations of them as they do for other Japanese students (Ogbu, 1992). Ogbu distinguishes between voluntary or immigrant minorities, who tend to succeed academically, and involuntary minorities who tend to experience academic difficulties. The former have immigrated to the host country with the expectation of a better life and generally have a positive orientation to the host community and no ambivalence or insecurity in regard to their own identities. Involuntary minorities, by contrast, were originally brought into the society against their will, for example, through slavery, conquest, colonization, or forced labor, and were often denied the opportunity for true participation in or assimilation into the mainstream society. The four major groups that experience disproportionate academic failure in the United States (African Americans, Latinos/Latinas, Native Americans, and Hawaiian Americans) clearly match the profile of involuntary minorities. Similarly, in the Canadian context, First Nations (Native) and minority francophone students underachieve academically in ways that would be predicted from Ogbu's dichotomy.

However, Ogbu's distinction is undoubtedly oversimplified. It fails to explain the underachievement of some immigrant minority groups in the Canadian context (e.g., Afro-Caribbean, Portuguese-speaking, and Spanish-speaking students). Similarly, it does not account for considerable within group variance in academic achievement nor the effect of variables such as socioeconomic status (Cummins, 1997; Gibson, 1997).

It is also likely that refugee students constitute a separate category that cannot easily be subsumed within the *voluntary-involuntary* distinction (Vincent, 1996).

In spite of its inability to account for the complexities of dominant-subordinated group relationships, Ogbu's distinction represents a useful starting point in conceptualizing the causes of underachievement among subordinated group students. It highlights important patterns of how coercive power relations operating in the broader society find their way into the structures and operation of schooling. The distinction must be conceived in dynamic rather than static terms. The status of groups may change rapidly from one generation to another in ways that a rigid dichotomy cannot accommodate.

For these reasons, I prefer to discuss the issues in terms of coercive and collaborative relations of power that encompass the important distinction that Ogbu has made as well as the other categories of difference that define inter-group power relations (e.g., racism, sexism, homophobia, discrimination based on language and/or cultural differences, etc.). This orientation also facilitates examination of how power relations in the broader society get translated into educational failure within the schools, and most importantly, how this process can be resisted and reversed.

The two diagrams (Figures 1 and 2) outline an analysis of the causes of school failure and the intervention model that forms the basis for the current theoretical framework. The framework (Figure 1) proposes that relations of power in the wider society (macro-interactions), ranging from coercive to collaborative in varying degrees, influence both the ways in which educators define their roles and the types of structures that are established in the educational system. Role definitions refer to the mindset of expectations, assumptions, and goals that educators bring to the task of educating culturally diverse students.

Coercive relations of power refer to the exercise of power by a dominant individual, group, or country to the detriment of a subordinated individual, group or country. For example, in the past, dominant group institutions (e.g., schools) have required that subordinated groups deny their cultural identity and give up their languages as a necessary condition for success in the "mainstream" society. For educators to become partners in the transmission of knowledge, culturally diverse students were required to acquiesce in the subordination of their identities and to celebrate as "truth" the perspectives of the dominant group (e.g., the "truth" that Columbus "discovered" America and brought "civilization" to its indigenous peoples).

Collaborative relations of power, by contrast, reflect the sense of the term "power" that refers to "being enabled," or "empowered" to achieve more. Within collaborative relations of power, "power" is not a fixed quantity but is generated through interaction with others. The more empowered one individual or group becomes, the more is generated for others to share, as is the case when two people love each other or when we really connect with children we are teaching. Within this context, the term *empowerment* can be defined as the *collaborative creation of power*. Students whose schooling experiences reflect collaborative relations of power participate confidently in instruction as a result of the fact that their sense of identity is being affirmed and extended in their interactions with educators. They also know that their voices will be heard and respected within the classroom. Schooling amplifies rather than silences their power of *self*-expression.

Educational structures refer to the organization of schooling in a broad sense that includes policies, programs, curriculum, and assessment. While these structures will generally reflect the values and priorities of dominant groups in society, they are not by any means fixed or static. As with most other aspects of the way societies are organized and resources distributed, educational structures are contested by individuals and groups.

Educational structures, together with educator role definitions, determine the micro-interactions between educators, students, and communities. These micro-interactions form an interpersonal space within which the acquisition of knowledge and formation of identity is negotiated. Power is created and shared within this interpersonal space where minds and identities meet. As such, these micro-interactions constitute the most immediate determinant of student academic success or failure.

Micro-interactions between educators, students, and communities are never neutral; in varying degrees, they either reinforce coercive relations of power or promote collaborative relations of power. In the former case, they contribute to the disempowerment of culturally diverse students and communities; in the latter case, the micro-interactions constitute a process of empowerment that enables educators, students and communities to challenge the operation of coercive power structures.

The relationships sketched in 1 are elaborated in Figure 2. The term *Exclusionary/Assimilationist* refers to the general orientation to education characteristic of most countries prior to the 1960s and still characteristic of many today. The goal of education was either to exclude certain groups from the mainstream of society or assimilate them completely. The term *Transformative/Intercultural* refers to the orientation

Figure 1
Coercive and Collaborative Relations of Power Manifested in
Macro- and Micro-Interactions

Coercive and Collaborative Relations
of Power Manifested in Macro-Interactions between
Subordinated Communities and Dominant Group Institutions

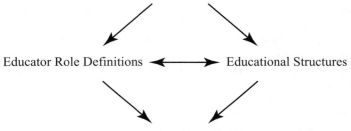

Educator Role Definitions ⟷ Educational Structures

Micro-Interactions between
Educators and Students

forming an

Interpersonal Space

within which

knowledge is generated
and
identities are negotiated

EITHER

Reinforcing Coercive Relations of Power

OR

Promoting Collaborative Relations of Power

required to challenge the operation of coercive relations of power in the school and wider society. This form of pedagogy entails interactions between educators and students that foster the collaborative creation of power; in other words, *empowerment*. Although *exclusionary* and *assimilationist* may appear to be opposites insofar as "exclusionary" focuses on segregation of subordinated groups from the mainstream of schools and society while "assimilationist" focuses on total integration into the society, in reality they are frequently two sides of the same coin: both orientations aspire to make subordinated groups invisible and inaudible. Minority groups constructed as "racially different" have historically been subjected to exclusionary rather than assimilationist policies for the simple reason that "disappearance" could not readily be achieved through assimilation. In addition, if assimilationist policies were applied to "racial" minorities, it would imply inter-marriage across "races" within the same "melting pot." This mixing of "races" would implode the myths of racial superiority that have characterized most dominant groups in societies around the world.

By contrast, *Transformative/Intercultural* orientations are based on principles of racial and cultural equality and a commitment to educate students for full participation within a democratic society. This implies providing opportunities for students to develop a form of critical literacy where they become capable not only of decoding the words, but also reading between the lines in order to understand how power is exercised through various forms of discourse (advertisements, political rhetoric, textbooks, etc.). The focus is on understanding not only what is said but also whose perspectives are represented and whose have been excluded.

The macro-interactions between dominant and subordinated groups in the wider society give rise to particular forms of educational structures that are designed to reflect the priorities of the society. Since dominant groups, almost by definition, determine the priorities of the society, education has historically tended to reproduce the relations of power in the broader society.

Examples of educational structures that reflect coercive relations of power are:

- submersion programs for bilingual students that actively suppress their L1 and cultural identity;

- exclusion of culturally-diverse parents from participation in their children's schooling;

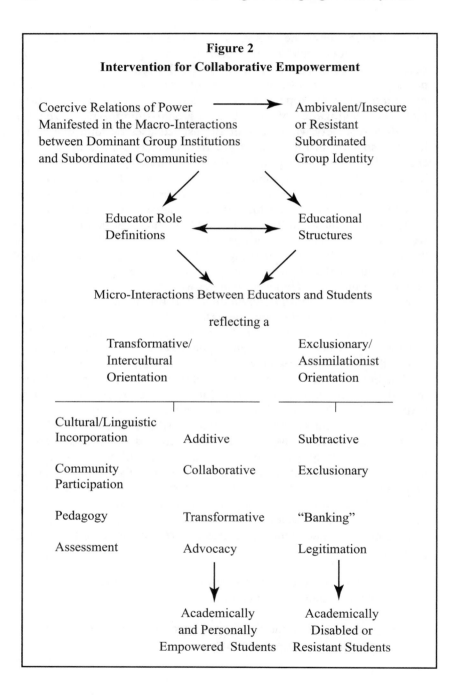

Figure 2
Intervention for Collaborative Empowerment

- tracking or streaming practices that place subordinated group students disproportionately in lower-level tracks;

- use of biased standardized tests for both achievement monitoring and special education placement;

- teacher education programs that prepare teachers for a mythical monolingual monocultural white middle-class student population;

- curriculum content that reflects the perspectives and experiences of dominant groups and excludes those of subordinated groups.

These educational structures constitute a frame that sets limits on the kinds of interactions that are likely to occur between educators and students. They constrict rather than expand the interactional space.

Societal macro-interactions also influence the ways in which educators define their roles in relation to culturally-diverse students and communities; in other words, they influence the mindset of assumptions, expectations and goals that educators bring to the task of educating students. The framework presented in Figures 1 and 2 argues that culturally-diverse students are empowered or disabled as a direct result of their interactions with educators in the schools. These interactions are mediated by the implicit or explicit role definitions that educators assume in relation to four organizational aspects of schooling:

- the extent to which students' language and cultural background are affirmed and promoted within the school; this includes the extent to which literacy instruction in school affirms, builds on, and extends the vernacular literacy practices that many culturally-diverse students engage in outside the context of school (see, for example, Hardman, 1998; Heath, 1983; Lotherington et al., 1998; Martin-Jones & Bhatt, 1998; Vásquez, Pease-Alvarez, & Shannon, 1994).

- the extent to which culturally diverse communities are encouraged to participate as partners in their children's education and to contribute the "funds of knowledge" that exist in their communities to this educational partnership

(Moll, Amanti, Neff, & González, 1992; Schecter & Bayley, 1998).

- the extent to which instruction promotes intrinsic motivation on the part of students to use language actively in order to generate their own knowledge, create literature and art, and act on social realities that affect their lives. The alternative is what Freire (1970) termed a *banking education* where the teacher defines her role as depositing information and skills in students' memory banks.

- the extent to which professionals involved in assessment become advocates for students by focusing primarily on the ways in which students' academic difficulty is a function of interactions within the school context rather than legitimizing the location of the "problem" within students.

These four dimensions namely, language/culture incorporation, community participation, pedagogy, and assessment represent sets of educational structures that will affect, but can also be influenced by, educators' role definitions.

It is important to note that students (and communities) do not passively accept dominant group attributions of their inferiority. Frequently, they actively resist the operation of the societal power structure as it is manifested in educational settings. An example is the three-day school boycott called by the Latino/Latina community in Santa Barbara when the school board voted to end the city's 25-year-old bilingual program in January 1998. Four hundred families set up their own alternative bilingual academy in a community center (Hornblower, 1998).

For some students, resistance can contribute to academic development (Zanger, 1994); students work hard to succeed in order to repudiate their teachers' low expectations. However, more typically, resistance takes the form of mentally withdrawing from a coercive educational relationship. Unfortunately, this withdrawal usually entails severe costs with respect to academic success and upward mobility (Fordham, 1990; Willis, 1977). Students find affirmation on the streets rather than in the classroom. Armando Vallejo, director of the Casa de la Raza in Santa Barbara which housed the alternative academy set up by the parents who boycotted the school expressed his view that abolishing bilingual classes amounts to cultural genocide: "Kids sit in the back of the classroom for a couple of years without understanding, and they get disillusioned. That's when they join gangs" (cited in Horn-blower, 1998).

In summary, a central principle of the present framework is that the negotiation of identity in the interactions between educators and students is central to students' academic success or failure. Our interactions with students are constantly sketching a triangular set of images:

- an image of our own identities as educators;

- an image of the identity options we highlight for our students; consider, for example, the contrasting messages conveyed to students in classrooms focused on collaborative critical inquiry (*transformative education*) compared to classrooms focused on passive internalization of information (Freire's *banking education*);

- an image of the society we hope our students will help form.

In other words, an image of the society that students will graduate into and the kind of contributions they can make to that society is embedded implicitly in the interactions between educators and students. These interactions reflect the way educators have defined their role with respect to the purposes of education in general and culturally diverse students and communities in particular. Are we preparing students to accept the societal status quo (and, in many cases, their own inferior status therein) or are we preparing them to participate actively and critically in the democratic process in pursuit of the ideals of social justice and equity which are enshrined in the constitutions of most democratic countries?

This perspective clearly implies that in situations where coercive relations of power between dominant and subordinated groups predominate, the creation of interpersonal spaces where students' identities are validated will entail a direct challenge by educators (and students) to the societal power structure. For example, to acknowledge that culturally diverse students' religion, culture and language are valid forms of *self*-expression, and to encourage their development, is to challenge the prevailing attitudes in the wider society and the coercive structures that reflect these attitudes.

In summary, empowerment derives from the process of negotiating identities in the classroom. Interactions between educators and culturally diverse students are never neutral with respect to societal power relations. In varying degrees, they either reinforce or challenge coercive relations of power in the wider society. Historically, subordinated group students have been disempowered educationally in the same way their communities have been disempowered in the wider society. In the same way as the attribution of inherent inferiority legitimated the brutalities of slavery, the slaughter of indigenous peoples, and the exploitation of colonized populations in countries around the world, definitions of subordinated group students as "genetically inferior" (e.g., Dunn, 1987; Jensen, 1969), "culturally deprived," or simply suffering cognitive confusion as a result of bilingualism have been used to explain their poor academic performance and justify their continued educational exclusion. It follows from this analysis that subordinated group students will succeed academically to the extent that the patterns of interaction in the school challenge and reverse those that have prevailed in the society at large.

Relationship between the Intervention Framework and Psycholinguistic Principles

The analysis of power relations operating in educator-student interactions within the school context is intended to address a different, although complementary, set of questions than the analysis of psycholinguistic issues. Understanding how power relations operate in the process of identity negotiation between educators and students points to some of the causes of underachievement among subordinated group students and provides general directions for reversing this process. The intervention framework provides a lens through which the learning process can be observed and assessed. It allows us to look at the deep structure of learning. What matters is not whether a program is called "bilingual," "ESL" "structured immersion" or "mainstream;" much more significant is what is being transacted in the interactions between educators and students. Some "bilingual" programs make little attempt to develop students' L1 literacy skills or to promote students' pride in their cultural and linguistic heritage. By contrast, some predominantly English-medium programs may operate largely on the *Transformative/ Intercultural* end of the continua in Figure 2 (See Schecter & Cummins, 2003, for one example).

It is doubtless much easier to promote students' bilingualism, involve parents (who may speak little or no English), and build on students' background experience, in the context of a genuine bilingual program than in a monolingual program. A shared language between teachers, students, and parents clearly facilitates communication. However, use of students' L1 for instructional purposes is no panacea. To be truly effective bilingual education should encompass a transformative/intercultural orientation to instruction that challenges the operation of coercive relations of power.

Essentially, the psycholinguistic principles are links in the causal chain that relate societal power relations to student outcomes. If it were the case that knowledge of two languages resulted in cognitive confusion and linguistic retardation (as some still appear to believe—for example, Dunn, 1987; Schlesinger, 1991), then any positive impact of bilingual education on students' sense of cultural identity would have to be weighed against the potentially negative cognitive consequences of bilingualism. Similarly, if less instructional time through English exerted adverse effects on the development of students' English academic skills (as most opponents of bilingual education claim), then bilingual education would indeed be a risky educational strategy.

The research data however, are unequivocal in demonstrating that additive forms of bilingualism are associated with positive linguistic and academic consequences. They also show clearly that literacy in two or more languages can be promoted by the school at absolutely no cost to students' academic development in English. Thus, the psycholinguistic research findings, and the theoretical principles that account for these findings, open up significant possibilities both for enriching the personal and academic lives of bilingual students and for challenging coercive relations of power in the wider society. Educators who encourage students to develop their L1 literacy skills are not only promoting learning in the narrow sense, they are also challenging the coercive discourse in the wider society which proclaims that "bilingualism shuts doors" and "monolingual education opens doors to the larger world" (Schlesinger, 1991, p. 109). The psycholinguistic research illuminates these views (and the discourse surrounding Proposition 227 in California) not only as factually wrong but as forms of racism designed to return the educational system to the exclusionary/assimilationist orientations characteristic of the pre-Civil Rights era in the United States.

Similarly, the distinction between conversational and academic language proficiency together with the time periods required to attain grade expectations in English academic tasks, refutes the assumption that most bilingual/EL students can catch up within a year of starting to learn English (as Proposition 227 claims). Again, the psycholinguistic data lay bare the coercive sociopolitical agenda that is at work in the claims of groups that oppose bilingual education.

In summary, although they were elaborated at different times and addressed to different questions, the psycholinguistic and sociopolitical theoretical constructs intersect in fundamental ways. Both sets of constructs are essential components of the theoretical framework. The psycholinguistic constructs are focused more on *knowledge generation* (i.e. learning) while the sociopolitical constructs focus on *identity negotiation* and its rootedness in societal power relations. The point of the framework is that one dimension cannot be adequately considered without the other. They are two sides of the same coin.

REFERENCES

Baker, C. (1996). *Foundations of bilingual education and bilingualism.* Clevedon, England: Multilingual Matters.

Banks, J. A. (1996). The canon debate, knowledge construction, and multicultural education. In J. A. Banks (Ed.), *Multicultural education, transformative knowledge & action: Historical and contemporary perspectives.* (pp. 3-29). New York: Teachers College Press.

Becker, W. C. (1977). Teaching reading and language to the disadvantaged: What we have learned from field research. *Harvard Educational Review, 47,* 518-543.

Becker, W., & Gersten, R. (1982). A follow-up of follow through: The later effects of the direct instruction model on children in the fifth and sixth grades. *American Educational Research Journal, 19,* 75-92.

Biemiller, A. (1999). *Language and reading success.* Cambridge, MA: Brookline Books.

Chall, J. S., Jacobs, V., & Baldwin, L. (1990). *The reading crisis: Why poor children fall behind.* Cambridge, MA: Harvard University Press.

Collier, V. P., and Thomas, W. P. (1999). Making U.S. schools effective for English language learners, Part 1. *TESOL Matters,* 9(4) (August/September), pp. 1 & 6.

Corson, D. (1997). The learning and use of academic English words. *Language Learning,* 47(4), 671-718.

Crawford, J. (1992). *Language loyalties: A source book on the Official English controversy.* Chicago: University of Chicago Press.

Cummins, J. (1976). The influence of bilingualism on cognitive growth: A synthesis of research findings and explanatory hypotheses. *Working Papers on Bilingualism*, 9, 1-43.

Cummins, J. (1979). Linguistic interdependence and the educational development of bilingual children. *Review of Educational Research,* 49, 222-251.

Cummins, J. (1981a). The role of primary language development in promoting educational success for language minority students. In California State Department of Education (Ed.), *Schooling and language minority students: A theoretical framework* (pp. 3-49). Los Angeles: Evaluation, Dissemination and Assessment Center, California State University.

Cummins, J. (1981b). Age on arrival and immigrant second language learning in Canada: A reassessment. *Applied Linguistics,* 1, 132-149.

Cummins, J. (1991). Interdependence of first- and second-language proficiency in bilingual children. In E. Bialystok (Ed.), *Language processing in bilingual children* (pp. 70-89). Cambridge, England: Cambridge University Press.

Cummins, J. (1997). Minority status and schooling in Canada. *Anthropology & Education Quarterly*, 28(3), 411-430.

Cummins, J., & Corson, D. (Eds.). (1997). *Bilingual education* (Vol. 5). Dordrecht, The Netherlands: Kluwer Academic Publishers.

Cummins, J., Swain, M., Nakajima, K., Handscombe, J., Green, D., & Tran, C. (1984). Linguistic interdependence among Japanese and Vietnamese immigrant students. In C. Rivera (Ed.), *Communicative competence approaches to language proficiency assessment: Research and application* (pp. 60-81). Clevedon, England: Multilingual Matters.

Dunn, L. (1987). *Bilingual Hispanic children on the U.S. mainland: A review of research on their cognitive, linguistic, and scholastic development.* Circle Pines, Minnesota: American Guidance Service.

Ehri, L. C., Nunes, S., Stahl, S. Willows, D. (2001). Systematic phonics instruction helps students learn to read: Evidence from the National Reading Panel's meta-analysis. *Review of Educational Research,* 71(3), 393-447.

Elley, W. B. (1991). Acquiring literacy in a second language: The effect of book-based programs. *Language Learning,* 41, 375-411.

Fielding, L. G., & Pearson, P. D. (1994). Reading comprehension: What works. Educational Leadership, 51(5), 62-68.

Fitzgerald, J. (1995). English-as-a-second-language learners' cognitive reading processes: A review of research in the United States. *Review of Educational Research,* 65, 145-190.

Fordham, S. (1990). Racelessness as a factor in Black students' school success: Pragmatic strategy or Pyrrhic victory? In N. M. Hidalgo, C. L. McDowell, & E. V. Siddle (Eds.), *Facing racism in education* (Reprint series No. 21, pp. 232-262): Harvard Educational Review.

Freire, P. (1970b). *Pedagogy of the oppressed.* New York: Continuum.

Gándara, P. (1999). *Review of research on instruction of limited English proficient students: A report to the California Legislature.* Santa Barbara: University of California, Linguistic Minority Research Institute.

Genesee, F. (1979). Acquisition of reading skills in immersion programs. *Foreign Language Annals,* 12, 71-77.

Geva, E. (2000). Issues in the assessment of reading disabilities in L2 children— Beliefs and research evidence. *Dyslexia,* 6, 13-28.

Gibson, M. A. (1997). Complicating the immigrant/involuntary minority typology. *Anthropology & Education Quarterly,* 28(3), 431-454.

Hakuta, K., Butler, Y. G., & Witt, D. (2000). *How long does it take English learners to attain proficiency?* Santa Barbara: University of California Linguistic Minority Research Institute.

Hardman, J. (1998). Literacy and bilingualism in a Cambodian community in the USA. In A. Y. Durgunoglu & L. Verhoeven (Eds.), *Literacy development in a multilingual context: Cross-cultural perspectives* (pp. 51-81). Mahwah, NJ: Lawrence Erlbaum Associates.

Heath, S. B. (1983). *Ways with words.* Cambridge: Cambridge University Press.

Hornblower, M. (1998) No habla español. *Time* (January 26), 44.

Jensen, A. R. (1969). How much can we boost I.Q. and scholastic achievement? *Harvard Educational Review,* 39, 1-123.

Klesmer, H. (1994). Assessment and teacher perceptions of ESL student achievement. *English Quarterly,* 26(3), 8-11.

Krashen, S. D. (1993). *The power of reading.* Englewood, CO: Libraries Unlimited.

Krashen, S. (2001, September/October/November). Are children ready for the mainstream after one year of structured English immersion? *TESOL Matters,* 11, 1, 4.

Kwan, A. B., & Willows, D. M. (1998, December). *Impact of early phonics instruction on children learning English as a second language.* Paper presented at the National Reading Conference, Austin, TX.

Lambert, W. E., & Tucker, G. R. (1972). *Bilingual education of children: The St. Lambert experiment.* Rowley, MA: Newbury House.

Lasagabaster, D. (1998). The threshold hypothesis applied to three languages in contact at school. *International Journal of Bilingual Education and Bilingualism,* 1(2), 119-133.

Lotherington, H., Ebert, S., Watanabe, T., Norng, S., & Ho-Dac, T. (1998). Biliteracy practices in suburban Melbourne. Australian Language Matters, 6(3), 3-4.

Martin-Jones, M., & Bhatt, A. (1998). Literacies in the lives of young Gujerati speakers in Leicester. In A. Y. Durgunoglu & L. Verhoeven (Eds.), *Literacy*

Development in a multilingual context: Cross-cultural perspectives (pp. 37-50). Mahwah, NJ: Lawrence Erlbaum Associates.

Moll, L. C., Amanti, C., Neff, D., & González, N. (1992). Funds of knowledge for teaching: Using a qualitative approach to connect homes and classrooms. *Theory into Practice*, 31(2), 132-141.

National Reading Panel. (2000). *Teaching children to read: An evidence-based assessment of the scientific research literature on reading and its implications for reading instruction.* Washington, DC: NICHD.

Nieto, S. (1999). *The light in their eyes: Creating multicultural learning communities.* New York: Teachers College Press.

Ogbu, J. (1978). *Minority education and caste.* New York: Academic Press.

Ogbu, J. U. (1992). Understanding cultural diversity and learning. *Educational Researcher*, 21(8), 5-14 & 24.

Ovando, C., & McLaren, P. (Eds.) (1999). T*he politics of multiculturalism and bilingual education: Students and teachers caught in the cross fire.* Boston: McGraw Hill.

Poplin, M., & Weeres, J. (1992). *Voices from the inside: A report on schooling from inside the classroom.* Claremont, CA: The Institute for Education in Transformation at the Claremont Graduate School.

Postlethwaite, T. N., & Ross, K. N. (1992). *Effective schools in reading: Implications for educational planners. An exploratory study.* The Hague: The International Association for the Evaluation of Educational Achievement.

Rand Reading Study Group. (2002). *Reading for understanding: Toward an R&D program in reading comprehension.* Report prepared for the Office of Educational Research and Improvement. Santa Monica: RAND. *(http://www.rand. org/publications/MR/MR1465/MR1465.pdf)*

Ricciardelli, L. A. (1992). Bilingualism and cognitive development in relation to threshold theory. *Journal of Psycholinguistic Research*, 21, 301-316.

Schecter, S. R., & Bayley, R. (1998). Concurrence and complementarity: Mexican-background parents' decisions about language and schooling. *Journal for a Just and Caring Education*, 4(1), 47-64.

Schecter, S. R. & Cummins, J. (Eds.). (2003). *Multilingual education in practice: Using diversity as a resource.* Portsmouth, NH: Heinemann.

Schlesinger, A. Jr. (1991). *The disuniting of America.* New York: W. W. Norton.

Sierra, J., & Olaziregi, I. (1991). *EIFE 3. Influence of factors on the learning of Basque. Study of the models A, B and D in second year Basic General Education.* Gasteiz: Central Publications Service of the Basque Country.

Snow, C. E., Burns, M. S., & Griffin, P. (1998). *Preventing reading difficulties in young children.* Washington, DC: National Academy Press.

Thomas, W., & Collier, V. (2002). *A national study of school effectiveness for language minority students' long-term academic achievement.* Santa Cruz, CA and Washington, DC: Center for Research on Education, Diversity & Excellence. Available: *http://www.crede.ucsc.edu/research/llaa/1.1_final.html*

Tizard, J., Schofield, W. N., & Hewison, J. (1982). Collaboration between teachers and parents in assisting children's reading. *British Journal of Educational Psychology, 52,* 1-15.

Vásquez, O. A., Pease-Alvarez, L., & Shannon, S. M. (1994). *Pushing boundaries: Language and culture in a Mexicano community.* New York: Cambridge University Press.

Venezky, R. L. (1998). An alternative perspective on Success for All. *Advances in Educational Policy,* 4, 145-165.

Verhoeven, L., & Aarts, R. (1998). Attaining functional literacy in the Netherlands. In A. Y. Durgunoglu & L. Verhoeven (Eds.), *Literacy development in a multilingual context: Cross-cultural perspectives* (pp. 111-134). Mahwah, NJ: Lawrence Erlbaum Associates.

Vincent, C. (1996). *Singing to a star: The school meanings of second generation Salvadorean students.* Doctoral dissertation, George Mason University, Fairfax, VA.

Wagner, D. A. (1998). Putting second language first: Language and literacy learning in Morocco. In L. Verhoeven & A. Y. Durgunoglu (Eds.), *Literacy development in a multilingual context* (pp. 169-183). Mahway, NJ: Lawrence Erlbaum Associates.

Willis, P. (1977). *Learning to labor: How working class kids get working class jobs.* Lexington: D. C. Heath

Wong Fillmore, L. (1992). Against our best interest: The attempt to sabotage bilingual education. In J. Crawford (Ed.), *Language loyalties: A sourcebook on the Official English controversy* (pp. 367-375). Chicago: University of Chicago Press.

Zanger, V. V. (1994). ḫNot joined inḫ: Intergroup relations and access to English literacy for Hispanic youth. In B. M. Ferdman, R.-M. Weber, & A. Ramírez (Eds.), *Literacy across languages and cultures* (pp. 171-198). Albany: SUNY Press.

Bilingual Education and
Second Language Acquisition Theory*

Stephen D. Krashen

Introduction

The impression one gets from the popular press is that bilingual education is a mess. We are told that "basic disagreements range across the entire field of bilingual education" (Trombley, 1980a), that the experts disagree on which programs are best, that those who are supposed to benefit from bilingual education often oppose it, that there is little information about how second languages are acquired, and that basic research on all of those issues is either contradictory or lacking.

While we cannot cover the entire field of bilingual education, we will examine some of these disagreements, certain central issues in bilingual education that appear to be unresolved. In the first section, we will briefly describe the issues, the points of contention. Following this, we will review what is known today about the process of second language acquisition. A third section will show how this new information, along with a considerable amount of excellent thinking and research in bilingualism and bilingual education, helps to resolve some of the issues facing parents and educators today. We will see that while bilingual education does have many unresolved problems, the situation is not nearly as bad as it may appear. Basic research and theory already exist that speak to many of the issues in the field today.

The Issues

The aim of this section is merely to present the issues. This is no easy task. There appear to be a bewildering variety of options and programs, each with its supporters and detractors. I will try to present some of these options and some of the points of debate. This will not be a complete survey; it will, however, cover those questions upon which current research and theory can shed some light. The presentation is in the form of definitions, done in the hope that consistent use of terms will alleviate at least some of the confusion that exists in bilingual education today.

*This paper owes a tremendous debt to the research and thinking of James Cummins. I would also like to thank Professors Merrill Swain and John Oller for a very helpful discussion of Professor Cummins' ideas and their relationship to second language acquisition theory, and to Robin Scarcella for her comments.

Bilingual Education Programs

While we could use bilingual education as a cover term for practically all of the programs described below, it will be useful to limit it here. Bilingual education refers to situations in which students are able to study subject matter in their first language (L1) while their weaker language skills catch up. This is Trombley's view of bilingual education: "Bilingual Education is intended to permit students who speak little or no English to learn reading, writing, arithmetic and other basic subjects in their primary language while they are acquiring proficiency in English" (1980b, p. 1). The theory behind bilingual education is that it allows non-English proficient (NEP) children to keep up in subject matter while acquiring English as a second language.

There are, of course, many varieties of bilingual education. Bilingual education programs vary in at least four ways:

1. Language use (manner). It is possible to present subject matter in the first language and leave it up to the English as a Second Language (ESL) component to provide practice in English (bilingual education + ESL). Most programs provide at least some subject matter in both languages, and there are several ways this can be done. Some provide some subjects in English and others in the first language; others use both languages for the same subject. Here again, there are several possibilities. A common method is speaking in first one language and then the other; an explanation is given in both the first language and in English during the same class hour. This is known as *concurrent translation*.

2. Amount of each language used. Not all programs provide exactly 50 percent exposure to each language. Legarreta (1979) informed us, for example, that in one concurrent translation class, Spanish was used 28 percent of the time and English 72 percent, while in a balanced bilingual class (some subjects in Spanish and others in English), the percentage was 50 percent Spanish and 50 percent English.

3. Type of ESL. There are many ways of teaching the second language. Methods include the still popular audiolingual system, which emphasizes repetition and memorization of phrases and sentences, as well as other grammar-oriented approaches, which stress the conscious understanding of rules of grammar, and more conversational methods.

4. Purpose. Bilingual programs vary with respect to whether they are intended to maintain the children's first language indefinitely (maintenance) or are only to help them ultimately adjust to an all-English program (transitional). It is important to note that the announced goals of both transitional and maintenance programs always include acquisition of the second language and subject matter education.

Alternatives to Bilingual Education

1. Submersion or "Sink or Swim"

In submersion programs, NEP children are simply placed in the same classroom as native English speakers and the regular curriculum is followed. There is no organized attempt to provide any special instruction or extra help for these children. Although sympathetic teachers often try to do something, all instruction is in English.

Many people feel that "Sink or Swim" is the best solution. Here are the two most commonly heard arguments for "Sink or Swim," as opposed to bilingual education:

a. Clearly, "Sink or Swim" provides more exposure to English, and the more exposure to English received, the better off children are. In letters to the *Los Angeles Times,* several writers claimed that bilingual education condemns children to second-class status since it fails to provide a full exposure to English, thus denying immigrant students full economic and social opportunity (September 19, 1980).

b. Many people, it is maintained, succeeded via "Sink or Swim." Since they had to learn English, and were surrounded by it, they learned, or so the argument goes.

We will return to these points of view later, after looking at theory and the empirical research.

2. Submersion + ESL

This option is often referred to simply as "ESL," which is a misnomer, since ESL in some form is nearly always a part of bilingual education programs. In submersion plus ESL, NEP children are usually given a separate ESL class for some prescribed period of time, usually an hour per day (termed "pull-out"). The rest of the day is spent in classes with native English speakers, and the NEP students attempt to follow the all-English curriculum.

Those who favor "Sink or Swim" usually support this program as well, on the grounds that it provides more English; more time spent exposed to English; the motivation to learn, since subject matter is taught in English; and the advantages of formal instruction. Lopez, in a letter to the *Los Angeles Times,* speaks for those who hold this view:

> Bilingual classes segregate these [non-English-speaking] students and thus seriously reduce their contact with [the] English speakers and, even more importantly, weaken their drive to communicate with others in English. If you have ever taught a class of immigrants, you know that only the most highly motivated will consistently respond in English if they know you speak their native language....You cannot learn

English well if you do not have the opportunity to interact
with English speakers in thousands of varied situations over a
period of years. This should take place not only in special
classes (English-as-a-second-language classes are the right
idea for immigrant students, but only for a limited time) but
also in regular classes as well as extra-class situations.
(September 19, 1980)

Lopez describes herself as one who had to learn English herself as a
young immigrant and as a bilingual teacher. Her view is shared by some
legislators and some members of the communities who are supposedly
served by bilingual education. According to Trombley:

Many parents think the key to success in the United States is
to learn English, and they do not believe the educators who
tell them their children will learn to speak English better in
bilingual classes. (September 4, 1980b)

Of course, many legislators, immigrants, and members of minority
language communities support bilingual education enthusiastically. We
will evaluate these arguments in a later section of this chapter.

3. *Immersion*

"Immersion" is often used as a synonym for "Sink or Swim," but this
term has been used in the professional literature to refer to a very different kind of program. Immersion typically refers to programs in which
majority language children (e.g., English-speaking children in the United
States and Canada) are instructed in a second language, that is, programs
in which subject matter is taught in a second language such as Spanish or
French. This need not always be the case, however; and theoretically immersion programs are possible for minority children as well.

Typically, immersion students receive all instruction in the second
language, with the exception of language arts in the first language. Many
programs, however, increase the amount of subject matter instruction in
the first language as children progress. Immersion students are also
"segregated," that is, native speakers of the second language are not
usually included in these programs; and immersion students do not
usually receive formal instruction in the second language.

In early immersion, the second language is used in kindergarten and
for most subjects starting from the first grade. In late immersion,
students may receive one or two years of formal instruction in the second
language before starting subject matter instruction in the L2. Late immersion programs begin around sixth grade, but here again there is variation. There are also partial immersion programs in which some subjects
are taught in the L2 and some in the L1 (Swain, 1978).

Immersion programs in Canada using French as the second language have been carefully followed by researchers. More recently, American immersion programs have been developed using Spanish and other languages.

With this definition of immersion, there really can be no conflict between bilingual education and immersion, since they are aimed at different populations. Nevertheless, immersion is a logical possibility for NEP children (i.e., subject matter instruction in English, segregated from native speakers with L1 language arts), a possibility discussed later.

We also see that immersion research is a rich source of information about second language acquisition for bilingual education specialists.

Table 1 reviews the differences between submersion programs and majority child immersion programs.

Table 1

COMPARISON OF SUBMERSION AND IMMERSION PROGRAMS

Submersion	*(Majority child) Immersion*
Children are mixed with native speakers of the L2	Children are linguistically segregated.
Language of instruction is the majority language.	Language of instruction is a minority language.
Instruction in L1 language arts is not provided.	Instruction in L1 language arts is provided.

Summary of Issues

The issues, then, are these:

1. Does bilingual education retard the development of English as a second language?
2. Are "Sink or Swim" (submersion) and/or ESL methods better than bilingual education?
3. How should ESL be taught?
4. Is there a place for "immersion" for the NEP child?
5. Which bilingual education options are better for language acquisition?

The answers to these questions, contrary to much popular opinion, are not obvious, and not merely a matter of common sense. They should not be resolved by vote but by consideration of empirically based theory and research. In the following section, we will review current second language acquisition theory, an exercise that will be of great use in discussing the issues listed above.

Second Language Acquisition Theory

Current second language acquisition theory will be discussed in terms of five hypotheses about second language acquisition:

1. The Acquisition-Learning Hypothesis

2. The Natural Order Hypothesis

3. The Monitor Hypothesis

4. The Input Hypothesis

5. The Affective Filter Hypothesis

These hypotheses are presented here without extensive supporting evidence, as this evidence has been published elsewhere (Krashen, 1981, 1982b, Dulay *et al.*, 1982).

The Acquisition-Learning Hypothesis

According to this hypothesis, second language acquirers have two distinct ways of developing ability in second languages. Language *acquisition* is similar to the way children develop first language competence. Language acquisition is a subconscious process in two senses: people are often not aware that they are acquiring a language while they are doing so. What they are aware of using the language for some communicative purposes. Also, they are often not aware of what they have acquired; they usually cannot describe or talk about the rules they have acquired but they have a "feel" for the language. Language *learning* is different. It is knowing about language or formal knowledge of a language. Language learning is thought to profit from explicit presentation of rules and from error correction. Error correction, supposedly, helps the learner come to the correct conscious mental representation of a rule. There is good evidence, however, that error correction does not help subconscious acquisition (Brown *et al.*, 1973).

In everyday terms, *acquisition* is picking up a language. Ordinary equivalents for *learning* include grammar and rules.

The Natural Order Hypothesis

The Natural Order Hypothesis states that students acquire (not learn) grammatical structures in a predictable order; that is, certain grammatical structures tend to be acquired early and others, late. For English, a very well-studied language, function words (grammatical morphemes) such as *-ing* (as in: John is going to work now.) and plural/s/ (as in: two boys) are among the earliest acquired. The third person singular ending/s/ (as in: He lives in New Jersey.) and the possessive /s/

(as in: John's hat) are acquired much later (in children's first language acquisition, possessive and third person endings may come as much as one year later). It appears that the order of acquisition for first language acquisition is not identical to the order of acquisition for second language acquisition, but there are some similarities. For grammatical morphemes in English, children's second language order is similar to adult second language order. There is thus a "first language order" and a "second language order" (Krashen, 1981).

Two disclaimers about order of acquisition and the Natural Order Hypothesis are necessary. First, linguists do not have information about the order of acquisition of every structure in every language. In fact, we have information only about a few structures in a few languages. As we shall see below, this does not present a practical problem. Also, the order is not rigidly obeyed by every acquirer; there is some individual variation. There is significant agreement among acquirers, however, and we can definitely speak of an average order of acquisition.

As we shall see later, the existence of the natural order does *not* imply that we should teach second languages along this order, focusing on earlier acquired items first and later acquired items later. Indeed, there is good evidence that language teaching aimed at acquisition should not employ a grammatical syllabus.

The Monitor Hypothesis

The Acquisition-Learning Hypothesis merely stated that two separate processes for the development of ability in the second language exist. The Monitor Hypothesis states the relationship between acquisition and learning. It seems that acquisition is far more important. It is responsible for our fluency in a second language, our ability to use it easily and comfortably. Conscious learning is not at all responsible for our fluency but has only one function: it can be used as an editor or monitor. This is illustrated in Figure 1.

Figure 1

**ACQUISITION AND LEARNING IN SECOND
LANGUAGE PRODUCTION**

We use conscious learning to make corrections, to change the output of the acquired system before we speak or write, or sometimes after we speak or write (as in self-correction).

Studies (reviewed in Krashen, 1981) suggest that it is not easy to use the Monitor efficiently. In order to use the Monitor Hypothesis, three *necessary* conditions need to be met. These conditions are *necessary* but not sufficient; that is, even if they are met, second language users may not use the monitor very well.

(1) *Time.* In order to use conscious rules, the performer has to have enough time. In normal conversation, there is rarely enough time to consult conscious rules.

(2) *Focus on form.* In order to use conscious rules, just having time is not enough. The second language performer must also be focused on form (Dulay and Burt, 1978) or thinking about correctness. Research has indicated that even when performers have time, as when they are writing, they may not fully use the conscious grammar, since they are more concerned with what they are expressing rather than how they are expressing it.

(3) *Know the rule.* This is a formidable condition, considering our incomplete knowledge of the structure of language. Linguists concede that they have described only fragments of natural languages, and only a few languages have been worked on to any extent. Teachers and students, of course, have access to only a fraction of the linguists' descriptions.

These three conditions place tremendous limits on the use of conscious grammar—and, again, all three must be met to allow effective grammar use—but even this is no guarantee. Research strongly suggests (Krashen, 1981; 1982b) that conscious grammar use is surprisingly light on anything short of a grammar test.

The Input Hypothesis

According to the first three hypotheses, acquisition has the central role in second language performance. If this is so, the crucial question becomes: How do we acquire? Stated in terms of the Natural Order Hypothesis, we can ask how we move from one stage to another, from stage 3, for example, to stage 4 (or more generally from stage i, our current level of competence, i + 1, the next stage that the acquirer is due to acquire, or ready to acquire).

The Input Hypothesis postulates that we acquire by understanding input containing i + 1; that is, by understanding language that contains input containing structures that are a bit beyond the acquirer's current level. We acquire structure by understanding messages and not focusing on the form of the input or analyzing it. We can do this, we can understand language that contains structures we do not "know" by utilizing context, extra-linguistic information, and our knowledge of the world. In second language classrooms, for example, context is often provided via visual aids (pictures) and discussion of familiar topics.

Our usual approach to second language teaching is very different from the Input Hypothesis. As Hatch (1978) has pointed out, we assume the opposite: We first teach students structures and then try to give them practice in "using" them in communication. According to the Input Hypothesis, on the other hand, we acquire structure not by focusing on structure but by understanding messages containing new structure.

The Input Hypothesis also claims that we do not teach speaking directly. Rather, speaking fluency emerges on its own over time. The best way to "teach" speaking, according to this view, is simply to provide "comprehensible input." Speech will come when the acquirer feels ready. This readiness state arrives at different times for different people, however. Also, early speech is typically not accurate; grammatical accuracy develops over time as the acquirer hears and understands more input.

A third part of the Input Hypothesis is the claim that the "best" input should not be "grammatically sequenced," that is, it should not deliberately aim at $i + 1$. We are all familiar with language classes that attempt to do this; there is a "structure of the day" (e.g., the aim of today's lesson is to "learn" the past tense), and both teacher and students feel that the aim of the lesson is to learn and practice this structure. Once the day's structure is mastered, we proceed on to the next. The Input Hypothesis claims that such deliberate sequencing is not necessary and may even be harmful! Specifically, it hypothesizes that if there is successful communication, if the acquirer indeed understands the message contained in the input, $i + 1$ will automatically be provided in just the right quantities. Acquirers will receive comprehensible input containing structures just beyond them if they are in situations involving genuine communication, and these structures will be constantly provided and automatically reviewed.

It may be useful to detail some of the disadvantages of grammatical syllabi, even those that present structures along the natural order. They assume, first of all, that all of our students are at the same level in a given class, that they are all ready for the same $i + 1$. This is hardly ever true. In most classes, a substantial percentage of students will have already acquired the structure of the day, while another large sub-group is nowhere near ready for it. Thus, a teacher's audience for any given structure is usually a small part of the class. Even if the structure of the day is the appropriate one, how do we know when we have provided enough practice? And what about students who miss the structure due to absence? Under current procedures, they often have to wait until the following year. A third problem is perhaps the most serious: It is practically impossible to discuss any topic of real interest in any depth when the hidden agenda is practice of a structure.

Genuinely interesting and comprehensible input solves these problems. According to the Input Hypothesis, if students can follow the general meaning of a discussion, i + 1 will be provided for all of them, different i + 1 for different students.   With natural comprehensible input, students need not worry about missing a class and thereby missing the past tense forever. It will come up again and again, both in the class discussion and in reading. Finally, there is no need to worry about contextualizing a different structure every unit. The focus, at all times, is on helping students understand messages and not rules of grammar.

In other words, input for acquisition need not focus only on i + 1, it only needs to contain it. Thus, i + 1 will be supplied, and naturally reviewed, when the acquirer obtains enough "comprehensible input."

Evidence supporting the Input Hyupothesis is given in some detail in other publications (Krashen, 1981; 1982b) but it is useful to briefly mention two phenomena in second language acquisition that are consistent with this hypothesis. The first is the presence of the *silent period,* a period of time before the acquirer actually starts to speak. The silent period is very noticeable in children's second language acquisition; six- and seven-year-olds, for example, in a new country, may not say anything (except for some memorized sentences and phrases) for several months. According to the Input Hypothesis, this is a time during which they are building up competence via input, by listening. When they are ready, they start to talk.

We generally do not allow adults to have a silent period but insist on production right away. When adults have to talk "too early," before they really have the acquired competence to support production, they have only one choice, and that is to fall back on their first language, an idea first proposed by Newmark (1966). Here is how this works: performers will "think" in their first language, that is, mentally produce the desired sentence in the first language and then fill in the words with second language vocabulary. If time permits, performers will note where the syntax or grammar of the sentence in L1 differs from how this sentence should look in the second language and will use the conscious monitor to make changes. For example, if one wishes to say in French:

(1) The dog ate them.

The learner would mentally produce a sentence similar to (1). Step ((2) would be to simply plug in French words, giving:

(2) *Le chien a mangé les.*

Some acquirers may consciously know that sentences like (2) are not correct and, given time, can make the necessary correction, giving:

(3) *Le chien les a mangé.*

According to this view, first language "interference" is not something "getting in the way." It is not interference at all but is the result of falling back on old knowledge. Its cure is more acquisition, or more comprehensible input. It is not restricted to adults but will happen in situations where production demands exceed current competence. It is a fairly common occurrence, and we occasionally see it even in acquisition-rich environments, although the number of first language-influenced errors is generally a small minority of the total number of errors children produce. Sentence (2), in fact, was observed in a child second language acquisition situation in an immersion class in Toronto (Selinker *et al.*, 1975).

Table 2 summarizes the Input Hypothesis:

Table 2

THE INPUT HYPOTHESIS

1. We acquire (not learn) language by understanding input that contains structures that are just beyond our current level of competence (i + 1).
2. Speech is not taught directly, but "emerges" on its own. Early speech is typically not grammatically accurate.
3. If input is understood, and there is enough of it, i + 1 is automatically provided. We do not have to deliberately program grammatical structures into the input.

The Affective Filter Hypothesis

The fifth and final hypothesis deals with the role of "affect," that is, the effect of personality, motivation, and other "affective variables" on second language acquisition. Briefly, the research literature in second language acquisition tells us that the following affective variables are related to success in second language acquisition:

1. *Anxiety*. Low anxiety relates to second language acquisition. The more the students are "off the defensive" (Stevick, 1976), the better the acquisition.

2. *Motivation*. Higher motivation predicts more second language acquisition. Certain kinds of motivation are more effective in certain situations, moreover. In situations where acquisition of the second language is a practical necessity, "instrumental" motivation relates to second language acquisition; in many other situations, such as those where acquisition of the second language is more of a luxury, "integrative" motivation predicts success in second language acquisition (Gardner and Lambert, 1972).[1]

---

[1] "Instrumental" motivation is defined as wanting to acquire another language for some practical purpose, e.g., for a profession. "Integrative" motivation occurs when the language is acquired in order to feel a closer sense of identity with another group.

3. *Self-confidence.* The acquirer with more self-esteem and self-confidence tends to do better in second language acquisition (Krashen, 1981).

I have hypothesized that these affective factors relate more directly to subconscious language acquisition than to conscious learning, because we see stronger relationships between these affective variables when communicative-types tests are used (tests that require the use of the acquired system) and when we test students who have had a chance to *acquire* the language and not just learn it in foreign language classes. Dulay and Burt (1977) have made this relationship more explicit and clear by positing the presence of an "affective filter." According to the Affective Filter Hypothesis, acquirers in a less than optimal affective state will have a filter, or mental block, preventing them from utilizing input fully for further language acquisition. If they are anxious, "on the defensive," or not motivated, they may understand the input, but the input will not enter the "language acquisition device." Figure 2 illustrates the operation of the filter.

Figure 2

THE AFFECTIVE FILTER

When the filter is "up," input may be understood but will not reach the language acquisition device; it will not strike "deeply" (Stevick, 1976).

The Causative Variable in Second Language Acquisition

We can summarize the five hypotheses with a single claim: People acquire second languages when they obtain comprehensible input and when their affective filters are low enough to allow the input in. In other words, comprehensible input is the only causative variable in second language acquisition. All other factors thought to encourage or cause second language acquisition only work when they are related to comprehensible input.

This hypothesis resolves may problems in the professional literature. For example, some studies seem to show that language teaching is beneficial, while others show that real-world use of the second language is superior (for a review, see Krashen, 1982b). This conflict is resolved by positing that language teaching helps second language acquisition by providing comprehensible input. It seems that language teaching is most efficient for students who have no other source of comprehensible input, that is, foreign language students who have no chance to interact with speakers of the target language and beginners who are not yet advanced enough to understand second language input outside class. Language teaching is of less value when rich sources of comprehensible input are available, e.g., for the intermediate student living in the country where the language is spoken.

The effects of *age* on second language acquisition also reduce down to comprehensible input plus the affective filter. The professional literature consistently supports these generalizations about age and second language acquisition: (1) Older acquirers progress faster in earlier stages (adults are faster than children; older children acquire faster than younger children), but (2) children outperform adults in the long run (Krashen *et al.*, 1979). It usually takes children about six months to one year to catch up to older acquirers (Snow and Hoefnagel-Hohle, 1978).

A possible explanation for these findings is as follows: Older acquirers are faster because they can use production strategies younger acquirers do not usually have. Specifically, older acquirers are able to "beat the system" and perform using a combination of the first language and the conscious grammar, as described earlier. While children also show occasional first language interference, adults appear to be more able to use the first language syntax as a strategy, and with their superior cognitive development, are better able to use the conscious grammar to bring their sentences into conformity with second language patterns. A good "learner" can use a combination of the first language and monitor to begin speaking fairly complex sentences very early, in a matter of hours. While this system has real drawbacks, i.e., it requires constant monitoring and vigilance, it allows the older acquirer to participate in conversation early and obtain more input.

Evidence also suggests (Scarcella and Higa, 1982) that older acquirers are more proficient at conversational management. While younger acquirers get what looks like simpler input, older performers are better able to make the input comprehensible; they ask native speakers for more help, are better at keeping the conversation going, etc.

Older acquirers also have the advantage of greater knowledge of the world—greater cognitive/academic language proficiency (CALP) (Cummins, 1980). This additional extralinguistic information gives older acquirers a greater chance to understand what they hear, both in and out of school.

An explanation for children's superiority in ultimate attainment is simply that the strength of the affective filter is sharply increased at puberty; adults may get sufficient quantities of input, but it does not all get in. The increase in filter strength at this time is due to the biological and cognitive changes the adolescent is going through at puberty (Elkind, 1970; Krashen, 1982a).

Table 3 summarizes explanations for age differences in second language acquisition.

Table 3

AGE DIFFERENCES IN SECOND LANGUAGE ACQUISITION

1. Older acquirers are faster in the early stages of second language acquisition because:
   a. They are better at obtaining comprehensible input (conversational management).
   b. They have superior knowledge of the world, which helps to make input comprehensible.
   c. They can participate in conversation earlier, via use of the first language syntax.
2. Younger acquirers tend to attain higher levels of proficiency in second languages than adults in the long run due to a lower affective filter.

Second Language Teaching

Before proceeding on to the implications of second language theory for bilingual education, it will be useful to examine the implications of theory for language teaching, since language teaching is usually considered one of the goals of bilingual education. While theory should not be the only element considered in language teaching practice (Krashen, 1982b), the five hypotheses given in the previous section have some very clear implications. They predict that any successful second language teaching program will have these characteristics:

1. It will supply input in the second language that is, first of all, comprehensible and, second, interesting and relevant to students. As discussed earlier, the goal of this input will not be to provide practice on specific points of grammar but to transmit messages of interest.

2. It will not force students to speak before they are ready and will be tolerant of errors in early speech. The theory implies that we improve in grammatical accuracy by obtaining more input, not by error correction. [Although error correction will work for some people (monitor users) some of the time (when they have time to think about form) and for some easy-to-learn rules.]

3. It will put grammar in its proper place. Some adults, and very few children, are able to use conscious grammar rules to increase the grammatical accuracy of their output; and even for these people, very strict conditions need to be met before the conscious knowledge of grammar can be applied, given the Monitor Hypothesis presented above. Children have very little capacity for conscious language learning and may also have little need for conscious learning, since they can come close to native speaker performance standards using acquisition alone.

Many different methods come very close to meeting these requirements. Asher's Total Physical Response Approach, Lozanov's Suggestopedia, Terrell's Natural Approach, and materials developed by Winitz are some examples (Krashen, 1982b). In addition, several non-methods also meet these requirements. For example, successful *conversation* with a speaker of the language you are trying to acquire may be the best lesson of all, as long as the speaker succeeds in modifying his or her speech so that you understand. According to the theory, acquirers profit directly not from what they themselves say, but from what native speakers say. Acquirer output makes an *indirect* contribution to acquisition by inviting comprehensible input. Also, pleasure reading or reading for content and intrinsic interest has the potential for supplying the necessary input for acquisition.

Subject Matter Teaching and Second Language Acquisition

Another clear potential source of comprehensible input is the subject matter classroom itself in which subject matter is taught using the second language as a medium of instruction (immersion classes).

Simply, the theory predicts that second language acquisition will occur in subject matter classes taught in the second language if the child can follow and understand the lesson. Language levels necessary for comprehension will differ, of course, for different subjects. It has been suggested, for example, that arithmetic does not require as much control of the second language as science. In the former, there is considerable extralinguistic help in understanding, fewer demands on students in terms of verbal responses, and a more restricted vocabulary (Cazden, 1979).

Applied linguistics research confirms this prediction and helps us see both the advantages and limitations of subject matter teaching as a means of encouraging second language acquisition. English-speaking immersion students, both in the United States and Canada, are in general able to follow the curriculum in a second language, that is, they learn subject matter as well as monolinguals do. Research has shown that they also do far better in acquiring the second language than students who study the second language only in formal classes. Researchers are careful to point out, however, that immersion students do not reach native-like levels in speaking and writing. Also, it takes several years for immersion students to attain these high levels of competence in the second language (see e.g., Lambert and Tucker, 1972; Swain, 1978, 1979). The classroom, thus, has its limits. Immersion students hear the language only from the teacher and not from peers. This may mean both a lack of certain kinds of input (conversational) and the existence of an affective filter.

Subject matter teaching, thus, has both advantages and limitations. It can provide comprehensible input and help second language acquisition; students exposed to the subject matter alone can achieve high levels of proficiency in certain kinds of second language usage. This takes time, however, and such students do not typically reach the native speaker level.

Before proceeding to implications, one major point about the success of immersion programs need to be made. Cohen and Swain (1976) point out that one of the reasons immersion programs succeed, where some kinds of bilingual programs fail, is because the immersion students are "segregated." In early immersion, they note, "all kindergarten pupils are unilingual in the L1. In essence, the successful program starts out as a segregated one linguistically" (p. 47). This linguistic segregation raises the chances of students receiving comprehensible input. The presence of native speakers in a class (submersion) ensures that a good percentage of the language heard by the non-native speaker will be incomprehensible, since teachers naturally will gear much of their speech to the native speakers in a native to native rather than a native to non-native speaker register.

Cohen and Swain (1976) point out several other factors that, in our terms, lead to a lower affective filter in immersion programs. The linguistic segregation "eliminates the kind of ridicule that students exert on less proficient performers" (p. 47), teachers have positive expectations, and the program is voluntary. Also, "in kindergarten, the children are permitted to speak in the L1 until they are ready to speak in the L2" (p. 48). Thus, a silent period in L2 is allowed.

Bilingual Education and Second Language Acquisition

We are now prepared to deal with some of the questions and issues raised in the first section. To do this, we first need to consider what requirements any program must meet in order to promote second language acquisition. From what we have learned from second language acquisition theory, there seem to be two major requirements.

I. Provide Comprehensible Input in the Weaker Language

Clearly, this requirement does not mean merely being exposed to the second language. There is a tremendous difference between receiving comprehensible, meaningful input and simply hearing a language one does not understand. The former will help second language acquisition, while the latter is just noise. It remains noise no matter how much exposure is provided. According to the theory, a small amount of comprehensible input, even one hour per day, will do more for second language acquisition than massive amounts of incomprehensible input.

There are several possible sources of comprehensible input for NEP children. The one that we traditionally turn to is classes in ESL. Simply, the theory predicts that ESL will help to the extent that it supplies comprehensible input. Not all teaching methods do this; some, in fact, supply amazingly little comprehensible input in a second language (e.g., grammar-translation and audiolingual type methods). Both theory and practical experience confirm that repetitive drill does very little for acquisition; and grammar approaches, shown to be ineffective for adults, are even less effective for small children. ESL can make a contribution when it supplies the necessary input to children who have few or no other sources of input (see Terrell, 1977, 1981 for some ideas on how this can be done).

A second source of comprehensible input for NEP children is interaction with other children outside of school, on the playground, and in the neighborhood. This can be an extremely rich source of input, and it may be the case that the availability of this source is responsible for the success of many people who succeeded without ESL or bilingual education.

It should be pointed out that even with informal playground interaction, acquisition of English or of any other language takes time. As mentioned earlier, children in informal environments typically show a silent period and may produce very little for several months. Thus, even under the best conditions, language acquisition is slow.

A third possible source of comprehensible input is subject matter, as discussed in the previous section. It will help second language acquisition if children understand enough of the second language to follow the lesson. Non-English proficient children, however, can make it to this level in "Sink or Swim" programs only if they get the comprehensible input somewhere else or if the linguistic level of the class is somehow lowered.

II. Maintain Subject Matter Education

A bilingual program needs to make sure that NEP children do not fall behind in subject matter. This entails, in many cases, instruction in subject matter using the first language as a medium of instruction. Contrary to the view of critics, this does not necessarily mean less acquisition of English as a second language. In fact, *it may mean more acquisition of English*. To see how this is so, we will describe what observance this requirement can do for NEP children.

First, the school system's basic responsibility is providing subject matter instruction so that NEP children can keep up and obtain the tools they need to live in and contribute to society. Second, subject matter instruction plays an important role in cognitive development. Children who fall behind in subject matter because they do not understand the language of instruction may also be missing the stimulation necessary for normal intellectual development.

The third reason is that subject matter knowledge and the cognitive/academic proficiency it encourages will help second language acquisition. It does this by giving children the context or background needed to understand academic input. In other words, children who are not behind in subject matter and who have normal cognitive development will simply understand more of what they hear, both in English language medium classes and in academic or intellectual discussions outside of class. If children understand more, they will acquire more of the language! Very simply, the more cognitively mature and knowledgeable children are about the *topic* of discussion, the better chance they have to acquire the language.

Anyone who has attempted to acquire a second language has had experiences that illustrate this phenomenon: We find it much easier to understand discussions of topics with which we are familiar and find it difficult to eavesdrop and come into conversations in the middle. (In my own case, I find it easy to read and understand discussions on familiar topics with my intermediate French and German, but I understand very little when I overhear a conversation in these languages.) This illustrates the powerful effect context and background knowledge have on our ability to understand a partially acquired language. The major point here is that understanding is a prerequisite for acquisition. Thus, the more context or background we can provide, the more acquisition will take place.

Children who are behind in subject matter and weak in the second language face double trouble. Their failure to understand will not only cause them to fall further behind but they will also fail to make progress in second language acquisition. Knowledge of subject matter, thus, has an indirect but very powerful effect on second language acquisition despite the fact that it may be provided in the students' first language.

Finally, it can be argued that maintaining subject matter, whether in the first or second language, leads to a better attitude toward school in general and higher self-esteem, factors that contribute to a lower affective filter and better acquisition of English, especially when English is presented in a school situation.

We can also suggest a third requirement for bilingual programs, not one motivated by considerations of second language acquisition but by independent motivations. As we shall see, this requirement may be met by programs that meet the first two requirements, at little or no additional cost.

III. Maintain and Develop Children's First Language

As with nearly all other issues in bilingual education, there is pro and con here as well. Some experts argue that we should make real efforts to maintain the first language. Reasons given include:

1. Speakers of languages other than English make a valuable contribution to our society. Since so few native English speakers successfully acquire a second language, it is foolish to waste this natural resource. Campbell expressed this view in a *Los Angeles Times* (September 5, 1980) interview:

> [The] emphasis on "transition" means we will systematically eradicate foreign languages in elementary school, then spend millions to try to develop these same skills in high school and college....That doesn't make much sense.

2. Maintaining the first language and culture of NEP children may help to build pride and counter negative attitudes members of a linguistic minority may have. There is evidence, in fact, that strongly suggests that those language acquirers who do not reject their own language and culture succeed better in second language acquisition than those who have negative attitudes toward their own group (Gardner and Lambert, 1972).

3. Cummins (1978; 1980) argues that in order to keep up in subject matter and maintain normal cognitive development, students need to develop high levels of first language competence. Specifically, they need to develop not only basic interpersonal and communicative skills in the first language (termed BICS) but also "cognitive competence," the ability to "use language effectively as an instrument of thought and represent cognitive operations by means of language" (Cummins, 1978, p. 397). A lack of development of this aspect of first language competence may explain problems some minority children have in school. When the first language is not used extensively and promoted at home, and is not supported at school, low first language skills, according to Cummins, can exert "a limiting effect" on the development of the second language. Majority language children in immersion programs do not have this problem, since their language is highly developed outside school (Cummins, 1978).

Cummins argues that education in the first language develops CALP (Cognitive/Academic Language Proficiency). CALP developed in one language contributes to CALP in any other, according to Cummins; that is, someone who is able to use Spanish for academic purposes will have developed an ability that will be useful in using any other language for academic purposes.

Arguments against first language maintenance have, in general, attempted to counter any of the above arguments but usually insist that since English is the official language of the United States, taxpayers should not have to support the maintenance or development of minority languages.

Another Look at the Options

We can now ask to what extent different programs meet the conditions described in the previous section. In this section, we will see that both theoretical predictions and empirical evidence show that some programs do satisfy the requirements while others do not and that this success or the lack of it depends not only on the program but also on the characteristics of the students. Most important, it will show that research exists, is not conflicting, and that real generalizations can be made about what works and what does not work in bilingual education. Table 4 presents this analysis.

1. We first consider submersion, or "Sink of Swim" programs. According to Table 4, "Sink or Swim" will satisfy the first requirement by providing comprehensible input in the weaker language only when extra ESL is provided (assuming a form of ESL that indeed provides comprehensible input) and/or when children have sufficient contact with input from the outside. In and of itself, "Sink or Swim" may not meet the first requirement, and children in such situations are in danger of not getting the input needed to acquire English. Such situations clearly exist in submersion programs that include children living in *barrios* where there is little if any social interaction among NEP and native English-speaking children.

The second requirement can only be met by "Sink or Swim" if the children's linguistic competence in English develops quickly enough. Children in "Sink or Swim" are playing a dangerous game of catch-up, hoping their competence in English will be high enough to do school work before they are hopelessly behind in subject matter. "Sink or Swim," even under the best conditions, is a risk.

No "Sink or Swim" program, by definition, attempts to meet the third requirement, development of the first language.

2. Immersion programs for majority children do meet all conditions. As discussed earlier, immersion programs have a better chance of supplying comprehensible input in subject matter classes than do "Sink or Swim" programs. Since all children are at the same linguistic level, there

Table 4
REQUIREMENTS TO BE MET BY PROGRAMS FOR NEP CHILDREN AND CURRENT OPTIONS

Requirements for Programs (predicted by theory)	SUBMERSION ("SINK OR SWIM")			IMMERSION		BILINGUAL EDUCATION	
	Only	+ Informal CI	+ ESL	Majority Child	Minority	Concurrent Translation	Ideal Bilingual
1. Comprehensible input in weaker language.	no	yes	yes [b]	yes	yes[c]	no[d]	yes[e]
2. Maintain subject matter.	no	?[a]	?[a]	yes	yes[c]	?[f]	yes
Additional: 3. Maintain and develop first language.	no	no	no	yes	no	?[f]	yes

a: This program will work if second language ability grows fast enough to reach subject matter threshold before children are too far behind.

b: Yes, if the ESL method supplies comprehensible input.

c: *De facto* immersion programs do not succeed as well as bilingual education, however. May be due to attitudes, teacher expectations, low development of first language, and inappropriate materials.

d: Students tune out weaker language in concurrent translation programs (Legarreta, 1979).

e: Yes, if second language skills are adequate for those classes taught in the second language.

f: Will not succeed unless there is adequate input in the second language.

CI = Comprehensible Input

Ideal Bilingual = Subject matter in primary language, plus comprehensible input in English, either as ESL and/or subject matter instruction in comprehensible English.

is less of a tendency to speak over the comprehension level of the students. This helps to satisfy the first and second requirements. The empirical evidence from the research programs evaluating immersion classes confirms that immersion children develop high levels of competence in the second language and do as well as monolinguals in subject matter.

Immersion programs for majority students also meet the third requirement through the use of language arts classes in the first language. Also, many programs provide for increasing use of the first language as a medium of instruction as children progress in school. Of great importance in meeting this requirement is that in immersion programs for majority students, children's first language is the language of the country, home, and playground; there is little chance that this language will be assigned a lower status.

One could argue that a solution for NEP children is an adaptation of the immersion model. This would entail a completely separate curriculum, all taught in English, to groups consisting only of NEP children. Assuming all children start at the same time and on an equal footing with respect to English competence, it would appear to have the linguistic advantage of having a better chance of supplying comprehensible input as compared to "Sink or Swim." Thus, theoretically, we could expect progress both in language acquisition (first requirement) and subject matter (second requirement) even if little or no contact with English-speaking children outside of school was possible. Judging from reports from majority immersion, we would not expect completely native-like English.

It can be maintained, however, that many "Sink or Swim" programs are already *de facto* immersion programs in that they often involve a majority of NEP children and, in some cases, are composed entirely of NEP children (e.g., in certain inner city areas and on American Indian reservations). These programs do not report overwhelming success. There may be good reasons why, however, reasons that explain why minority-child immersion may look good on paper but may not always work.

First, NEP students who enter immersion programs late will face nearly the same problems they face in "Sink or Swim"; they will not understand and may thus fall behind in subject matter and not improve in English. (Late entering bilingual education students will not have this problem; they can be taught in the first language at least until their English develops sufficiently.)

Also, minority immersion teachers may not have the same kinds of expectations as do majority immersion teachers. They may be less able or willing to make input comprehensible and may set higher standards for second language acquisition than are possible under the circumstances. As Cohen (1976) points out, we have a double standard:

> People applaud a majority group child when he can say a few words in the minority language (e.g., at the beginning of an immersion program) and yet they impatiently demand more English from the minority group child. (p. 85)

Thus, many *de facto* immersion programs look more like "Sink or Swim," with inappropriate materials and input that is too complex and incomprehensible.

3. We turn now to the programs categorized as Bilingual Education in Table 4. Let us first consider the program labeled concurrent translation. In this kind of program, concepts are explained in one language and then repeated in the second. This kind of program may not meet the first requirement for the simple reason that children need not pay attention to the explanation in the second or weaker language, and there is no motivation for teachers to attempt to simplify explanations in the second language. Legarreta (1979) noted that in the concurrent translation program, "Teachers reported that the Hispanic students tune out the English and wait to hear the material explained in Spanish" (p. 533). (This phenomenon also predicts, and correctly I think, the failure of bilingual TV to teach the second language. In many programs, a given character will speak either Spanish or English, but it is quite possible to follow the story line by attending only to one language. Similarly, it predicts that Americans will not acquire centigrade temperature systems from the practice of announcing the temperature in both centigrade and fahrenheit. Most people will simply listen to the version they understand.) Concurrent translation can theoretically meet the second and third requirements, however, since subject matter can be explained in the first language and continued use of the L1 helps to ensure its maintenance. In practice, however, concurrent translation often fails to meet these requirements. This is because, despite its intentions, concurrent translation input in many programs often is incomprehensible, most materials are in English, and primary language input often is provided by under-trained aides or Anglophone teachers who have not fully mastered the children's first language.

The Ideal Bilingual program, shown in Table 4, is one in which subject matter is taught in the primary language and some source of comprehensible input in the second language is supplied. This can be in the form of ESL or comprehensible subject matter instruction using English (as in the balanced bilingual program discussed earlier). Such programs have the potential for satisfying all three requirements, even for children who have little access to English outside of school. Balanced bilingual programs will be successful according to the predictions of the theory, especially if the subject matter classes given in the second language are those where more extra-linguistic context is available to aid comprehensible (e.g., math), while those dealing with more abstract topics—topics that typically employ fewer physical props (e.g., social sicence and language arts)—are taught at first in the primary language (Cazden, 1979).

Empirical Evidence

Our analysis based on the three requirements derived from language acquisition theory bring us to these conclusions:

1. "Sink or Swim" programs will not be effective for children with no extra source of comprehensible input.
2. Adding ESL to "Sink or Swim" will help but will not be as effective as bilingual education in encouraging acquisition of English.
3. Bilingual programs in which subject matter is taught in the first language, and a source of comprehensible input is provided in the second language, whether ESL or not, will succeed best.

Despite years of discussion of bilingual education in the professional literature and many studies of different aspects of bilingualism, little research speaks directly to these three predictions. The research that is available, however, is fully consistent with them.

Legarreta (1979) examined the acquisition of English in kindergarten children in three kinds of bilingual programs (balanced, concurrent translation, and concurrent translation + ESL) and two kinds of "Sink or Swim" programs [with and without ESL where the ESL component consisted of "daily, sequenced lessons in English structure and use, presented orally to small groups" (p. 523)]. The overall exposure time was seven months—relatively short for this kind of study, as Swain (1979) points out—and the number of subjects involved was not large. The results, however, are very interesting.

1. Children in all bilingual education programs outperformed "Sink or Swim" children in listening comprehension and conversational competence[2] tests of English, despite the fact that the "Sink or Swim" children had more exposure to English.

---

[2] The test of conversational competence asked children to use the language in real communication; it thus demands more than knowledge of vocabulary and grammar but also tests abilities such as "the ability to be only as explicit as a situation demands, to elaborate, to make inferences about a situation, to be sensitive to social rules of discourse..." (Legarreta, 1979, p. 525).

2. The balanced bilingual program produced the greatest overall gains in both the second language and the first language (Spanish).
3. "Sink or Swim" with ESL outperformed "Sink or Swim" without ESL on listening comprehension testing but not on the test of conversational competence.

Legarreta (1979) concluded that the use of audiolingual style ESL training is "marginally facilitative" (p. 534), while "an alternate immersion bilingual program, with balanced Spanish and English input, really facilitates both Spanish and English acquisition" (p. 534). This appears to be so, but her data support a deeper generalization: Bilingual programs will work when they supply comprehensible input in the second language and adequate, comprehensible subject matter instruction in either language. The balanced program does this, but so do other versions.

Rosier and Farella (1976) report results from a different context that conform to the same underlying principles. They report of the success of bilingual education for Navajo children at the Rock Point Community School in the heart of the Navajo reservation. In 1960, according to Vorih and Rosier (1978), Rock Point ranked at the bottom of eight Indian schools in student achievement. The introduction of intensive ESL in 1963 helped somewhat, but Rock Point sixth graders were still two years behind national norms. In 1967, bilingual education was introduced, with kindergarten children receiving 70 percent of their instruction in Navajo and first and second graders receiving 50 percent in Navajo. Third through sixth graders had 75 percent of their instruction in English. English is taught in early grades "by TESL methods" (Vorih and Rosier, 1978, p. 264). The program can thus be classified as Bilingual Education + ESL.

Analysis of the Rock Point program confirms the validity of our requirements: Students in the bilingual program, with subject matter in the first language, outperformed non-bilingual education students on a reading test of English. Again, the bilingual students actually had *less* exposure to English but apparently acquired more, confirming that it is comprehensible input and not mere exposure that counts.

Research cited by Cummins (1980) provides even more confirmation. As Cummins (1980) reports it:

> Carey and Cummins (1979) reported that grade 5 children from French-speaking home backgrounds in the Edmonton Catholic School System bilingual program [Canada] (80% French, 20% English from K-12) performed at an equivalent level in English skills to anglophone children of the same IQ in either the bilingual or regular English programs. A similar

finding is reported in a large-scale study carried out by Hébert *et al.* (1976) among grades 3, 6 and 9 francophone students in Manitoba. At all grade levels there was a significant positive relationship between percentage of instruction in French (PIF) and French achievement, but no relationship between PIF and English achievement. In other words, francophone students receiving 80% instruction in French and 20% instruction in English did just as well in English as students receiving 80% instruction in English and 20% in French. (p. 184)

Conclusions

We are now ready to return to the issues raised in the first section of this chapter and attempt to give some answers.

1. Does Bilingual Education Retard the Development of English as a Second Language?

Both theory and empirical research tell us that proper bilingual education need not retard the development of second language competence and should, in fact, promote it. Classes taught in the first language help children grow in subject matter knowledge and stimulate cognitive development, which in turn helps second language acquisition by providing children with the extra-linguistic context necessary for comprehension.

2. Are "Sink or Swim" (Submersion) and/or ESL Methods Better?

Obviously, "Sink or Swim" children have more exposure to English, but they do not necessarily have more comprehensible input; it is comprehensible input, not merely "heard" language, that makes language acquisition happen. Thus, "Sink or Swim" classes, at worst, may be providing children only with noise. The results of this are doubly tragic: Children will fall behind in subject matter and will not acquire the second language.

"Sink of Swim" with ESL will fare somewhat better but will work only if children acquire English fast enough, before they are hopelessly behind in subject matter. It may be that in most cases where "Sink or Swim" worked, children had rich comprehensible input from playmates outside the classroom.

3. How Should ESL Be Taught

Second language acquisition research strongly suggests that methodology *per se* is not the issue: By whatever name, children need comprehensible input to acquire English. This can come in the form of ESL classes taught according to a method that provides such input (e.g., Terrell's Natural Approach) or subject matter taught in comprehensible English.

4. Is There a Place for Immersion for NEP Children?

Theoretically, immersion for NEP children appears to meet the three requirements. Yet, results of *de facto* immersion programs in the United States are not encouraging. This could be due to several factors, including inadequate development of the first language, as suggested by Cummins (1978), differing teacher expectations the failure of late-entering students to obtain comprehensible input, and inappropriate materials.

5. Which Bilingual Education Options Are Better for Language Acquisition?

There are several bililngual education options that will satisfy the requirements given in Table 4 and earlier in the chapter. Balanced bilingual education programs will do this as long as those subjects taught in the second language are comprehensible. There is nothing magic, however, in the 50 percent figure: It need not be the case that exactly one-half of the program be in one language and one half in the other. What counts is that the requirements are met and that NEP students receive enough comprehensible input to improve in their weaker language. This has happened with as little as 20 percent input in the second language in some programs.

Several issues of course remain unsolved, and in a real sense they always will be. As is typical of scientific reasoning, we have discussed hypotheses and some evidence that supports them. We have not provided proof, nor can we. What we have tried to show is that there is substantial information available about how language is acquired, that it is certainly enough to formulate hypotheses, that these hypotheses shed light on some of the basic issues in bilingual education, and that the field is not in a state of helpless confusion. Researchrs are evaluating children's progress, adding to their knowledge of language acquisition, and using this knowledge to better serve the children they study and those who will come after them.

REFERENCES

Brown, R., Cazden, Courtney, & Bellugi, U. (1973). The child's grammar from I to III. In C. Ferguson, & D. Slobin (Eds.), *Studies in child language development* (pp. 295-333). New York: Holt, Rinehart and Winston.

Campbell, Russell (1980, September 5). *Los Angeles Times.*

Cazden, Courtney B. (1979). Curriculum language contexts for bilingual education. In Eugéne J. Briere (Ed.), *Language development in a bilingual setting* (pp. 129-138).

Cohen, Andrew D. (1976). The case for partial or total immersion education. In António Simões (Ed.), *The bilingual child* (pp. 65-89). New York: Academic Press.

Cohen, Andrew D., & Swain, Merrill (1976, March). Bilingual education: The "immersion" model in the North American context. *TESOL Quarterly, 10*(1), 45-53.

Cummins, James (1978). Educational implications of mother tongue maintenance in minority language groups. *The Canadian Modern Language Review, 34,* 395-416.

Cummins, James (1980, June). The cross-lingual dimensions of language proficiency: Implications for bilingual education and optimal age issue. *TESOL Quarterly, 14*(2), 175-187.

Dulay, Heidi C., & Burt, Marina K. (1977). Remarks on creativity in second language acquisition. In Marina K. Burt, Heidi C. Dulay, & M. Finnochiaro (Eds.), *Viewpoints on English as a second language* (pp. 95-126). New York: Regents.

Dulay, Heidi C., & Burt, Marina K. (1978, June). Some guidelines for the assessment of oral language proficiency and dominance. *TESOL Quarterly, 12*(2), 177-192.

Dulay, Heidi C., Burt, Marina K., & Krashen, Stephen (1982). *The language two.* New York: Oxford University Press.

Elkind, David (1970). *Children and adolescents: Interpretive essays on Jean Piaget.* New York: Oxford University Press.

Gardner, Robert C., & Lambert, Wallace E. (1972). *Attitudes and motivation in second language learning.* Rowley, MA: Newbury House.

Hatch, Evelyn M. (1978). Discourse analysis and second language acquisition. In E. Hatch (Ed.), *Second language acquisition: A book of readings.* Rowley, MA: Newbury House.

Krashen, Stephen (1981). *Second language acquisition and second language learning.* London: Pergamon Press.

Krashen, Stephen (1982a). Accounting for child-adult differences in second language rate and attainment. In Stephen Krashen, R. Scarcella, & M. Long (Eds.), *Child-adult differences in second language acquisition.* Rowley, MA: Newbury House.

Krashen, Stephen (1982b). *Principles and practice in second language acquisition.* New York: Pergamon Press.

Krashen, Stephen, Long, Michael A., & Scarcella, Robin C. (1979, December). Age, rate and eventual attainment in second language acquisition. *TESOL Quarterly, 13*(4), 573-582.

Lambert, Wallace E., & Tucker, Richard G. (1972). *Bilingual education of children: The St. Lambert experiment.* Rowley, MA: Newbury House.

Legaretta, Dorothy (1979, December). The effects of program models on language acquisition by Spanish-speaking children. *TESOL Quarterly, 13*(4), 521-534.

Lopez, Rosa Maria (1980, September 19). *Los Angeles Times.*

Los Angeles Times. (1980, September 19).

Newmark, L. (1966). How not to interfere with language learning. *International Review of American Linguistics, 40,* 77-83.

Rosier, Paul, & Farella, Merilyn. (1976, December).   Bilingual education at Rock Point—Some early results. *TESOL Quarterly, 10*(4), 379-388.

Scarcella, Robin, & Higa, C. (1982). Input and age differences in second language acquisition. In Stephen Krashen, Robin Scarcella, & Michael A. Long (Eds.), *Child-adult differences in second language acquisition.* Rowley, MA: Newbury House.

Selinker, Larry, Swain, Merrill, & Dumas, Guy (1975, June). The interlanguage hypthesis extended to children. *Language Learning, 25*(1), 139-152.

Snow, Catherine E., & Hoefnagel-Hohle, Marian (1978, December). The critical period for language acquisition: Evidence from second language learning. *Child Development, 49*(4), 1114-1128.

Stevick, Earl W. (1976). *Memory, meaning, and method.* Rowley, MA: Newbury House.

Swain, Merrill (1979). Bilingual education: Research and its implications. In C. Yorio, K. Perkins, & J. Schachter (Eds.), *On TESOL '79.* Washington, DC: TESOL.

Swain, Merrill (1978, May). French immersion: Early late or partial? *Canadian Modern Language Review, 34,* 577-585.

Terrell, Tracy D. (1977, November). A natural approach to second language acquisition and learning. *Modern Language Journal, 41*(7), 325-337.

Terrell, Tracy D. (1981). The natural approach in bilingual education. In *Schooling and language minority students: A theoretical framework* (1st ed.), Los Angeles, CA: Evaluation, Dissemination and Assessment Center, California State University, Los Angeles.

Trombley, William (1980a, September 7). Bilingual education: Even the experts are confused, *Los Angeles Times.*

Trombley, William (1980b, September 4). Is bilingual education able to do its job? *Los Angeles Times.*

Vorih, Lillian, & Rosier, Paul. Rock Point community school: An example of a Navajo-English bilingual elementary school program. *TESOL Quarterly, 12*(3), 263-269.

Part Two
Strategies for Implementation

Communicative Approaches to Second Language Acquisition: From Oral Language Development into the Core Curriculum and L₂ Literacy

Alan N. Crawford

Theoretical Bases

English-as-a-second-language instruction is the keystone of programs to meet the academic needs of language minority students. It is especially important where only small numbers of students speak the same mother tongue or where a lack of trained personnel and appropriate instructional materials prevents the implementation of programs of bilingual education. It is also the major element of those full bilingual education programs where the native language is used for academic instruction while students develop sufficient English to benefit from academic instruction in their new second language.

The foundation for communicative approaches to second language acquisition is based on concepts, theories, and hypotheses that have converged around the interaction of constructivist notions about making meaning. Vygotsky (1978) defined the zone of proximal development as "the distance between the actual developmental level as determined by independent problem solving and the level of potential development as determined through problem solving under adult guidance in collaboration with more capable peers" (p. 86). This key concept emphasizes the social dimension of learning that results from the support of parents, teachers, older siblings, and other caregivers. The collective wisdom of the cooperative learning group has an obvious role here, as well.

The concept of scaffolding involves the temporary support provided by teachers when students are engaged in a task within the zone of proximal development. Bruner (1978) described scaffolding as a temporary launching platform designed to support and encourage children's language development to higher levels of complexity. Pearson (1985) described the temporary nature of scaffolding as the gradual release of responsibility. Good teachers intuitively use such scaffolding strategies as questioning, prompts, illustrations and other visual resources, demonstrations, dramatization, gestures, comprehension monitoring, graphic organizers, and rephrasing. These strategies enable students to sustain participation in learning activities.

Approximation is a related process in which students imitate language and test hypotheses about it. The process of approximation underlies oral and written language in that students are acquiring new skills and understandings within the context of authentic wholes. Students exhibit behaviors in which they approximate the language behavior of their models, growing closer and closer to their levels of proficiency. In his view of successive approximation, Holdaway (1979) described the process as one in which Vygotsky's adults and more capable peers use the output from learner responses to construct, adjust, and finally eliminate the scaffolding that permits learning to progress.

It is also important to examine the dichotomy between skills-based and constructivist models of instruction. Skills-based models focus on the disassembly or fragmentation of curricular elements so that isolated skills and concepts can be mastered within a linear paradigm, referred to as direct instruction. A constructivist view of instruction conversely focuses on the construction of meaning, using what the learner already knows and combining it with new ideas to be integrated. It is learner-based, an important factor in working with the students from diverse backgrounds who are often at-risk in any case. Within the constructivist view, language acquisition is embedded in function. Skills are taught, as needed, within a meaningful context, not in an isolated, artificial, and fragmented manner.

The purpose of this chapter is to link the constructivist paradigm to communicative approaches to second language acquisition and to related instructional strategies for English language learners. In addition, we will extend the third stage of Terrell's natural approach, the emergence of speech, into more advanced levels of language development. This will include access to the core curriculum through sheltered instruction in English, which is referred to as specially designed academic instruction in English (SDAIE) in California.

Finally, the development of literacy in English will be examined. The approach and strategies presented will reflect a constructivist view of reading instruction. They will be consistent with communicative approaches to second language acquisition and with Krashen's underlying hypotheses about that process. The processes of second language acquisition, content/language integration in the core curriculum, and a constructivist view of literacy and the language arts are unified in this convergence.

A Historical Perspective

Until recent years, most students in the public schools have tried to learn a second language using such grammar-based approaches as the grammar-translation and audiolingual methods. The grammar-translation approach is most familiar to us as the one used in the foreign language courses in high school and college in the 1950's and even later (Chastain, 1975). Vocabulary was learned in terms of the first language from lists where teachers paired words in the foreign language with their English counterparts. Students studied the grammar of the new language again in terms of their own. The first language was always the window through which students viewed, and contrasted, their new second language. Students rarely became functional in that language because of the classes they took. At best, they scored well on tests of grammar, translated with difficulty, and read with halting comprehension.

The audiolingual approach is rooted in structural linguistics and behavioral psychology. This combination results in a methodology based on a grammatical sequence, with mimicry and the memorization of pattern drills, but without the heavy grammatical analysis of the grammar-translation approach (Chastain, 1975). The audiolingual approach is characterized by the following:

- Based on the unconscious mastery of sequenced grammatical forms

- Learning as the result of teaching patterned oral drills

- Emphasis is on correct oral production of grammatical forms in response to oral stimuli

- Language skills acquired in the natural sequence of listening, speaking, reading, and writing

- No reference to the primary language during instruction (Finocchiaro, 1974)

The typical audiolingual lesson consists of a dialogue followed by a series of related pattern drills. The purpose of the dialogue is to present the meaning of the vocabulary or grammatical element being taught within the context of a real situation. For example, a dialogue to introduce the grammatical concept of prepositions of position might appear as follows:

Rosa: *Where is the ball, Diego?*

Diego: *It's on the table, Rosa.*

Rosa: *No, it fell under the table.*

Diego: *Pick it up and put it in the box, Rosa.*

This dialogue would be taught using a repetition drill, illustrating it with pictures or dramatizing with actual objects and students. Students would then practice the new elements using pattern drills that develop a habitual response through repetition. Based upon a stimulus or cue from the teacher, the students respond, making one incremental change in the pattern at a time. They usually begin by responding as a total group. As they gain confidence, smaller groups respond separately, until individual students are confident enough to respond alone. The result is usually an artificial and boring program based on a grammatical continuum that does not reflect the sequence in which elements are naturally acquired.

The findings of recent research have resulted in major changes in educators' conceptions of how a second language is acquired and how this acquisition is best promoted in the elementary and secondary classroom. There has been a major paradigm shift away from the grammar-based approaches to language acquisition and toward those we call *communicative*. This change has been particularly apparent in the second language acquisition of English language learners.

Underlying Principles of Communicative Approaches

Krashen's Hypotheses

Krashen (1982) has offered five important hypotheses that underlie current practice in most communicative approaches to second language acquisition.

The Acquisition-Learning Hypothesis. In his acquisition-learning hypothesis, Krashen illustrates the difference between the infant's subconscious acquisition of the primary language and the high school foreign language student's conscious learning of a second language. We acquire language subconsciously, with a *feel* for correctness. Learning a language, on the other hand, is a conscious process that involves knowing grammatical rules. Of course, the infant is almost always successful in acquiring language, while the high school foreign language learner is usually not.

Gee (1992) has expanded Krashen's concept of acquisition by incorporating a social factor that encompasses Vygotsky's "zone of proximal development" and also the concept of approximation:

> Acquisition is a process of acquiring something subconsciously by exposure to models, a process of trial and error, and practice within social groups, without formal teaching. It happens in natural settings that are meaningful and functional in the sense that acquirers know that they need to acquire the thing they are exposed to in order to function and that they in fact want to so function. (p. 113)

The Natural Order Hypothesis. According to Krashen's natural order hypothesis, grammatical structures are acquired in a predictable sequence, with certain elements usually acquired before others. He has concluded that the orders for first and second language acquisition are similar, but not identical. It is important to note, however, that Krashen does not conclude that sequencing the teaching of language according to this natural order is either necessary or desirable. The content of grammatical approaches to second language acquisition is organized around sequences of grammatical structures. The content learned when the primary language is acquired in infancy is whatever the infant needs and is interested in at that time.

The Input Hypothesis. Among Krashen's most important contributions is his input hypothesis. He concludes that growth in language occurs when we receive comprehensible input, or input that contains structure at a slightly higher level than what we already understand. The input hypothesis corresponds to Vygotsky's zone of proximal development. The context of the input provides clues to maintain the integrity of the message. According to the input hypothesis, a grammatical sequence is not needed. The structures are provided and practiced as a natural part of the comprehensible input that the learner receives, much as it occurs with infants acquiring their primary language. Krashen characterizes this comprehensible input as caretaker speech about the *here and now.*

The Monitor Hypothesis. Krashen's related monitor hypothesis describes how the learner's conscious monitor or editor functions to make corrections as language is produced in speaking or writing. Several conditions are necessary for the application of the monitor: (a) time to apply it, a situation not present in most ordinary oral discourse, especially in classroom settings; (b) a focus on the form or correctness of what is said, rather than on the content of the message; and (c) knowledge of the grammatical rule to be applied. These conditions serve to illustrate why so few students learn to understand and speak a foreign language in a grammar-translation or audiolingual high school or university foreign language course.

The Affective Filter Hypothesis. In his affective filter hypothesis, Krashen concludes that several affective variables are associated with success in second language acquisition. These include high motivation, self-confidence and a positive self-image, and low anxiety in the learning environment. Krashen (1981) relates the input hypothesis to the silent period, the interval before speech in either the primary or second language in which the learner listens to and develops an understanding of the language before beginning to produce language.

Other Underlying Principles

Results from recent research have led to other major changes in educators' conceptions of how a second language is acquired and how this acquisition is best facilitated in the elementary and secondary classroom.

Similarities between Primary and Second Language Acquisition

An important similarity between primary and second language acquisition is the formation of an incomplete and incorrect interlanguage by both primary and second language learners (Selinker, Swain, & Dumas, 1975). Most children move through similar stages of development in this incomplete language. It is often called telegraphic speech because it resembles the incomplete patterns we use to carry meaning in telegrams (Terrell, 1982). Selinker, Swain and Dumas point out the danger that this interlanguage may become fossilized, stopping short of its continued development into fluency in the absence of native language speakers.

In a related study, Ervin-Tripp (1974) conducted a meta-analysis of research comparing first and second language acquisition. She found that the development of syntax by second language learners parallels the order of development of primary language learners. Dulay and Burt (1974b) similarly found that learners from diverse language backgrounds tend to acquire English grammatical structures in approximately the same order. Chinese and Spanish-speaking children, for example, acquired the copula at approximately the same stage of language development, even though the copula is present in Spanish, but not in Chinese. Their conclusions lead to questions about the actual effects of interference from the primary language. In a related study, they found that fewer than 5% of children's errors in the second language could be attributed to interference from the primary language (Dulay & Burt, 1974a). This leads us to additional reservations about the use of an ESL curriculum based on grammatical sequences.

Chamot (1981) pointed out another similarity, the lack of student interest in abstract language concepts. Instead, students should use language for functional purposes based upon immediate needs and interests, just as infants do.

The role of correction is also similar in both primary and second language acquisition. According to Terrell (1982) and Krashen and Terrell (1983), we should view correction as a negative reinforcer that can raise the affective filter and the level of anxiety in a language classroom, whether with children or adults. When there is no interference with comprehension, the correction of errors has no more place in the second language acquisition program than it does when infants acquire their primary language. Caregivers may expand incorrect or incomplete forms, such as *Kitty gots four feets*, and say *Yes, Kitty has four feet*. There is little evidence, however, that this expansion has any positive effect.

These similarities between primary and second language acquisition are not consistent with either the grammar-translation or the audiolingual approach. Children learning their first language don't rely on grammatical rules or on systematic acquisition of vocabulary. With its emphasis on early production instead of a silent period, on correct production instead of an acceptable, though immature and incomplete, interlanguage, and on grammatical sequence instead of function and communicative competence, the audiolingual approach bears little resemblance to the way primary or second languages are successfully acquired.

Other Factors Associated with Second Language Acquisition

Krashen, Long and Scarcella (1979) found that adults developed second language proficiency faster than children, that older children developed faster than younger children, and that those who had natural exposure to second languages during childhood tended to be more proficient than those who began as adults. Cummins (1980) also concluded that older students acquired second language cognitive/ academic language proficiency (CALP) more rapidly than younger students because of the greater development of CALP in the primary language and its interdependence with CALP in the developing second language.

Collier (1987) examined the relationship between the age of English language learners and their acquisition of English. She found that students who entered the ESL program at ages eight to eleven were the fastest achievers and that they reached the 50th percentile in all subject areas within two to five years. The lowest achievers entered the program at ages five to seven, and they were one to three years behind students from eight to eleven years of age. Students from twelve to fifteen years of age had the most difficulty acquiring English. It was projected that they would need from six to eight years of instruction to reach grade-level norms in academic achievement.

When Collier (1989) later analyzed other research on age and academic achievement in English, she found that students who had primary language academic instruction, whether in English or another native language, generally required from four to seven years to reach national norms on standardized tests in reading, social studies, and science, and as little as two years in mathematics and language arts, including spelling, punctuation, and grammar. She also found that those students from ages eight to twelve who brought at least two years of schooling from their home country in their primary language needed from five to seven years to reach the same levels of achievement in English reading, social studies, and science, and two years in mathematics and language arts. Young students with no schooling in the primary language from either the home country or the new host country needed seven to ten years of instruction in reading, social studies, and science. Adolescent students with no second language instruction and no opportunity for continued academic work in the primary language were projected, in the main, to drop out of school before reaching national norms, both those with a good academic background and those with interrupted schooling.

Ervin-Tripp (1974) concluded that older language learners are more effective because they take advantage of the generic similarities of languages in learning the second one. They learn new symbolic representations for concepts and ideas they already have in their primary language. They have better skills in managing memory heuristics, and they have greater capacity to solve problems and form generalizations.

Communicative Approaches to Second Language Acquisition

The implications of Krashen's hypotheses and of related similarities between first and second language acquisition are that approaches to second language acquisition should provide comprehensible input, focus on relevant and interesting topics instead of grammatical sequences, and provide for a silent period without forcing early production. There are approaches to second language acquisition that meet these criteria. They are categorized as communicative approaches, and those most appropriate for elementary and secondary classrooms include the total physical response method and the natural approach.

The Total Physical Response Method

Asher's (1969; 1979; 1982) total physical response or TPR method is an important communicative approach in the initial stages of second language acquisition. The TPR method provides for comprehensible input, a silent period, and a focus on relevant content, rather than on grammar or form. The focus of TPR is on physical responses to verbal commands, such as *Stand up* and *Put your book on the desk.* Because little emphasis is given to production, the level of anxiety is low.

Lessons can be given to small groups or to an entire class. In the beginning, the teacher models one-word commands. This is done first with a few students, then with the entire group, then with a few students again, and finally with individual students. The teacher would say, for example, *Sit,* and then model by sitting down. Later, the teacher would issue the command without modeling. As the students' levels of language increase, the teacher begins to use two and three-word commands, such as *Stand up* and *Bring the book. The students* demonstrate their understanding by physically carrying out the commands. The order of commands is varied so that the students cannot anticipate which is next. Old commands are combined with new ones in order to provide for review. Whenever the students do not appear to comprehend, the teacher returns to modeling. After a silent period of approximately ten hours of listening to commands and physically responding to them, a student then typically reverses roles with the teacher and begins to give those same commands to other students. It is important for the teacher to maintain a playful mood during classroom activities.

The total physical response approach can be extended to higher levels of proficiency by using the technique of nesting commands. The teacher might say the following:

Manuel, take the pencil to Enrique, or open the door.

Esperanza, if Manuel took the pencil to Enrique, stand up. If he opened the door, close your eyes.

A high level of understanding is necessary to carry out such commands, but no oral production is needed. Parents of young children will recognize that their infants can understand and carry out such commands long before they begin to speak themselves.

The Natural Approach

Terrell's (1977) original concept of the natural approach provided for three major characteristics: (a) classroom activities were focused on acquisition, that is, communication with a content focus leading to an unconscious absorption of language with a feel for correctness, but not an explicit knowledge of grammar; (b) oral errors were not directly corrected; and (c) learners could respond in the target language, the native language, or a mixture of the two.

Krashen and Terrell (1983) later presented four principles that underlie the natural approach to language acquisition. The first is that comprehension precedes production, which leads to several teacher behaviors: the teacher always uses the target language, focuses on a topic of interest to the students, and helps the students maintain comprehension.

The second principle is that production emerges in stages ranging from non-verbal responses to complex discourse. Students can begin to speak when they are ready, and speech errors are not corrected unless they interfere with communication.

The third principle is that the curriculum consists of communicative goals. Topics of interest comprise the syllabus, not a grammatical sequence. Finally, activities must lead to low anxiety, a lowering of students' affective filter. The teacher accomplishes this by establishing and maintaining a good rapport and friendly relations with and among students.

Terrell's (1981) natural approach is based on three stages of language development: (1) preproduction (comprehension); (2) early production; and (3) emergence of speech.

The Preproduction Stage. The teacher provides topical, interesting, and relevant comprehensible input in the first stage, which closely parallels Asher's TPR approach. The teacher speaks slowly, using gestures to maintain comprehension. Students may respond with physical behaviors, shaking or nodding their heads, pointing at pictures or objects, or saying yes and no. It is important that input is dynamic, lively, fun, and comprehensible. Using a pet turtle, the teacher might say:

> *This is a turtle. His name is Herman. Is he red? Who wants to hold him?* [Hand to student.] *Who has the turtle? Does Tran have the turtle? Yes, he does. Does Rosa have the turtle? No, she doesn't.*

This basic input can be repeated with other objects in the classroom. We can also use large-format illustrations and posters. For example:

> *Here is a picture of a circus. Are there animals in the picture? Yes. How many animals are there? Yes, four. Point to the lion. Where is the elephant?*

If each student in the group is given a different illustration, the teacher might provide such input as:

> *Who has a picture of a boat? Yes, Eloy, you do. Is the boat large? Eloy, give your picture to Zipour. Who has a picture of an airplane? Yes, Araceli has a picture of an airplane.*

These examples include three primary preproduction techniques: using TPR, using TPR and naming objects, and pictures. The required responses include movement, pointing, nodding or shaking the head, and using the names of other students in the group. We should remember that nodding the head for an affirmative response and shaking it for a negative one are not appropriate in all cultures. Students may also have to acquire these nonverbal behaviors.

Since the emphasis at this stage is on listening comprehension, verbal responses in the primary language are also acceptable. This may be a problem if the teacher is unable to understand the students' mother tongue, but they usually find a way to help the teacher understand.

Classroom props allow for relevant expansion of this and subsequent stages of the natural approach. Any manipulative or concrete object is helpful, including flannel boards and puppets. Large colorful illustrations, such as those in travel posters and big books, are also very helpful. Sources of free color illustrations include calendars, outdated or otherwise, large posters available from textbook and trade book publishers, food group posters available from the National Dairy Council, and colorful illustrations in the annual reports of many large corporations, usually available on request through announcements in major business magazines.

The Early Production Stage. In the stage of early production, the student begins to produce one-word utterances, lists, and finally two-word answers, such as *little dog* and *in house.* Some of the latter, such as *me like* and *no want,* are grammatically incorrect or incomplete. Krashen and Terrell (1983) indicate that error correction has a negative effect that raises anxiety level and is not helpful. According to Crawford (1986), we should view these errors as immature language, not incorrect language. In the presence of good models, most of these errors will disappear in time, just as they do among infants developing their primary language.

Several types of questions can be used to elicit the one and two-word responses within the reach of students as they transition into the early production stage:

Question Type	Question
Yes/no	*Are you hungry?*
Here/there	*Where is the picture of the boat?*
Either/or	*Is this a pen or a book?*
One-word	*How many apples are there?*
Two-word	*What animals are in the picture?*

As in the preproduction stage, these strategies should be integrated into activities that permit a variety of responses, ranging from physical responses from those not ready for production, to brief oral responses from those who are.

> *Does Jaime have a picture of a tree? [Yes.] Is the tree red? [No.] Who has a picture of an airplane? [Rigoberto.] Does it go fast or slow? [Fast.] Where is the picture of the tree? [There.] Look at Bo-Gay's picture. How many children are there? [Three.] What are they doing? [Playing ball.]*

As the students begin production, conversations should increasingly require one-word responses. Within the same conversation, the teacher can address questions calling for longer responses to those children who are ready.

> *Sven, show us your picture. What is in Sven's picture? [Hamburger.] Yes, it is a hamburger. What is on the hamburger? [Catsup.] Is there apple on the hamburger? [No. Laughter.] What else is on the hamburger? [Lettuce, mayonnaise.] How does it taste? [Good.] What do you like with a hamburger? [French fries. Soda.] I like a milk shake with mine.*

Terrell suggests other formats to elicit language from the students.

Activity	Example
Add-on sentence	*I like ice cream.*
	I like ice cream and cake.
	I like ice cream, cake, and . . .
Open-end sentence	*Playing basketball is . . .*

He also recommends the use of oral lists, interviews, and the discussion of charts, tables, graphs, newspaper advertisements, and pictures.

The Emergence of Speech Stage. During the stage of emergence of speech, students begin to produce structures that are longer, more complex, richer in vocabulary, and more correct. This production proceeds from three-word phrases to sentences, dialogue, extended discourse, and narrative. At this stage, Terrell recommends such activities as preference ranking, games, group discussions, skits, art and music, radio, TV, filmstrips, pictures, readings, and filling out forms.

Terrell (1981) suggests three general techniques to focus students in this stage on using language instead of on form: games; affective-humanistic activities; and problem-solving tasks. Games are helpful for providing comprehensible input in low anxiety situations. He recommends some of the affective-humanistic activities suggested by Galyean (1977; 1980) (see section below), including dialogues about personal topics, such as weekend activities, interviews, preference ranking, and the preparation of personal charts, tables, and graphs. An example of a chart that incorporates preference ranking follows below:

Favorite Sandwiches

Name	Peanut butter	Tuna	Lunch meat	Mayonnaise	Mustard	Jelly	Cheese
Mae Lin	X					X	
Duc		X		X			
Alfredo			X				X
Rousanna							
Inna			X				X

Does Duc like tuna? [Yes.] What kind of sandwich does Inna like? [Lunchmeat with cheese.] How many like cheese on their sandwich? [Two, Alfredo and Inna.] How does Rousanna like her sandwich? [She doesn't like sandwiches.] Which students like the same kind of sandwich? [Alfredo and Inna.] Is there something that no one likes? What is it? [Yes. Mustard.] How do we know? [Nobody wants mustard.]

Not only is the chart a valuable source of comprehensible input, but the process of gathering the data for the chart is, as well.

Krashen and Terrell (1983) describe several other problem-solving activities. One is a task analysis of a daily activity, such as washing a car or getting ready for school. Teachers and students can organize other information into charts and tables for problem-solving activities, including student class schedules, physical characteristics and clothing, airline, bus and train schedules, and department sale information. Maps of the community are particularly effective and also very useful for preparing students to live in a new environment. In addition, students can work on developing speech for particular situations, such as ordering food in a restaurant, purchasing clothing, and making appointments. Analyzing advertisements is another worthwhile problem-solving activity. Terrell (1981) also suggests that we can provide comprehensible input in such a way that students can acquire extensive English proficiency through studying science, social studies, music, art, and mathematics.

The Curriculum of a Communicative Program

Teachers who would advocate teaching the first person present indicative tense to a child in a second grade classroom would be incredulous at the suggestion that a parent teach the same concept to a three-year-old at home. Of course, both children can use the tense correctly, and neither as the result of instruction. This leads us to conclude, as do Krashen, Terrell, Galyean, and others, that the content of second language acquisition programs should be based primarily on content, not on grammatical sequence.

Topical Curricula

Under the assumption that needed language structures will emerge and be acquired naturally within the context of topical lessons, a communicative ESL curriculum is usually organized around a set of topics in order to ensure the introduction of new vocabulary and concepts of interest and utility to the students. Grammatical sequences also appear as a subcategory of some communicative curricula, as we shall see below.

Terrell (1981) has suggested that, at the elementary and secondary levels, a grammatical continuum is not appropriate in the language acquisition process. He recommends the use of a topical curriculum that de-emphasizes the form or correctness of the message and that emphasizes instead its content. He suggests that the content should be limited to the following until students demonstrate production of more than one-word responses: following commands for classroom management; names of articles in the classroom; colors and description words for articles in the classroom; words for people and family relationships; descriptions of students; clothing; school areas; school activities; names of objects in the school that are not in the classroom; and foods, especially those eaten at school.

Later in the acquisition process, topics of interest to students would include the students' families, their homes and neighborhoods, their favorite activities, and pleasant experiences they have had. They also enjoy discussing their preferences about food, colors, television programs and films, and other aspects of their lives.

Like Terrell, Asher (1982) advocates the use of a topical curriculum. He suggests, however, that it should be organized into behaviors, objects that these behaviors are acted upon, and qualifiers or modifiers, such as adverbials and adjectivals, as outlined below:

Behaviors	Objects	Qualifiers
action verbs	nouns	adverbials
		prepositions
		adjectivals
		possessives

For example, the teacher might use the behavior *put*, the object book, and the qualifier *on the table* to produce the command, *Put the book on the table*. According to Asher, these elements can be combined and presented in a variety of creative and interesting ways.

Chamot (1983) offers several recommendations that very effectively tie the ESL program to the core curriculum. She suggests that vocabulary and concepts from content areas of the curriculum be used in ESL activities and that reading and writing instruction in English be increased for older students, especially those with literacy skills in the native language. Instead of focusing on the correct pronunciation of words in oral reading, teachers should emphasize silent reading comprehension, including extensive experiences with expository text in the content areas of the core curriculum.

Grammar in the Communicative Approach Curriculum

In spite of the advocacy of topical curricula by most authorities in the communicative approaches, some do find a place for grammatical structures. In his most recent work, Terrell (1991) reexamined the place of grammar in communicative approaches with respect to adults. He postulated that, instead of relying on input to produce language following the silent period, many adults rely on output, indicating that grammar may have more importance than previously thought in their language development. Indeed, most of us who work in fields related to language acquisition recognize our own need for references to the grammar of any language we attempt to acquire.

Terrell concluded that, for some adults, we should consider using grammar instruction as an advance organizer to help language learners make sense of input. He also recommended using meaning-form focus in activities that contain many examples of a single grammatical relationship, that is, activities in which one grammatical concept is intentionally exemplified repeatedly, as described by Rutherford and Sharwood-Smith (1985). Terrell further suggested that, by using the monitor, learners might acquire their own output, instead of only acquiring comprehensible input from others. Although he addressed this discussion to adults, it has obvious implications for more capable secondary school English language learners. Teachers should give serious consideration to the expressed wishes of those of their students who request some type of referencing to grammar.

Access to the Core Curriculum through Sheltered Instruction in English (SDAIE)

A major issue in the acquisition of English as a second language is the extent of access to the core curriculum during that process. In a study of programs for limited-English-proficient students in California, Berman et al. (1992) concluded that most English language learners, especially those at the intermediate and senior high school levels, did not have access to aspects of the core curriculum that would permit them to receive a diploma. Instead, they were clustered in what was characterized as "a steady diet of ESL classes."

Many communicative strategies can be adapted to provide access to this core curriculum through a scaffolding process called sheltered instruction in English. It is referred to as specially designed academic instruction in English (SDAIE) in California. The topics treated in this highly contextualized instruction are the important content areas of the core curriculum. It should be emphasized that sheltered instruction is a strategy to be used with intermediate English language learners. If it were used as a beginning strategy, it would be submersion instruction.

Strategies for Providing Access to the Core Curriculum

Sheltered instruction in English in the content areas of the curriculum adds substantially to the knowledge and vocabulary that students need as a base for comprehension as they read and think in any language (Krashen, 1985). These strategies are consistent with the philosophy of communicative approaches to second language acquisition, and they additionally provide access to academic areas of the curriculum in such a way that communication is maintained.

Cummins (1981) provides a set of intersecting continua that are very useful for conceptualizing the issue of balancing the complexity of curriculum content with demands on language proficiency. The vertical continuum extends from cognitively undemanding to cognitively demanding, ranging, for example, from a conversation about what students ate for lunch on the cognitively undemanding side to a third grade mathematics lesson about the distributive principle of multiplication on the cognitively demanding side.

Cummins' intersecting horizontal continuum extends from context-embedded to context reduced, ranging, for example, from a science lesson on classification taught with concrete manipulatives on the context-embedded side to an abstract lecture/discussion about the principles of democracy on the context-reduced side. Sheltered instruction in English will be most effective in subject areas of the curriculum that can be presented concretely, such as mathematics, science, art, music, and physical education. Although there are aspects of social studies that can be taught concretely, such as geography and map skills, there are so many abstract concepts taught that instruction in this area might well be delayed until students acquire additional English proficiency.

The purpose of the sheltered instruction approach to the core curriculum in English is to provide a focus on context-embedded activities, ensuring that comprehensible input is provided while treating increasingly cognitively demanding aspects of the core curriculum. The Los Angeles Unified School District (1985) prepared a set of English-language teaching strategies that provide the necessary scaffolding in content areas for intermediate English language learners. They recommend that teachers simplify input by speaking slowly and enunciating clearly, using a controlled vocabulary within simple language structures. Where possible, they should use cognates and avoid the extensive use of idiomatic expressions. They suggest that teachers make frequent use of nonverbal language, including gestures, facial expressions, and dramatization. They also recommend the use of manipulatives and concrete materials, such as props, graphs, visuals, overhead transparencies, bulletin boards, maps, and realia. Comprehension should be maintained through extensive use of gestures, dramatization, illustrations, and manipulatives. Teachers should check frequently for understanding by asking for confirmation of comprehension, by asking students to clarify, repeat, and expand, and by using a variety of questioning formats. Schifini (1985) recommends a focus on student-centered activities, especially at the secondary level where lecturing and textbook use predominate.

Richard-Amato and Snow (1992) provide valuable strategies for content-area teachers of English language learners. For mainstream teachers, they recommend providing a warm learning environment, recording lectures and talks on tape for later review, rewriting some key parts of text material at lower levels, asking native-English-speaking students to share notes with English language learners, and avoiding competitive grading until students have achieved sufficient English proficiency to complete successfully with native speakers. In addition to strategies suggested by LAUSD and Schifini above, they recommend that teachers reinforce key concepts frequently, that they establish consistent routines in the classroom, that they provide sufficient wait time for students to respond to questions, that corrections be in the form of expansion and mirroring in correct form, and that they avoid forcing students to speak until they are ready. They also suggest that teachers frequently summarize and review, demonstrate that they acknowledge and value the language and culture that students bring to the classroom, and make effective use of teaching assistants or aides who speak their students' native language.

There are several other strategies that provide scaffolding for English language learners in sheltered instruction activities in English. The highly contextualized interactions that take place in cooperative learning can make the difference between what Krashen (1985; 1991) describes as submersion, or sink or swim, and immersion, the type of scaffolded subject-matter instruction described above. Cooperative learning is most effective when, in the words of Vygotsky, more capable peers, that is, stronger speakers of English, are included in groups with English language learners at various levels.

It benefits all students when no one has all of the information or skills needed to complete a task, but rather when all have an opportunity and a need to contribute. According to Hamayan and Perlman (1991), assigning a function to each student, such as materials director, time-keeper, supervisor to keep the group on task, or recorder, helps ensure that each has a role and is actively involved.

Johnson (1988) suggests creating cross-language pairs in which a group of English language learners is taught in English to do something, such as an art activity. Each of them must each then teach the activity to an English-speaking student. This creates a need to communicate, making

English functional and goal-oriented. In addition, the English language
learner has the status of the person who knows how to accomplish the
task, while the English speaker does not. Doughty and Pica (1986) also
reported that interaction in small groups could be greatly increased by
ensuring that group members needed to know each other's information
in order to complete a task.

Cathcart-Strong (1986) has found that a sufficient amount of time is
needed in group activities so that English language learners can elicit
needed comprehensible input from English-speaking peers. They also
need abundant opportunities to initiate interaction with adults. These
are most likely to occur in problem-solving situations within small
groups.

Krashen and Terrell (1983) describe several useful grouping techniques for acquisition activities. Teachers can form restructured groups
according to some arbitrary criterion, such as the amount of money students have in their pockets, the color of their shirts, or the time they
went to bed the night before. In a one-centered group, a single student
becomes the focus of the activity. For example, one student might think
of something, and the other students ask questions in order to guess
what it is. A unified group activity is one in which everyone in the group
has a part of the information needed to solve a problem. Therefore,
everyone must participate. Dyads or buddy groups are those in which
two students work together. Finally, some activities can be conducted
with an entire class or with a large group of students in the class. In all
of these activities, the focus is on the message transmitted, not on its
form.

A Structure for Integrating English Language Learners:
The Eastman Model

English language learners are often organized into classrooms for the
purpose of providing native language instruction, a practice that tends to
segregate them from English-speaking students unless other arrangements are made. The isolation of English language learners from
English-speaking students can lead to fossilization, a stopping-in-place
of language development caused by a lack of comprehensible input from
expert English speakers. Krashen and Terrell (1983) indicate that exposure to the interlanguage, that is, the incorrect or incomplete structures of
English language learners, in the classroom should not be a problem if it
is not the only input to which they are exposed.

The Eastman model (Krashen & Biber, 1988) of the Los Angeles Unified School District effectively alleviates this problem at the elementary level. Spanish-speaking students are organized for native language instruction in reading and the language arts during the morning, along with a natural approach program of ESL. In the afternoon, Spanish-speaking students are mainstreamed with English-speaking students in art, music, and physical education. As Spanish-speaking students gain English proficiency, they begin to receive sheltered instruction in English in the more concrete areas of the curriculum, such as mathematics and science. Social studies in English is introduced later.

Finally, we should reinforce once again the idea that students should learn academic content from the core curriculum in the native language until they are ready for sheltered instruction in English when they reach a level of *intermediate* fluency in English. Schifini (1985) describes these intermediate learners as those who can engage in extended discussion in English. This instruction follows that provided in the primary language when students have enough background in the new second language to benefit from content instruction in it with the support inherent in what Krashen (1985) termed a sheltered approach.

Teachers will find that students who have mastered a numeracy concept in the native language, for example, will find the same concept to be much more comprehensible in the second language than for the student who is learning the concept for the first time. It is for the latter student, in fact, that primary language instruction in that subject area is vital. Students who have developed language proficiency at an academic level in the primary language will gain more both in the further development of the numeracy concept and in the second language development that will surely accompany it in sheltered instruction in English.

There is, however, a situation in which sheltered instruction in English may be the preferred mode, or even the only mode, for teaching. It is the case of students who speak a primary language in which instruction cannot be provided. This may result from a lack of personnel proficient in the language, of materials, or of sufficient numbers of students to support such a program.

Extending Communicative Approaches into L$_2$ Literacy

A few years ago, it was commonly held that English language learners should not begin learning to read and write in English until they had reached an intermediate level of English fluency. We now recognize that the processes of reading and writing in English can begin earlier in the acquisition process, especially for those students who have developed literacy skills in the primary language. In *Preventing Reading Difficulties in Young Children*, Snow, Burns, and Griffin (1998) recommended teaching children to read in their mother tongue before teaching them to read in English, wherever possible. In a major five-year developmental study, Thomas and Collier (2002) provided additional evidence to support this point of view. Many mother tongues were represented in their study of over 210,000 students in five school districts in Texas, Oregon, and Maine; however, most students were Spanish-speaking. They reported that enrichment one-way or dual language bilingual education programs that were 90-10 or 50-50 (the percentage of mother tongue instruction) were the only programs in which students reached the fiftieth percentile in both languages. In addition, those programs had the fewest dropouts. Some parents refused bilingual education programs for their children, insisting instead on English only, and their children had much lower achievement. The most significant predictor of English language achievement was the amount of formal mother tongue instruction. They reported that the highest achievement in bilingual education programs was associated with those that offered a natural learning environment in school, with rich oral and written language in both mother tongue and English, problem-solving, group student activities, media-rich learning, challenging thematic units, and use of the students' bilingual-bicultural knowledge to access new knowledge.

In addition, literacy can play a major role in support of the acquisition of English as a second language. Krashen and Terrell (1983) describe reading in the second language as an important source of comprehensible input. In the same way that we find parallels between communicative approaches to second language acquisition and sheltered instruction in English, we can identify many aspects of communicative approaches that parallel access to literacy in students' new second language—English.

Communicative Approaches and a Constructivist View of Literacy

The convergence between communicative approaches to second language acquisition and literacy is particularly prominent in a constructivist or whole language view of literacy. Coote and Stevens (1990) define whole language as "the interplay of all aspects of language needed to communicate with others, or when others, present or past, communicate with us," a definition that encompasses second language acquisition, including literacy.

Goodman (1986) views learning as proceeding from whole to part, without any basis in a sequence of skills. He places the major focus on authentic language use in the real world. Smith (1989) reinforces the importance of authenticity in stating that "literacy is a social phenomenon. Individuals become literate not from the formal instruction they receive, but from what they read and write about and who they read and write with." We can readily interchange listening and speaking for reading and writing in the Smith citation.

Rigg (1991) has identified major purposes of language within this constructivist view, including the construction of knowledge and the creation and communication of purposeful and authentic meaning. Freeman and Freeman (1988) describe it as whole to part; as learning-centered; as having meaning and purpose; as including the four modes of listening, speaking, reading, and writing; and as reflecting high teacher expectations for students. Finally, Altwerger, Edelsky, and Flores (1987) describe the constructivist view as a set of beliefs or a perspective about language, not as a method.

These mutually supporting concepts about a constructivist view of literacy are entirely consistent with the underlying principles of communicative approaches to second language acquisition. Before we examine some approaches and strategies to reading and writing that promote second language acquisition and reading comprehension within this perspective, we should consider the growing use of direct instruction programs that are characterized by a heavy and single-minded focus on phonemic awareness and phonics at the earliest stages of reading, by the use of so-called decodable text that is absent of meaning, and by linear scripted programs that address all children in the same way, regardless of language background or difficulties they may be having with reading. The research cited to support these types of programs is highly questionable, and outcomes do not indicate changes in the all-important factor of reading comprehension (Allington, 2001; Coles, 2000).

The increasing diversity of our classrooms seems to bring with it an increase in the numbers of children who are struggling to read, and this is exacerbated by the presence of large numbers of English language learners. Duffy-Hester (1999) examined several model reading programs and found common guiding principles that should serve teachers well who are working with struggling readers. Among these guiding principles are the following:

- Reading programs should be balanced, not drawing on only a single theoretical perspective. A one-size-fits-all approach to reading instruction inevitably seems to miss meeting the needs of some children, especially English language learners. A balanced program addresses all of the learning modalities that diverse groups of children bring to the classroom

- Every element in a balanced reading program should have a well-supported role. Some currently popular direct instruction reading programs, for example, make heavy use of decodable text, fragments of unconnected text in which the students practice word recognition elements they have been studying. There is little research to support the use of such text, although there is abundant research to support the use of connected text, especially in the promotion of reading comprehension (Allington, 1997).

- Word recognition, comprehension, and vocabulary development should not be taught in isolation, but rather within the context of authentic reading and writing activities.

- Teacher read-aloud activities serve to build background knowledge and vocabulary, preparing children to understand their own reading of the text later.

- Authentic assessment yields valuable information that teachers can use to inform their instruction. We should consider that some assessment does not provide this type of information and instead takes up valuable time that can be used for children to read and write. We should heed an important traditional dictum about assessment: "You don't fatten a pig by weighing it."

- Teachers should use what they have learned in their professional preparation to make instructional decisions about reading programs they use.

- Staff development activities for teachers should provide time for reflection and opportunities to share experiences about best practices.

- The learner-centered goals and strategies most effective for troubled readers will serve other children well, too, including English language learners.

Early Literacy Experiences. Most English language learners have had some emergent literacy experiences at home and in the community—recognizing cereal and soft drink labels, knowing brands of automobiles, being read to, and watching a parent read, referring to a calendar, or writing a check. They have begun to understand the underlying concept of print representing spoken ideas, even in the second language they are only beginning to understand.

A print-rich environment in the classroom is an important step toward providing meaningful material to read. Students don't need to know letter names or sound/symbol correspondences to begin recognizing and discussing labels, their own names, and other forms of print to which they are exposed. Surrounding them with sources of print in the classroom will serve to supplant missing or inadequate experiences.

The Key-Vocabulary and Language Experience Approaches to Reading. The language experience approach is a major source of written language for providing authentic, meaningful, early literacy experiences in English for English language learners. If students have an extremely limited background in the language of initial instruction, especially if it must be English as a second language, then the key-vocabulary approach of Veatch, Sawicki, Elliott, Flake, and Blakey (1979) may serve well to bridge to literacy from a strong, communicatively-based second language acquisition program.

As a part of the natural approach, Terrell (1981) recommends that key words be written on the chalkboard in the second language for older students who are literate in their native language. In the early production stage of Terrell's natural approach, students may express themselves quite appropriately in one or two word utterances as they begin to acquire a second language. It is altogether proper that they also begin to read key vocabulary that they have expressed for their teacher to write for them. They may later produce lists of related ideas, such as foods to eat at a carnival or fair, words that describe a favorite friend, or things to do after school. These topics and this output reflect the oral language common in the early production phase of Terrell's natural approach to language acquisition.

During an individual meeting with the teacher, each student in the key-vocabulary approach selects a word of personal importance. The teacher writes it on a card. After the student traces the word with a finger, the teacher records it in a key-word book and also records a sentence or phrase that is dictated by the student about the word. The student then reads the dictation back to the teacher and illustrates it. Finally, the student copies the word and the sentence.

Most bilingual teachers who teach reading in the mother tongue recognize that student motivation to begin reading and writing in English early is strong. Although it is most beneficial for students to learn to read and write in the native language (Cummins, 1986; Cummins, 1989; Krashen & Biber, 1988; Snow, Burns, and Griffin, 1998; Thomas and Collier, 2002), where possible, teachers can begin an early introduction to literacy in English in order to take advantage of that motivation. The use of the key-vocabulary and language experience approaches should be done with caution to ensure that the second language acquisition program does not evolve into an English literacy program presented before the student is ready. Being able to read and write in the mother tongue is always the most desirable base from which to establish literacy in English later because of the positive transfer of literacy skills to English.

Moving from the dictation of key vocabulary to predictable language patterns in the language experience approach (LEA) is a natural step, and one that quickly leads to more traditional LEA strategies (Heald-Taylor, 1986). A dictation about foods to eat at the fair might result in each of several students dictating an idea conforming to this predictable pattern:

I eat hot dogs at the fair.

I eat popcorn at the fair.

I eat cotton candy at the fair.

And so on.

Using the language experience approach in the second language is an excellent way to initiate students into reading print of interest and relevance to them (Dixon & Nessel, 1983; Moustafa & Penrose, 1985; Nessel & Jones, 1981). According to Crawford (1993), LEA also provides a means through which students can experience literature in their second language that is above their ability to read and comprehend. A teacher or aide can tell or read a story aloud. The students can then dictate the story back, that is, retell it for the teacher or aide to record, although probably in a less complicated version than the original. Peck (1989) found that listening to stories in this way helps students develop a sense of story structure, which should be reflected in the dictated version and in enhanced abilities to predict in this and other stories. The dictated text allows students to think, talk, read, and write about the piece of literature and to be exposed to its valuable cultural content. At the same time, they are actively interacting with the text at a level of comprehension and of English language proficiency appropriate for their stage of development. They will be able to activate background knowledge from this experience that will transfer positively into the second language when they later read the literature for themselves in their new second language.

Beginning an LEA activity with a piece of literature or a story will often result in a better structured dictation than the random list of sentences that sometimes results from LEA dictations stimulated by an illustration, a manipulative, or other prompts. Heller (1988) describes a process for eliciting dictations that incorporates aspects of story grammar and supports the composing process. She recommends adding several components to traditional LEA procedures, including the activation of background knowledge, the setting of a purpose and identification of a target audience for the dictation, the discussion of a model LEA dictation, the modeling of metacognitive strategies by teachers who describe their thoughts about creating an interesting story, and asking the students to make notes about the story they will dictate. They can then discuss, edit, and rewrite the dictated story in much the same way that the writing process would be applied in independent writing.

Many LEA activities can be adapted for English language learners. For example, multiple readings of the text can be helpful to them (Crawford, Allen, & Hall, 1995). Using a copy of the text with some words left out and with empty spaces where words are missing, children can practice reading the text as an oral cloze procedure. Let the children know that some words are missing and ask if they can predict what should be in the space. The teacher reads the text with the children, pausing briefly when encountering a missing word and filling in the missing words as the children identify them.

Children will learn many new words, and these collections can serve as their personal word files. After they have learned fifteen or twenty words, they can engage in sorting activities with their word files (Bear,

Invernezzi, Templeton, & Johnston, 2000). Finding words that start with the same letter and sound is a way some children learn to associate letters and sounds, allowing them to learn best about letters and sounds from these words that they already know. They can look for words that are names of people, places, animals, colors, foods, and clothing.

As children collect more and more words that they can read, they can begin to build sentences with them. The teacher should demonstrate before asking them to try it, and the teacher should read their sentences to them if they cannot read them independently. Children can also try to reassemble the same sentences they have used in their dictated texts.

Shared Reading. Another valuable form of written text for English language learners early in the reading process is the big book, particularly those big books with predictable or repetitive language patterns. Teachers read to students, who then read with them and finally back to them, although this reading may consist of telling the story while looking at the illustrations (Trachtenburg & Ferruggia, 1989). Using big books provides an opportunity for the teacher to model so that students can clearly see what they will later do in their own independent reading. In addition, students begin to notice correspondences between letters in familiar texts and the sounds they represent (Holdaway, 1979).

According to Lynch (1986), the shared reading process begins with consideration of the book language that has probably already been acquired by students whose parents or siblings read to them. For those who lack this experience, shared reading takes on increasing importance. English language learners will tend more than other students to come from homes where printed material is scarce or where parents' own literacy skills may be limited. We cannot make assumptions about the conceptual knowledge about print that they bring to the classroom (Crawford, 1993).

By looking at the cover and at illustrations inside a book together, students begin to understand that they can make predictions based on what they already know, their background knowledge, and what they think the author wants to say to them. As the teacher begins to read the story to them, they will note and discuss connections between their predictions and the story line.

Many teachers are concerned about how students can begin to read a big book or a predictable book before they have learned to read, that is, to decode or call the words. Smith (1988) describes the process as one of demonstration in which the teacher or parent reads the big book to the student, who in turn reads it back to the teacher or parent. As students gain confidence through this early successful experience with reading and through a process of approximation, they begin to read with increasing accuracy and faithfulness to the actual text. When students read to the teacher as a group, a process that Peetoom (1986) calls echoic reading, there is even a greater sense of success because individual errors are not noted. Students can either correct themselves or go right on, with a correspondingly low level of anxiety about reading. This process is very much parallel with the need for a low level of anxiety in the acquisition of a second language and with the role of correction in that process.

Students soon begin to identify which parts of the text tell about corresponding parts of the story, and they begin to recognize certain words of interest to them. In terms of the frequency of their appearance in primary texts or in the number of syllables they contain, these words are not necessarily easy words from an adult's point of view. They are instead easy from a student's point of view in terms of interest and utility. Such easy words as *elephant* and *yellow* are more likely to be readily remembered and identified on second or third reading than more difficult words, such as come and me.

As Lynch (1986) points out, repetition of familiar stories leads to increased success, not to boredom on the part of the students. Their abilities to predict will grow, and they will increase the kind and variety of cues they use to predict, moving from illustrations and background knowledge of a story to familiar words and other visual cues. The later use of graphophonic cues, the phonics and structural analysis skills of so much concern to some educational decision-makers, emerges then as a result of this process, not as its cause (Smith, 1988).

Strategies to Promote Reading Comprehension. In recent years, we have moved away from the controlled environment of the traditional basal reader into authentic children's literature, including fiction and non-fiction trade books. According to Crawford (1993), students are exposed to oral and written ideas that demand higher levels of background knowledge, vocabulary, and language proficiency. In their work with English language learners, teachers face great challenges in providing for the equitable access of all students to quality literature while helping them make progress in reading and writing.

We have tended to place these at-risk students in perpetual compensatory or remedial programs where we expect them to learn to read and write by acquiring isolated skills through interaction with incomplete fragments of language. These students rarely move successfully into the mainstream curriculum, more frequently leaving these programs when they leave school, all too often as dropouts.

Whether or not English language learners read literature from the primary or from the second language, we can organize a set of strategies to support their reading comprehension into three categories: prereading strategies, guided reading strategies, and postreading strategies. The contrast between these recommended strategies and those ordinarily used for English language learners is significant. The recommended strategies resemble most closely the enrichment or additional activities that teachers of English language learners never have time for because they are busy installing the isolated skills that the students seem to lack. We need to develop those skills directly and, within the context of language, in an authentic mode.

The recommended strategies are those that will provide the underlying support or scaffolding needed for reading comprehension. It is the isolated skills that teachers should set aside. We should view skill development as an outcome of learning to read, not as its cause (Samuels, 1971; Smith, 1985). Only on those rare occasions when a student's needs suggest that a directed skill lesson is needed should teachers seek out an appropriate one in the teachers' editions and workbooks of traditional reading and language arts programs.

Prereading Strategies

Background Knowledge. There is increasing recognition of the importance of bringing background knowledge to bear on making sense of new information (Smith, 1988). The activation of this background knowledge, and often its development, constitutes a vitally important prereading activity. The background knowledge that we have acquired about the world forms the structure through which we assess new information and incorporate it. We use this knowledge to make and verify predictions about the new information to which we are exposed. According to Krashen (1991), background knowledge also makes second language input more comprehensible and therefore facilitates second language acquisition.

All students have acquired background knowledge, but there is often a discontinuity between the background knowledge a student has and the assumptions that teachers, authors, and textbook publishers make about that knowledge. This discontinuity must be assumed to be deeper when the student comes from a language or culture different from that of the student for whom the materials are designed or intended. A story about a birthday leads most American children to activate background knowledge about a party, a cake with candles and gifts. While a Mexican child activates background knowledge of a birthday and thinks about a piñata, children from Senegal and Morocco don't think about birthdays at all because they are not celebrated in their cultures. If children who lack a schema for a birthday cake are to read a literature selection in which the American celebration plays a significant role, then background knowledge must be activated or developed as a pre-reading activity.

Group Discussion. The activation or development of background knowledge in students without previous exposure can often be accomplished through a sharing of the group's knowledge. Although no individual student may know a great deal about a topic, many children in a group will have some knowledge (María, 1989). A skillful teacher can lead a group discussion to elicit the information to be shared.

Semantic Mapping. A useful strategy for providing structure to the development of background knowledge is semantic mapping (Heimlich & Pittelman, 1986). Knowledge is activated from long-term memory, shared with other students, and discussed in terms of needed vocabulary. It is then recorded in a graphic format that promotes organizing schemata so that relationships become more clear. The resulting semantic map may also serve as an advance organizer that will promote reading comprehension when the students later read the selection.

A teacher might write a word on a chart, chalkboard, or transparency and ask students to tell what they know about that concept. Although most students won't know much about the concept, many will know something. The process of discussing and systematically recording their background knowledge on a semantic map permits them to share what they know while the teacher organizes it into logical categories. Semantic maps are widely used to develop vocabulary in the same way.

According to Crawford (1993), semantic mapping is not a strategy to use with English language learners every day. The nature of the literature selection, the desirability of formally structuring the background knowledge into a semantic map, and the existing background knowledge of the students should all be factors in deciding when and if the gains from devoting a considerable amount of instructional time to the activity are warranted.

Ordinarily, a semantic map for activating background knowledge or vocabulary is developed and completed during one or two related lessons and is not referred to subsequently. Teachers often find, however, that they are dealing with such concepts as feelings on repeated occasions. It can be useful to return to a semantic map on such a topic, to add to it, and to consider new additions in contrast with earlier ones. We can identify this elaborated strategy as the cumulative semantic map.

In Figure 1, for example, a teacher might introduce the new word *furious* from a piece of literature and ask students where it should be added to an existing cumulative semantic map for words about feelings. At that point, the students can discuss how angry *furious* is as compared to *miffed, enraged,* and *upset,* which were added to the semantic map on earlier occasions. When written on removable self-stick notes, the various words can be arranged and rearranged in ascending order of increasing anger as students negotiate their meaning with each other.

Figure 1
CUMULATIVE SEMANTIC MAP

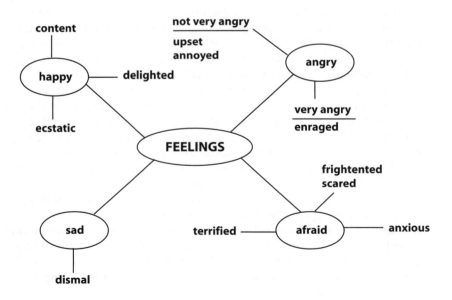

In a later writing assignment, students can again refer to the cumulative semantic map when they want to select just the right word to convey the degree of anger they have in mind. Discussing the choice of word with the teacher or other students will be particularly helpful. When students are ready to add yet another synonym for angry a week or a month later, they will have the opportunity to review other words or expressions for the same feeling, but within a context of known or somewhat familiar vocabulary. The original semantic map seen in Figure 1 would now appear elaborated, as seen in Figure 2. We can view a well-developed cumulative semantic map as a graphic thesaurus. Other suitable topics for cumulative semantic maps might include seeing (stare, peek, glare, etc.), motion (crawl, creep, dawdle, dash, poke along, lope, etc.), and touching (poke, tap, jab, stroke, etc.).

Figure 2
AN ELABORATED CUMULATIVE SEMANTIC MAP

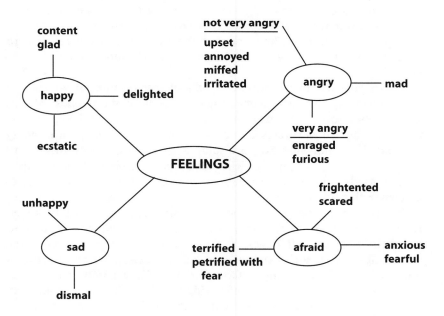

Advance Organizer. The advance organizer is another useful tool for activating background knowledge. It is perhaps most common to find advance organizers provided in content area textbooks, but they can also be a useful addition to literature readings, whether prepared by authors and publishers or by teachers. Some stories or literature selections provide a brief summary, often on a book jacket or on the back cover of a soft-cover book. Occasionally, this includes a question or comment designed to entice the reader into reading the selection. Teachers can use these to interest their students in stories, to activate background knowledge, and to help them make predictions about the story. Even an adult will rarely purchase a paperback novel without examining the advance organizer or publisher's teaser on the back cover, not to mention the illustration on the front cover.

Vocabulary Development. When English language learners read in their second language, the lack of vocabulary knowledge is often an obstacle to comprehension. This can be a problem in the primary language, as well, because they may have insufficient academically-related background knowledge and the primary language vocabulary development that would accompany it. We can consider vocabulary as an aspect of background knowledge, but we will treat it separately here in order to examine several concepts that relate more specifically to vocabulary.

Let us consider two different aspects of the question of vocabulary development for English language learners. One is the richness of language that surrounds them. It is well recognized that students become familiar with the meanings of words when those meanings are highly contextualized, not when they are studied in isolation as new vocabulary words. It follows, then, that a richer language environment should result in increased exposure to contextualized vocabulary and, therefore, to understanding of their meanings.

We often postpone or even eliminate instruction for English language learners, however, in the very areas of the curriculum where new vocabulary words will be offered in the most highly contextualized ways—in science, social studies, art, music, health, and other areas of the curriculum. According to Crawford (1993), we must ensure that these areas of the curriculum are provided for English language learners and that they are presented so that contextualized exposure to a rich vocabulary is promoted. Instruction in these areas should include the use of cooperative learning, problem solving, and other vocabulary-rich strategies.

In a study by Nagy, Anderson and Herman (1987), they found that, although the proportion of words learned was low, a major factor in vocabulary development by third, fifth, and seventh grade students was the sheer volume of reading that students did and the amount of vocabulary to which they were exposed. Stanovich (1986) elaborated this idea further in his treatment of individualized differences and the *Matthew effect*, the idea that those who read more (the rich) read better (get richer). In a related vein, Smith (1986) observed that good readers read, and poor readers take tests and do drill sheets.

Another aspect of vocabulary is the issue of direct instruction. Although many vocabulary words will be acquired incidentally, some literature or content selections will contain a few vocabulary words that must be clearly grasped if the text is to be understood. There will be other words not known to the students that need not be addressed through direct instruction because they are not critical to understanding the selection or because they can be quickly analyzed through the context in which they appear.

Many of the strategies recommended for the activation or development of background knowledge constitute direct approaches to vocabulary instruction. Semantic mapping is one of these strategies, but its application should be limited to those key and conceptually difficult vocabulary terms that are more in the realm of background knowledge. Otherwise, there will be little time left for reading after prereading activities are completed.

The teacher may analyze some words through brief discussion following read-aloud activities. They will have been presented in context, and someone in the group will likely have some knowledge of most vocabulary words. Others may be analyzed by reviewing the illustrations in a story or an appropriate illustration, manipulative, or visual aid provided by the teacher. Because illustrations provide important visual information, paging through a selection and discussing them provides an opportunity for presenting new vocabulary and also for making predictions about the text. A partial or complete read-aloud of a literature selection as a prereading activity is equally productive.

Guided Reading Strategies

According to Smith (1985), we learn to read by reading. This fundamental and obvious idea should underlie our thinking as we consider how English language learners' time is spent during reading instruction. Rather than having students study about reading by mastering skills, we must instead maximize the amount of reading they do. Some obvious counterproductive strategies are pencil-and-paper exercises and the still-common round-robin oral reading, which usually results in one student laboriously reading aloud a passage never before read, even silently, while the rest of the students in the group pretend to listen or read along.

From our own experiences with second language acquisition, we should also recall the importance of reading for comprehension, as opposed to word calling. Most of us had the experience of being asked to read aloud in a high school or university foreign language class. We read with great intensity, attempting to correctly soften the intervocalic *d* in Spanish or accurately pronounce the difficult initial *r* of French. When we finished, the teacher asked us to tell about the content of what we read in our own words. Of course, we had little idea, because we had been focusing on pronunciation. We must remember that communication and comprehension are the focus of reading and writing, just as they are in a communicative approach to oral language development. There are many guided reading strategies that will help us ensure that students focus on comprehension instead of only on correct pronunciation.

When students begin to read themselves, they may benefit from having their teacher read to them from the selection first. Occasionally, the teacher may find that presenting the entire selection as a read-aloud is helpful. When a parallel version of a text is available in the students' primary language, a teacher or aide may read it aloud before the students read later in English. Students in school are not bored or disturbed by several exposures to the same literature selection, any more than a three-year-old objects to hearing the same story before bed every night. The familiarity of a story that is an old friend becomes a real comfort. Familiarity with the background knowledge and structure of a story permits a student to read with good comprehension and with fewer time-consuming visual cues, especially for students' early literacy experiences in English. The teacher's read-aloud also provides the teacher with the opportunity to model predicting, thinking about context, and other strategies by talking through some of the metacognitive processes used during the teacher's oral reading.

With beginning readers, their first reading may take the form of group echoic reading with a teacher or lead reader, usually following a read-aloud by the teacher (Peetoom, 1986). As the lead reader reads very expressively, the time gap between that person and the group of students will diminish. When an individual or a part of the group stumbles, the lead reader should take charge and read until the group is together again. This activity lowers anxiety about oral reading because students' approximations, a very natural aspect of early reading, are not noticeable and comprehension is maintained. Most important, everyone is reading.

Peetoom (1986) also describes timed and repeated readings in which students read aloud passages of about 150 words from carefully selected literature. With practice, students read them more accurately and in less time. Dowhower (1987) has reported that such repeated and rehearsed readings can result in gains in the reading rate, accuracy, and comprehension of second grade students, with some evidence of transfer to unpracticed passages, as well. As a part of her study, students read along with an audiotape until they read easily, or they practiced reading a passage until they could read at a pre-established set rate. This may be an especially useful independent activity for student dyads working together. Again, they will be reading instead of completing written drill and practice activities on skill development. Samuels (1979) associated repeated readings with the development of automaticity, the stage at which students read and recognize words unconsciously, permitting their full attention to focus instead on meaning. Automaticity in reading seems to parallel the process of oral production without employing the monitor in language acquisition. It also has much in common with Terrell's (1986) concept of *binding*, where a linguistic form evokes meaning without any delay.

Middle and upper grade elementary students and secondary students should read silently on an extensive basis. It is through more rapid silent reading that students can read for the most practice and be exposed to the most background knowledge and contextualized vocabulary. It is more difficult for teachers to provide extra support to English language learners, however, because their need for it may be less obvious during the largely independent activity of reading silently.

One strategy for providing this support during the silent reading of literature selections is to direct or structure students' reading with questions. Some teachers would decry this as an annoying and unnecessary strategy that is destined to destroy any enjoyment of the selection by the student. That may indeed be the case for some students. The reality is, however, that many English language learners struggle to read, and their many failure experiences can result in a lack of motivation and interest in reading. Their teachers often have difficulty reading themselves during silent sustained reading (SSR) because of their need to supervise closely the reading of their sometimes reluctant students.

According to Crawford (1993), guiding students' reading with questions provides valuable support in maintaining comprehension. It brings key story concepts to their attention as they read, and, perhaps more important, it provides moral support, interest, and motivation from someone who cares about them. Students who cannot, or will not, read a lengthy selection alone may do so a page or two at a time within the security of a supportive teacher-directed group. Their reading can be structured by questions that elicit predictions, with timely resolution of those predictions through discussion and any needed mediation.

Beck and McKeown (1981) reported that having students develop a story map of the major events or ideas of a selection was even more effective if questions were developed to guide them toward identifying unifying events and ideas. Peetoom (1986) suggests chunking stories by having students read them in manageable and comprehensible sections. Questions can be used very effectively and naturally to accomplish this chunking.

Although there is considerable debate about the value of teaching reading comprehension skills through direct instruction, there are sufficient other reasons to guide silent reading with questions. A teacher will take no longer to formulate and ask a higher order comprehension question than a low-level recall question before asking students to read to find the answer. It is often said that teachers have low expectations for English language learners. Guided silent reading provides an opportunity for students to make inferences and predictions, identify cause and effect relationships, and apply other higher order critical thinking skills when their comprehension is supported (Crawford, 1993).

Postreading Strategies

After students read, there are other opportunities to provide scaffolding. We have already considered the retelling of stories told or read to students as a means of producing text through LEA for them to read themselves. Retelling is also an excellent postreading activity. An oral retelling provides students with the opportunity to negotiate with each other about the meaning of the selection. It is often through this process that students can incorporate new information gained through reading into existing background knowledge. Koskinen, Gambrell, Kapinus, and Heathington (1988) found that the verbal rehearsal that occurs in the retelling process also serves to improve the reading comprehension of less proficient readers. Some students may elect to retell in their primary language what they read or heard in their second language. Brown and

Cambourne (1990) observed that retelling also promotes multiple read-ings of text as a part of the negotiation process.

Retelling also provides a means for integrating writing into the pro-gram. Either through a cooperative learning process or through individ-ual or paired writing, students can prepare a written retelling (Strickland & Feeley, 1985). As a result of their earlier discussion, of the knowledge they gained through reading, and of such prereading activities as seman-tic mapping and the examination of story grammar, students are better prepared to write a well-structured retelling. Like the modeling that teachers provide during reading, teachers should also model retelling with an actual example.

The most obvious postreading activity should not be overlooked—more reading. If we are successful in providing quality literature that students will choose to read and also in supporting their comprehension, then we should expect gains in all areas of the English language arts. Krashen (1985; 1993) has concluded that reading is more powerful than direct instruction in developing vocabulary, grammar, spelling, and reading comprehension. He advocates extensive free voluntary reading with messages that are understood in low-anxiety situations. Finally, he feels that good writing is promoted more by extensive reading than by writing.

Adapting Phonics and Decoding Strategies for English Language Learners

In a developmental view of learning, children unify what they already know about the world with new information they gain through authentic experiences. Even in the largely synthetic process of learning about the isolated letters and sounds of a language, teachers will find that English language learners have background knowledge about the sound system of their mother tongue, phonemic awareness, and usually some knowledge about the symbols that represent those sounds, as well. Phonics, then, is the process of unifying that knowledge of sounds and letters in an authentic experience that permits children to generate new knowledge, that is, how to pronounce the sound of a letter or combina-tion of letters in an unknown word. When this is accomplished within the context of what children already know, then instruction in phonics can be taught in a whole-part-whole mode.

English language learners bring phonemic awareness of sounds in the mother tongue to the classroom. In the best of worlds, they should first learn phonics in the mother tongue out of the context of words they already recognize on sight, usually from their print environment and from language experience charts and big books. English language learners who learn phonics in the mother tongue generally have a much easier time learning phonics in English than children who must learn phonics first in English. There are some languages, such as Spanish and Korean, that are very regular in their sound/letter relationships. Phonics is not only easier to learn in these languages, but children have more confidence in the process than children learning to read in a language where sound/letter relationships are not regular, such as English.

We have seen that the language experience approach and shared reading are holistic strategies for teaching reading. In these strategies, teachers do not begin with phonics. But learning about the associations between letters and sounds (phonics) is a part of learning to read in all methods, including these. In a developmental approach to teaching about letters and sounds, children should develop a concept of print first. After dictating many LEA charts and reading them, children quickly learn to read some 100-200 words on sight. They should have many shared book reading experiences, and then they are ready to learn about letters and sounds using words they already know in English.

When English language learners must learn phonics in English first, they face a real dilemma. Although they may have learned to speak and understand English, they still lack the phonemic awareness skills in English of a native speaker. A native Spanish-speaking child will speak the 43 sounds of English using the 25 sounds of Spanish. There are fifteen vowel sounds in English, but only five in Spanish. This accounts for the difficulty that Spanish-speaking children have when they attempt to pronounce short vowels in English, including the schwa. They have similar difficulty in "reading" (correctly pronouncing) these sounds in a phonetic approach to reading. There are variations in the differences between other languages and English, but similar difficulties arise for children from most other languages. For those who learn phonics in their mother tongue, the process of learning English phonics is much easier because they already know how the process of reading works. The process transfers from the mother tongue, even if many of the sounds do not.

Sleeter and Grant (1999) remind teachers that they need to distinguish between mechanics and meaning when teaching students whose mother tongue is not English or standard American English. They concluded that teachers should not be bogged down in remediation whenever they encountered gaps in student learning that related more to mechanics than to understanding. This concept is particularly important in the area of word attack skills for English language learners.

The Writing Process

A major principle of the constructivist view of literacy is the interdependence of listening, speaking, reading, and writing. Hudelson (1984) observed that second language learners address the four language processes as a totality, not as separate entities. According to Fitzgerald (1993), writing begins when children can draw, and there is no need to wait for reading. We can certainly extend these ideas to English language learners, who should be encouraged to write in English early, especially if they have writing skills in their native language. The errors they make should be viewed in the same way that we view errors in oral production, as a part of the natural process of acquisition.

In keeping with the constructivist orientation of this chapter, Ferreiro (1991) described the process of writing as one of making meaning through construction and reconstruction. Samway (1993) reinforced this idea in her study of how a sample of non-native-English-speaking elementary students in grades two through six evaluated their own writing and that of others. Although these high-risk students were experiencing difficulties in school, they tended to focus on meaning in their evaluative comments. Most of their comments were categorized as Crafting, how well a story had been developed, or Understanding, making sense of the text.

For English language learners, we have already seen that writing flows out of a variety of language acquisition activities, including the key-vocabulary and language experience approaches to reading and the postreading strategy of written retellings. The structuring of their writing or their selection of vocabulary may be supported through the use of semantic maps and cumulative semantic maps.

Writing Workshop

Samway (1992) describes the writing workshop as an important strategy for providing a writing program for ESL learners. She describes writing as both a solitary and a social act in which students write for real audiences in a collaborative mode. She advocates the establishment of classroom work stations for editing, illustrating, and publishing. Among the activities one might see during that part of the day set aside for writing workshop are: whole class meetings for minilessons; children writing, with some beginning a first draft, while others are revising or editing; conferences among students or with the teacher; children searching for writing topics; research, such as reading, watching a film, or interviewing another student; illustrating; publishing final, clean copies; word-processing on a computer; making book covers; and sharing their writing, often from a place of honor called the author's chair.

In a typical writing workshop cycle (Samway, 1992), students would begin on the first day with a minilesson to generate topics. Supporting prewriting activities might include listening to literature, brainstorming, clustering and mapping activities, storytelling, interviewing and opinion surveys, and field trips. After modeling by the teacher, individual students list topics, select one of interest, and then write for ten to twenty minutes. On the second day, students read their pieces aloud to each other in dyads, describing their purpose, what they liked best about it, and any problems they had. They confer with each other, maintaining mutually supportive roles. At the end of the session, some of the students share their progress with the entire class.

On the third day, students consider the comments of their dyad partner and revise accordingly. On the fourth day, the teacher might model editing with a piece of personal writing in a minilesson. Students then edit their own work for clarity, mechanics, word use, and spelling. At the end of the session, some students share their progress with the class. On the fifth day, students publish their completed work. As a result of the five-day cycle, students have written for a real audience, conferred about their writing, and published their work.

In a six-month observational study of six upper elementary grade Southeast Asian students, Urzúa (1987) found that feedback between children in the writing process caused them to develop a sense of audience. Their peers asked them questions and made suggestions about their writing. The students also developed a sense of voice, preferring to select their own writing topics. Finally, she observed that they developed a sense of power in language as they learned to add to their writings, to discuss vocabulary with each other, and to take risks as they manipulated language.

Teachers should employ a variety of other writing activities to maintain interest in the process. Bromley (1989) suggests that at-risk students keep a buddy journal, a diary in which two students write back and forth to each other. Similarly, Arthur (1991) recommends the use of dialogue journals to promote authentic communication for ESL learners at the middle school level.

Invented Spelling

Consistent with the communicative approach principle of minimizing error correction and with the developmental nature of second language acquisition and literacy, teachers should accept the invented spellings of their students as a very natural aspect of their growth in writing. Gentry (1981, 1982) describes five developmental stages of spelling. In the precommunicative stage, students demonstrate some knowledge of letter forms, but no knowledge of letter-sound correspondences. Teachers will be unable to decipher their efforts, but children can usually "read" them to the teacher, at least at the time they are written.

In the semiphonetic stage, students begin to approximate an alphabetic orthography and to conceptualize the alphabetic principle. They begin to demonstrate the relationship between sound and letter, and they sometimes use letter names as words. They begin to understand the left-to-right convention of English, and they may begin to segment words. Consonants tend to predominate over vowels.

In the phonetic stage, students begin to map letter-sound correspondences in reference to sounds, but not to conventions. They generally segment words appropriately. At this point, teachers can decipher their writing with only occasional difficulty. During the transitional stage, students follow basic spelling conventions, with vowels in most syllables. They use morphological features and a larger number of learned (and correctly spelled) words.

In the correct stage, students have learned most basic rules of the English orthographic system. They are aware of such word structures as prefixes, suffixes, contractions, compound words, and homonyms, and they continue to learn some less common spelling patterns and rules. It is at this stage that they begin to recognize when a word *looks* correct, a phenomenon that corresponds to the natural approach characteristic in which English language learners begin to recognize when something *sounds* right or *feels* right. They are able to spell a large number of words automatically.

Nathenson-Mejia (1989) found that, in their English writing, Spanish-speaking students in the beginning stages of English spelling made extensive use of their Spanish pronunciation in their invented spellings in English. Edelsky (1982) made the same observation in a more generic sense. She took the positive point of view that students are applying some primary language writing skills to writing in the second language, rather than the negative point of view that it reflects interference from the first language to the second.

The Role of Evaluation in the Communicative Program

Current views of the scope of second language acquisition include not only listening and oral communicative competency, but they now also extend into sheltered instruction in English through content/language integration in the core curriculum and into literacy in English. Assessment must be considered in a similarly broad scope. The issue of assessment is further complicated by conflicts between the need for data to meet legal and fiscal requirements and those needed to make instructional decisions.

If a second language curriculum were designed to teach grammar, then the assessment tool to evaluate outcomes would logically consist of discrete point measures of the mastery of grammatical elements. Within the topical curriculum advocated by most proponents of communicative approaches, and in keeping with their advocacy of language being functional and authentic, we would expect wide variation in the acquisition of competence with respect to these topics and in related measures of assessment.

According to Terrell (1977), evaluation in the communicative second language acquisition program must focus on oral competence. He states that instruction should focus first on the transmittal of the message, second on the use of appropriate vocabulary, third on form or correctness, and last on pronunciation. Accordingly, we would expect evaluation to be a very dynamic and individualized process, depending on the topics of interest to individual students and on their stages of development in communicative competence.

Krashen and Terrell (1983) focus on global communicative competence, in contrast to discrete point linguistic competence. In the area of listening comprehension, they suggest such strategies as answering questions after listening to a recorded dialogue, a narrated story, a radio or TV program, a song, or a film. They suggest that teachers can evaluate speaking proficiency by holistically scoring performance in conversational interchanges, recounting events, giving directions, reports in class, and, at the higher levels, in debate and argumentation.

McGroarty (1984) concluded that communicative competence may refer to many different aspects of language for students with different needs and reasons for enrollment in programs. She found that English language learners in elementary and secondary schools need a diverse set of language skills, including literacy, in order to make normal school progress. One of the greatest needs she saw was for students to master and use context-reduced language.

Saville-Troike (1991) recognized the need for language assessment that provided information about the English language learner's readiness for success in a regular English-medium classroom. She recommended using standardized reading tests already in use with English language learners to assess academic language proficiency. Because of its strong generic relationship to academic progress, she emphasized the use of the vocabulary subtest score for children beyond the third grade.

Crawford (1982) suggested that the informal reading inventory (IRI) shows promise as a measure of English proficiency when used as a test of listening comprehension or reading capacity. The teacher can use the IRI to determine readiness for reading instruction in given materials by reading a selected passage aloud to the student. Crawford reported that students who respond correctly to 75% of comprehension-level questions about the material usually have sufficient English language proficiency to read it with support from the teacher. According to Antonacci (1993), story retelling is an important tool for assessing students' formation of story concept in the reading process.

Pierce and O'Malley (1992) proposed a series of what they characterize as alternative assessments. They defined alternative assessment as any method of determining what a student knows or can do, as criterion-referenced, as authentic in reflecting typical classroom and real-life tasks, as integrative of language skills, and as including the incorporation of teacher observation, performance assessment, and student-self assessment. They referred to performance assessment as an exercise in which students demonstrate specific skills and competencies in relation to a continuum, as judged by a professional rater. Finally, they recommended the use of portfolios as a record of student work over time and in various modes to show depth, breadth, and development, with possibilities for adding student reflection and self-monitoring.

Pierce and O'Malley's concept of assessment might be difficult to accommodate to the need for the formal classification and reclassification of students. It is, however, ideal for monitoring student placement and progress in programs. It is also appropriate for providing data for informed instructional decisions, particularly within the philosophies underlying communicative approaches to second language acquisition, to content/language integration in sheltered instruction in English in the core curriculum, and to related holistic approaches to literacy.

An assessment strategy that is very consistent with the constructivist paradigm underlying both communicative approaches to second language acquisition and a whole-part-whole approach to literacy is the portfolio. It is authentic and holistic, and it represents a developmental view of students' progress. Pierce and O'Malley (1992) suggest that portfolio assessment be used for making instructional decisions about moving students into mainstream programs. The materials included in the portfolio should therefore reflect the criteria used for making such decisions. They indicate that portfolio assessment can also be used for diagnosis

and placement, monitoring student progress, feedback on the effectiveness of instruction, communication with other teachers, feedback to students, and communication with parents.

The contents of the portfolio may vary widely, depending on its purpose. Teachers should consider including a log of personal reading, perhaps in the form of a response journal. A personal writing log, accompanied by periodic samples of students' published writing, is a useful component. Videotapes or audiotapes of students' reading, storytelling, and other language development activities provide a valuable record of student's progress in English, as well as in the primary language.

Summary and Conclusions

Communicative approaches to second language acquisition reflect Vygotsky's zone of proximal development, Bruner's concept of scaffolding, and Holdaway's concept of approximation in that teachers or others provide just enough support to maintain comprehension while students acquire language subconsciously. The natural approach is the most widely applied communicative approach. It is consistent with Krashen's hypotheses in that it involves providing comprehensible and meaningful input from a topical curriculum with a low anxiety level. Early production, correction, and the use of grammatical sequences are minimized. This is the language learning environment of the infant, who is almost always successful in effortlessly learning the mother tongue.

When English language learners have intermediate English proficiency, they should have access to the full core curriculum through the careful application of communicative approach strategies in sheltered instruction in English. The focus of this instruction should be on maintaining comprehension through the pacing of teacher input and through the extensive use of nonverbal language and of props and illustrations.

At an appropriate time, English language learners should receive instruction in English reading and writing through strategies that ensure continued comprehension and communication. Whole-part-whole strategies are very consistent with communicative approaches to second language acquisition. They focus on constructing meaning, they proceed from whole to part, they use authentic, relevant, and functional language, and they are learner centered.

In the early stages of literacy, teachers will find that the key-vocabulary and language experience approaches can provide English language learners with access to print that is consistent with their stage of production. When they are able to begin reading simple text, we should provide scaffolding through prereading activities that develop background knowledge and vocabulary. We should support reading comprehension through guided silent reading and postreading activities, such as oral and written retelling. Extensive silent sustained reading is potentially the most valuable activity for continued growth in English language development in the areas of vocabulary, reading comprehension, grammar, spelling, and writing.

Student progress in English language acquisition, in the core academic curriculum, and in literacy is enhanced for students who have developed a high level of proficiency in the primary language, including listening, oral language, reading, and writing skills at cognitive/academic levels. In addition, background knowledge they develop from the core curriculum in the primary language provides a strong base for learning in English.

REFERENCES

Allington, R. L. (2001). *What really matters for struggling readers: Designing research-based programs.* New York, NY: Addison Wesley Longman.

Allington, R. L. (1997). Overselling phonics. *Reading Today*, 14, 15

Altwerger, B., Edelsky, C., & Flores, B. M. (1987). Whole language: What's new? *The Reading Teacher*, 41, 144-154.

Antonacci, P. A. (1993). Natural assessment in whole language classrooms. In A. Carrasquillo & C. Hedley (Eds.), *Whole language and the bilingual learner* (pp. 116-131). Norwood, NJ: Ablex.

Arthur, B. M. (1991). Working with new ESL students in a junior high school reading class. *The Journal of Reading,* 34, 628-631.

Asher, J. J. (1982). The total physical response approach. In R. W. Blair (Ed.), *Innovative approaches to language teaching* (pp. 54-66). Rowley, MA: Newbury House.

Asher, J. J. (1979). Motivating children and adults to acquire a second language. *SPEAQ Journal,* 3, 87-99.

Asher, J. J. (1969). The total physical response approach to second language learning. *Modern Language Journal,* 53, 3-17.

Bear, D. R., Invernizzi, M., Templeton, S., & Johnston, F. (2000). *Words their way: Word study for phonics, vocabulary, and spelling instruction.* Upper Saddle River, NJ: Merrill.

Beck, I. L., & McKeown, M. G. (1981). Developing questions that promote comprehension: The story map. *Language Arts,* 58, 913-917.

Berman, P., Chambers, J., Gandara, P., McLaughlin, B., Minicucci, C., Nelson, B., Olsen, L., & Parrish, T. (1992). *Meeting the challenge of language diversity.* Berkeley, CA: BW Associates.

Bromley, Karen D'Angelo (1989). Buddy journals make the reading-writing connection. *The Reading Teacher,* 43, 122-129.

Brown, H., & Cambourne, B. (1990). *Read and retell: A strategy for the whole-language/natural learning classroom.* Portsmouth, NH: Heinemann.

Bruner, J. (1978). The role of dialogue in language acquisition. In A. Sinclair, R. J. Jarvella, & W. M. Levelt (Eds.). *The child's conception of language* (pp. 241-256). New York, NY: Springer-Verlag.

Cathcart-Strong, R. L. (1986). Input generation by young second language learners. *TESOL Quarterly,* 20, 515-530.

Chamot, A. U. (1983). Toward a functional ESL curriculum in the elementary school. *TESOL Quarterly,* 17, 459-471.

Chamot, A. U. (1981). Applications of second language acquisition research to the bilingual classroom. *Focus: National Clearinghouse for Bilingual Education,* 1-8.

Chastain, K. (1975). *Developing second-language skills: From theory to practice. Chicago,* IL: Rand McNally College Publishing Company.

Coles, G. (2000). *Misreading reading: The bad science that hurts children.* Portsmouth, NH: Heinemann.

Collier, V. P. (1989). How long? A synthesis of research on academic achievement in a second language. *TESOL Quarterly,* 23, 509-539.

Collier, V. P. (1987). Age and rate of acquisition of second language for academic purposes. *TESOL Quarterly,* 21, 617-641.

Coote, P., & Stevens, R. *Whole language: A New Zealand approach.* Christchurch, NZ: Christchurch College of Education.

Crawford, A. N. (1993). Literature, integrated language arts, and the language minority child: A focus on meaning. In A. Carrasquillo & C. Hedley (Eds.), *Whole language and the bilingual learner* (pp. 61-75). Norwood, NJ: Ablex.

Crawford, A. N. (1986). Communicative approaches to ESL: A bridge to reading comprehension. In M. P. Douglass (Ed.), *Claremont Reading Conference Yearbook* (pp. 292-305). Claremont, CA: Claremont Reading Conference.

Crawford, A. N. (1982). From Spanish reading to English reading: The transition process. In M. P. Douglass (Ed.), *Claremont Reading Conference Yearbook* (pp. 159-165). Claremont, CA: Claremont Reading Conference.

Crawford, A. N., Allen, R. V., & Hall, M. (1995). The language experience approach. In A. N. Crawford (Ed.), *A practical guidebook for adult literacy programmes in developing nations* (pp. 17-46). Paris: UNESCO.

Cummins, J. (1989). *Empowering minority students.* Sacramento: California Association for Bilingual Education.

Cummins, J. (1986) Empowering minority students: A framework for intervention. *Harvard Educational Review, 56,* 18-36.

Cummins, J. (1981). The role of primary language development in promoting educational success for language minority students. In California State Department of Education (Ed.), *Schooling and language minority students: A theoretical framework* (pp. 3-49). Los Angeles: Evaluation, Dissemination and Assessment Center, California State University, Los Angeles.

Cummins, J. (1980). The cross-lingual dimensions of language proficiency: Implications for bilingual education and the optimal age issue. *TESOL Quarterly, 14,* 175-187.

Dixon, C. N., & Nessel, D. (1983). *Language experience approach to reading and writing): LEA for ESL.* Hayward, CA: Alemany Press.

Doughty, C., & Pica, T. (1986). "Information gap" tasks: Do they facilitate second language acquisition? *TESOL Quarterly, 20,* 305-325.

Dowhower, S. L. (1987). Effects of repeated reading on second-grade transitional readers' fluency and comprehension. *Reading Research Quarterly, 22,* 389-406.

Duffy-Hester, A. (1999). Teaching struggling readers in elementary school classrooms: A review of classroom reading programs and principles for instruction. *The Reading Teacher, 52,* 480-495.

Dulay, H. C., & Burt, M. K. (1974a). Errors and strategies in child second language acquisition. *TESOL Quarterly, 8,* 129-143.

Dulay, H. C., & Burt, M. K. (1974b). Natural sequences in child second language acquisition. *Language Learning, 24,* 37-53.

Edelsky, Carole (1982). Writing in a bilingual program: The relation of L_1 and L_2 texts. *TESOL Quarterly, 16,* 211-228.

Ervin-Tripp, S. M. (1974). Is second language learning like the first? *TESOL Quarterly, 8,* 111-127.

Ferreiro, E. (1991). La construcción de la escritura en el niño. *Lectura y Vida, 12,* 5-14.

Finocchiaro, M. (1974). *English as a second language: From theory to practice.* New York, NY: Regents.

Fitzgerald, J. (1993). Literacy and students who are learning English as a second language. *The Reading Teacher, 46,* 638-647.

Freeman, D., & Freeman, Y. (1988). Whole language content lessons. Elementary *ESOL Education News,* 11, 1-2.

Galyean, B. (1980). *My language is me: A confluent program in English for K-3 NES/LES students* (Publication No. 3725). Los Angeles: Los Angeles Unified School District, Instructional Planning Division.

Galyean, B. (1977). A confluent design for language teaching. *TESOL Quarterly,* 11, 143-156.

Gee, J. P. (1992). *The social mind: Ideology and social practice.* New York, NY: Bergin & Garvey.

Gentry, J. R. (1982). An analysis of developmental spelling in GNYS AT WRK. *The Reading Teacher,* 36, 192-200.

Gentry, J. R. (1981). Learning to spell developmentally. *The Reading Teacher,* 34, 378-381.

Goodman, K. (1986). *What's whole in whole language?* Portsmouth, NH: Heinemann.

Hamayan, E. V., & Perlman, R. (1991). *Helping language minority students after they exit from bilingual/ESL programs.* Washington, DC: National Clearinghouse for Bilingual Education.

Heald-Taylor, G. (1986). *Whole language strategies for ESL students.* San Diego: Dormac.

Heimlich, J. E., & S. D. Pittelman (1986). *Semantic mapping: Classroom applications.* Newark, DE: International Reading Association.

Heller, M. F. (1988). Comprehending and composing through language experience. *The Reading Teacher,* 42, 130-135.

Holdaway, D. (1979). *The foundations of literacy.* Sydney: Ashton Scholastic.

Hudelson, S. (1984). Kan yu ret an rayt en Ingles: Children become literate in English as a second language. *TESOL Quarterly,* 18, 221-238.

Johnson, D. M. (1988). ESL children as teachers: A social view of second language use. *Language Arts,* 65, 154-163.

Koskinen, P. S., Gambrell, L. B., Kapinus, B. A., & Heathington, B. S. (1988). Retelling: A strategy for enhancing students' reading comprehension. *The Reading Teacher,* 41, 892-896.

Krashen, S. (1993). *The power of reading.* Englewood, CO: Libraries Unlimited, Inc.

Krashen, S. D. (1991). *Bilingual education: A focus on current research.* Washington, DC: National Clearinghouse for Bilingual Education.

Krashen, S. D. (1985). *Inquiries and insights: Second language teaching, immersion & bilingual education, literacy.* Hayward, CA: Alemany Press.

Krashen, S. (1982). Theory versus practice in language training. In R. W. Blair (Ed.), *Innovative approaches to language teaching* (pp. 15-30). Rowley, MA: Newbury House.

Krashen, S. D. (1982). *Principles and practice in second language acquisition.* New York, NY: Pergamon Press.

Krashen, S. D. (1981). Bilingual education and second language acquisition theory. In California State Department of Education (Ed.), *Schooling and language minority students: A theoretical framework* (pp. 51-79). Sacramento, CA: Office of Bilingual Bicultural Education, California State Department of Education.

Krashen, S., & Biber, D. (1988). *On course: Bilingual education's success in California.* Sacramento, CA: California Association for Bilingual Education.

Krashen, S. D., Long, M. A., & Scarcella, R. C. (1979). Age, rate and eventual attainment in second language acquisition. *TESOL Quarterly*, 13, 573-582.

Krashen, S. D., & Terrell, T. D. (1983). *The natural approach: Language acquisition in the classroom.* New York, NY: Pergamon/Alemany.

Lenneberg, E. (1967). *Biological foundations of language.* New York, NY: Wiley.

Los Angeles Unified School District (1985). *Strategies for sheltered English instruction.* Los Angeles: Los Angeles Unified School District.

Lynch, P. (1986). *Using big books and predictable books.* New York: Scholastic.

María, K. (1989). Developing disadvantaged children's background knowledge interactively. *The Reading Teacher*, 42, 296-300.

McGroarty, M. (1984). Some meanings of communicative competence for second language students. *TESOL Quarterly*, 18, 257-272.

Moustafa, M., & Penrose, J. (1985). Comprehensible input PLUS the language experience approach: Reading instruction for limited English speaking students. *The Reading Teacher*, 38, 640-647.

Nagy, W., Anderson, R. C., & Herman, P. (1987). Learning word meanings from context during normal reading. *American Educational Research Journal*, 24, 237-270.

Nathenson-Mejia, S. (1989). Writing in a second language: Negotiating meaning through invented spelling. *Language Arts*, 66, 516-526.

Nessel, D. D., & Jones, M. B. (1981). *The language-experience approach to reading.* New York, NY: Teachers College Columbia University.

Pearson, P. D. (1985). Changing the face of reading comprehension instruction. *The Reading Teacher*, 38, 724-738.

Peck, J. (1989). Using storytelling to promote language and literacy development. *The Reading Teacher*, 43, 138-141.

Peetoom, A. (1986). *Shared reading: Safe risks with whole books.* Richmond Hill, Ontario, Canada: Scholastic.

Pierce, L. V., & O'Malley, J. M. (1992). *Performance and portfolio assessment for language minority students.* Washington, D. C.: National Clearinghouse for Bilingual Education.

Richard-Amato, P. A., & Snow, M. A. (1992). Strategies for content-area teachers. In P. A. Richard-Amato & M. A. Snow (Eds.), *The multicultural classroom: Readings for content-area teachers* (pp. 145-163). White Plains, NY: Longman.

Rigg, P. (1991). Whole language in TESOL. *TESOL Quarterly*, 25, 521-542.

Rutherford, W., & Sharwood-Smith, M. (1985). Consciousness raising and universal grammar. *Applied Linguistics*, 6, 274-282.

Samuels, S. J. (1979). The method of repeated readings. *The Reading Teacher*, 32, 403-408.

Samuels, S. J. (1971). Letter-name versus letter-sound knowledge in learning to read. *The Reading Teacher*, 24, 604-608.

Samway, K. D. (1993). "This is hard, isn't it?": Children evaluating writing. *TESOL Quarterly*, 27, 233-257.

Samway, K. D. (1992). *Writers' workshop and children acquiring English as a non-native language.* Washington, DC: National Clearinghouse for Bilingual Education.

Saville-Troike, M. (1991). *Teaching and testing for academic achievement: The role of language development.* Washington, DC: National Clearinghouse for Bilingual Education.

Schifini, A. (1985). *Sheltered English: Content area instruction for limited English proficient students.* Los Angeles: Los Angeles County Office of Education.

Selinker, L., Swain, M., & Dumas, G. (1975). The interlanguage hypothesis extended to children. *Language Learning*, 25, 139-152.

Sleeter, C. E. & Grant, C. A. (1999). *Making choices for multicultural education.* Upper Saddle River, NJ: Merrill.

Smith, F. (1989). Overselling literacy. *Phi Delta Kappan,* 70, 352-359.

Smith, F. (1988). *Understanding reading.* Hillsdale, NJ: Erlbaum

Smith, F. (1986). Keynote address, California Reading Association, Fresno, California.

Smith, F. (1985). *Reading without nonsense.* New York: Teachers College Press.

Snow, C. E., Burns, M. S., & Griffin, P. (Eds.) (1998). *Preventing reading difficulties in young children.* Committee on the Prevention of Reading Difficulties in Young Children. Commission on Behavioral and Social Sciences and Education, National Research Council. Washington, DC. National Academy Press.

Snow, C. E., & Hoefnagel-Höhle, M. (1978). The critical period for language acquisition: Evidence from second language learning. *Child Development*, 49, 1114-1128.

Stanovich, K. E. (1986). Matthew effects in reading: some consequences of individual differences in the acquisition of literacy. *Reading Research Quarterly*, 21, 360-406.

Strickland, D. S., & Feeley, J. T. (1985). Using children's concept of story to improve reading and writing. In T. L. Harris & E. J. Cooper (Eds.), *Reading, thinking and concept development* (pp. 163-173). New York: College Entrance Examination Board.

Terrell, T. D. (1991). The role of grammar instruction in a communicative approach. *Modern Language Journal*, 75, 52-63.

Terrell, T. D (1986). Acquisition in the natural approach: The binding/access framework. *Modern Language Journal*, 70, 213-227

Terrell, T. D. (1982). The natural approach to language teaching: An update. *Modern Language Journal*, 66, 121-132.

Terrell, T. D (1981). The natural approach in bilingual education. In California State Department of Education (Ed.), *School and language minority students: A theoretical framework* (pp. 117-146). Los Angeles: Evaluation, Dissemination and Assessment Center, California State University, Los Angeles.

Terrell, T. D. (1977). A natural approach to second language acquisition and learning. *Modern Language Journal*, 6, 325-337.

Thomas, W. P., & Collier, V. P. (2002). *A national study of school effectiveness for language minority students' long-term academic achievement final report: Project 1.1.* Santa Cruz, CA: Center for Research on Education, Diversity & Excellence.

Trachtenburg, P., & Ferruggia, A. (1989). Big books from little voices: Reaching high risk beginning readers. *The Reading Teacher*, 42, 284-289.

Urzúa, C. (1987). "You stopped too soon": Second language children composing and revising. *TESOL Quarterly*, 21, 279-304.

Veatch, J., Sawicki, F., Elliott, G., Flake, E., & Blakey, J. (1979). *Key words to reading: The language experience approach begins.* Columbus, OH: Merrill.

Vygotsky, L. S. (1978). *Mind in society.* Cambridge, MA: Harvard University Press.

Primary Language Instruction: A Bridge to English Language Development

Marguerite Ann Snow

Introduction

One of the greatest challenges currently facing American schools is educating the burgeoning population of students who do not speak English. While English language learners have traditionally been clustered in the states of Arizona, California, Colorado, Florida, Illinois, New Jersey, New York, New Mexico, and Texas, they can be found in classrooms throughout the country. Many states in the Midwest and South such as Nebraska, Minnesota, Tennessee, and North Carolina have seen dramatic increases in recent years in the numbers of students who come to school speaking little or no English. It is now accurate to state that virtually all teachers, regardless of where they teach, will have English language learners in their classes at some point in their careers. How best to teach these elementary and secondary language minority students is the subject of much debate. This chapter makes a case for the use of the primary language in the schooling of English language learners by exploring relevant research in the second language acquisition and language education literature and suggesting ways in which teachers can support the use of the primary language while their students are developing their English language skills.

Any discussion of effective schooling for language minority students must first begin with an understanding of who these students are. The language minority population in American schools is a very complex mosaic of languages, native countries and cultures, familial circumstances, and educational experiences. Given this complexity, it is difficult to characterize this diverse school-age audience. Yet an understanding of this profile provides a critical backdrop in this chapter for discussion of the role of the primary language in the schooling of these students.

English language learners in the United States represent a linguistically and culturally diverse group that falls roughly into three broad categories: (1) recent immigrants; (2) early immigrants; and (3) U.S. born students. Profiles of these three types of students differ along a number of key dimensions, perhaps the most critical of which is the degree to which they have been exposed to literate practices or have developed literacy skills in their native language either in the home or at school. In fact, Williams and Snipper (1990) classified language minority students according to the degree to which they can read and write in their native language. In their scheme, language minority students are labeled as preliterate, literate, or postliterate.

Age of arrival is also a key variable. Early immigrants may have left their home countries in the early primary grades and schooling in the first language may have been interrupted. Collier (1987) found that children who arrive in the U.S. at ages 4 to 7 and are schooled exclusively in English may need up to five years to reach the same levels of academic achievement as older English language learners who have had some instruction in their primary language. Recent immigrants, on the other hand, have typically developed academic language proficiency in their native language and, in some cases, initial proficiency in English in their home countries, but need assistance in transferring concepts and skills learned in their first language to English.

The U.S.-born child, of course, comes to school with no prior schooling and, particularly for those living in ethnic communities, often little exposure to English in their daily lives. Depending upon literacy practices in the home, these children may or may not read and write in their native language. For these language minority students, schooling in the U.S. represents the only opportunity for native language literacy development.

Indeed the profile is even more complex. Other factors such as socioeconomic status, previous academic achievement, immigration status, family support and expectations, language proficiency, and social challenges shape these students' needs and school successes (Walqui, 2000). Furthermore, students coming from rural, poor, or war-torn countries may have experienced gaps in their education. Especially for secondary school immigrants, these gaps often mean little or poor literacy in the native language. Because their schooling has been disrupted, they may lack basic study skills and knowledge of school culture to fall back on as they learn English in the American school setting. Their difficulties are compounded by the fact that the level of cognitive complexity and sequential content knowledge of high school subject matter is very dependent on prior knowledge. Once in the U.S., other factors, such as the high transiency of students from migrant worker families, the tensions of being in undocumented status, work pressures on students helping to support their families financially, family responsibilities like caring for younger siblings, and trips back to the native country can create problems in school which are difficult for these students to overcome. For these older students, the amount of time remaining in school is a critical factor. Collier (1989) found that, for the late immigrant, if academic work in the primary language is not continued at home or at school while these students are learning English, there may not be enough time left in secondary school to make up for the lost periods of academic instruction. To counter the time factor, many school districts have created "newcomer schools" in an attempt to give English language learners more time to work through the secondary curriculum, five years in some sites, or have forged links with community adult schools for students who can no longer legally attend high school because of their age.

Even for those students who have had the benefit of consistent, high quality instruction in their home countries, these students, once in the U.S., may find the adjustment process difficult. Walqui (2000) noted that secondary students, in many cases, must deal with fragmented school days, departmentalized schools, course tracking, age-grade inflexibility, and complicated systems for obtaining course credit that, taken together, create many structural obstacles. Although these learners may have been successful students in their home countries, the transition may not be as smooth as expected. In addition, English language learners often encounter very different kinds of teaching styles (possibly more student-centered than teacher-centered) and learning styles (less need for rote memorization and more emphasis on analytical thinking), and emphasis on different skills (e.g., focus on writing rather than on grammar instruction). Moreover, these older students must deal with the adjustment to a new language, culture, and school setting, all while undergoing the inevitable growth pains experienced by teenagers. All this takes place in the typically impersonal setting of the American high school where, for the newly-arrived immigrant, the school day may seem like a whirlwind of ever changing classrooms, subjects, and teachers.

Older U.S.-born and early immigrants, increasingly referred to as "Generation 1.5" students in the literature, often have characteristics that lie somewhere between first and second generation immigrants (Rumbaut & Ima, 1988). As these students move through the U.S. educational system, they become increasingly English-dominant, yet by the time they exit U.S. high schools, they reflect a ". . . tremendously diverse student population along continua of language proficiency, language affiliation, and academic literacy backgrounds" (Harklau, Losey, & Siegal, 1999, p. 5), putting pressure on postsecondary institutions to develop appropriate placement and programmatic options, particularly in regard to students' writing skills.

In short, educators must recognize the tremendous heterogeneity to be found among our language minority students. We know that all students do not bring the same kinds of knowledge, language habits, and strategies for learning to school and we must take responsibility for presenting all students with a range of options for using language and organizing knowledge. Heath and Mangiola (1991) offer a strategy for dealing with the linguistic and cultural variety in our classrooms: "Let us then not think of students of diverse backgrounds as bringing 'differences' to school, but instead as offering classrooms 'expansions' of background knowledge and ways of using language" (p. 17). Diversity, in their view, is an opportunity, not a problem. Furthermore, Garcia (1991) helps us take a hopeful position, noting that these students "display a portrait of unrealized academic success" (p. 1). The perspective taken in this chapter is that primary language instruction is a bridge to academic literacy, a key link in assisting language minority students to realize success in English language development.

Primary Language Instruction: Can It Be Justified?

This section of the chapter will provide a rationale for instruction in the primary language. Justification comes from several perspectives, including the need for a language competent society and the positive benefits of bilingualism.

A Language Competent Society

Clearly the goal of our educational system is to produce students who are proficient in English in all realms of use—at home, at school, and on the job. Consider the paradox, however, when it comes to the lack of commitment to preserve these students' native language skills. Why do we offer foreign language instruction to monolingual English-speaking students while our school system, in general, is set up to eradicate the home language of the language minority students who come into American schools? In fact, Campbell and Lindholm put this paradox in bold perspective. They calculate that the Defense Language Institute in Monterey, California, each year provides instruction in more than 40 languages to 6,000 full-time students who are members of the U.S. military. Graduates of a 47 week course in Korean, for example, achieve lower levels of oral proficiency in Korean than that which a five-year old native speaker of Korean brings to school (in Crawford, 1989, p. 164).

Former U.S. Senator Paul Simon of Illinois was one of the first at the national level to recognize this potential crisis. In his 1980 book *The Tongue-Tied American*, Simon noted:

> Because of our rich ethnic mix, the United States is home to millions whose first language is not English. One of every fifty Americans is foreign-born. We are the fourth largest Spanish-speaking country in the world. Yet almost nothing is being done to preserve the language skills we now have or to use this rich linguistic resource to train people in the use of a language other than English. (p. 4)

Marcos (1999, para. 1) made a similar observation some twenty years later:

> One of our national ironies is that United States is short on the language expertise needed for national defense, international business, and local government services at the same time that unprecedented numbers of immigrants are arriving in the United States thoroughly fluent in languages other than English. As the children of these immigrants move through the educational system, their English language skills grow and improve (as they must), but their native language skills often fall by the wayside. In an ever more global economy, we cannot afford to let slip away the linguistic resources we already possess.

Put even more forcefully, Barr (2002) states that the shortage of foreign language expertise has ". . . adversely affected agency operations and hindered U.S. military, law enforcement, intelligence, counter terrorism, and diplomatic efforts" (in Brecht & Ingold, 2002, para. 1).

Bilingualism in most countries around the world is considered a fact of life—a resource for daily activities, a symbol of educational attainment, and a necessity in the global marketplace. In countries as diverse as Sweden, China, and Canada, societal bilingualism is commonplace and education in more than one language is supported by the government. Tucker (2003) underscores this point: ". . . available data indicate that there are many more bilingual or multilingual individuals in the world than there are monolingual. . . . In many parts of the world

bilingualism or multilingualism and innovative approaches to education
which involve the use of one or more languages constitute the normal
everyday experience" (p. 464).

Historically in the U.S, there has been a tradition of bilingual edition.
More than a dozen states offered instruction in such languages as German, French, Italian, Polish, Spanish, and Yiddish in the nineteenth century (Fishman, 2001). World War I and the attitudes of nationalism it
brought contributed to the decline in language instruction and the value
placed on bilingualism. The War's aftermath of isolationism exacerbated this decline. World War II, in contrast, brought a renewed interest
in language study with government recognition of the importance of language study for defense needs. This effort was followed by even greater
emphasis on language study with the launching of Sputnik in 1957 and
the commitment to narrow the perceived educational gap with the then
Soviet Union (Thompson, Christian, Stansfield, & Rhodes, 1990).

More recently, bilingualism has become a highly politicized national
issue. Ballot initiatives in several states have banned bilingual education,
and the English-Only movement aims to make English the official language.[1] Despite the on-going controversy surrounding issues of bilingualism, there are some bright spots. The longstanding efforts of foreign
language educators to teach Americans to speak foreign languages have
been augmented by action at the grassroots level in many ethnic communities, schools, and colleges to preserve so-called "heritage languages"
(Peyton, Ranard, & McGinnis, 2001). In the U.S., heritage language education refers to interest in the study, maintenance, and revitalization of
non-English languages. The profile of heritage language speakers is typically varied and complex; however, all have in common an historical or
personal connection to the language—for example, the language of their
grandparents or the language of their religious community. More specifically, Valdes (2001), defines a heritage language speaker as someone
". . . who is raised in a home where a non-English language is spoken,
who understands the language, and who is to some degree bilingual in
that language and in English" (p. 38). This growing interest in heritage
language education is leading to initiatives to develop appropriate curricula and materials for heritage language students and to offer professional

---

[1] See, for example, James Crawford's treatment of the English-Only versus
English-Plus debate in the U.S. in *Language Loyalties: A Source Book on the
Official English Controversy (1992)* and *At War with Diversity: U S Language
Policy in an Age of Anxiety* (2000).

development training to heritage language teachers through conferences and institutes. While the earliest efforts concentrated on the teaching of Spanish to native speakers (The American Association of Teachers of Spanish and Portuguese, 2000), there is increasing activity in heritage language education for speakers of Armenian, Arabic, Chinese, Creole, Khmer, Korean, Russian, and Vietnamese (Webb & Miller, 2000; Peyton, Ranard, & McGinnis, 2001).

In sum, calls for a language competent American society (cf., Tucker, 1984, 1990) continue to resonate and have, perhaps, taken on a greater sense of urgency in the post-September 11th era in the U.S. Paralleling foreign and heritage language education efforts, the schooling of language minority students in their primary language offers one more avenue to promote the rich natural resource these students bring to the American classroom. Tucker (2003) captures these benefits succinctly: "The graduates of such programs should be culturally rich, linguistically competent and socially sensitive individuals prepared to participate actively in our increasingly global economy" (p. 470).

The Positive Consequences of Bilingualism

Research has revealed that there are many benefits to being bilingual. In this section, the cognitive, academic, and socio-cultural benefits of bilingualism will be examined.

Studies of the relationship between intelligence and bilingualism offer two contrasting pictures. Early research on the cognitive consequences of bilingualism was consistently negative.[2] For instance, Thompson (1952) wrote:

> There can be no doubt that the child reared in a bilingual environment is handicapped in his language growth. One can debate the issue as to whether speech facility in two languages is worth the consequent retardation in the common language of the realm. (p. 367)

Similarly, Darcy (1953) reviewed 110 studies in the literature and found either adverse effects or no effects on intelligence associated with bilingualism.

---

[2] See Legarreta-Marcaida (1981) and Hakuta (1986) for reviews of these studies.

The tide began to shift when a widely cited UNESCO document entitled *The Use of the Vernacular Languages in Education* (1953) reported on successful programs around the world that used the native language as the medium of instruction. Perhaps the major turning point in the debate occurred with the publication of a study by Canadian researchers Peal and Lambert (1962) whose findings stood in stark contrast to many of the earlier suppositions. Based on their research, they described a bilingual as:

> a youngster whose wider experiences in two cultures have given him advantages which a monolingual does not enjoy. Intellectually his experience with two language systems seems to have left him with a mental flexibility, a superiority in concept formation, a more diversified set of mental abilities. . . . In contrast, the monolingual appears to have a more unitary structure of intelligence which he must use for all types of intellectual tasks (p. 20).

Peal and Lambert concluded that bilingualism facilitated mental flexibility, abstract thinking, concept formation, and allowed for the transfer of knowledge between the bilingual's two languages. Macnamara (1966) underscored this change in perspective on the value of bilingualism in a critical review of the early studies. He found them so fraught with methodological irregularities, such as failure to control for socio-economic status, sampling techniques which were questionable, and use of instruments which were not valid, that the early findings could no longer be considered credible.

More recent work confirms that children who grow up bilingual or become bilingual at an early age demonstrate advantages in several areas of cognitive functioning over children who are monolingual (Snow, 1990). One type of advantage is in the area of metalinguistic awareness, the ability to analyze the form as well as the content of language and the knowledge of how to talk about language. Certain kinds of metalinguistic skills, such as the realization that words have no intrinsic connection to the objects to which they refer, develop much earlier in bilingual children than in their monolingual counterparts. Interestingly, the metalinguistic skills so critical in learning to read, which are typically developed by monolingual children who come from highly verbal homes, can also be seen in bilingual children from families of low income and low educational backgrounds. These advantages do not appear for low income monolingual peers and seem to take place only when language minority students use their bilingual skills over an extended period of time in what Lambert (1980) first called "additive" language learning environments. In contrast, the "subtractive" bilingual model where the home language is replaced by the school language ". . . does not provide for any period of stable bilingualism during which the positive consequences of being bilingual can emerge" (Snow, 1990, p. 65). Bialystok's (1987) research provides further evidence for the positive benefits of bilingualism. In a comparison of the reading ability of four and five-year-old children, she found that the bilingual children were superior in understanding the symbolic meaning of print. Bolstering the arguments for the positive benefits of bilingualism, Cummins (2000) concluded that close to 150 empirical studies conducted during the past 30 years have reported a positive association between additive bilingualism and students' linguistic, cognitive, or academic growth.

Highlighting another kind of benefit, Krashen and Biber (1988) maintained that ". . . possibly the most important advantage of full bilingualism is that it can help lead to a healthy sense of biculturalism" (p. 27). In contrast, many language minority students perceive the negative messages about their language and culture that emanate from school and society at large and develop what Cummins has called "cultural ambivalence." A strong primary language component in school can mitigate these negative images, validating language minority students' home language and culture and helping to develop a strong sense of self-identity as these students adjust to life in a new country, a new language, or a new school culture. As Snow (1990) pointed out: "Schools should be operated in ways that maximize the self-esteem of their students—because that is a worthy goal in itself, but also because students with high self-esteem work harder, learn better, and achieve more" (p. 64).

Bilingual Education: An Overview

Faltis and Hudelson (1998) made the following claims about bilingual education: (1) Children learn best in a language they understand and use for communication; (2) Schools have a social, moral, and legal responsibility to educate all children regardless of their English proficiency; and (3) Schools that do nothing to assist the learning of non-English speaking students are discriminating against these students, and thus are in violation of Title VI of the Civil Rights Act of 1965 (pp. 14-15). Since the passage of, the Bilingual Education Act in 1968, school districts across the U.S. have developed a variety of approaches to bilingual education in an effort to meet the needs of English language learners. These approaches can best be described as varied and variable, due to contextual factors such as age of students, program length, type of curriculum and materials, teacher qualifications and availability, and financial and administrative support.[3] McGroarty (2000), in fact, makes the interesting observation that: "Programs are labeled bilingual for a variety of reasons, only some of which reflect the actual language of instruction" (p. 346).

Program Types

Bilingual education approaches range from programs which offer no special assistance to language minority students (traditionally referred to as "submersion"), to programs in which the development of students' native language is a key objective (typically labeled "maintenance" bilingual education). Other models include transitional bilingual programs (with either early- or late exit options) where the goal is to use the native language for instruction only to the point at which students have acquired sufficient oral and literacy skills to be schooled entirely in English. ESL "pull-out" programs are also a common program option. In this model, English language learners attend a separate class or classes for English language instruction usually taught by an ESL teacher. Pull-out programs can be found at both the elementary and secondary levels.

More recently, two other models have emerged which offer very disparate underlying philosophies for the education of language minority students. Starting in the mid-1980's, "dual language" or "two-way" immersion programs have been implemented, drawing on features of both maintenance bilingual education for language minority students and the immersion model of the type developed in Canada to teach French to language *majority* students (i.e., English speakers).[4] In this model of bilingual education, language minority and language majority students are integrated for instruction in the target language for some

---

[3] For more detailed discussions of bilingual education program models, see Carrasquillo & Rodriguez (2002), Faltis & Hudelson (1998), and Kuhlman & Murray (2000).

[4] See Genesee (1987) and Johnson and Swain (1997) for more in-depth descriptions of the Canadian model of immersion education.

portion of the school day—thus, the "two-way" notion. For example, in a Spanish two-way program, language minority students receive a significant amount of instruction daily in their first language (Spanish) while the language majority, English-speaking students, are schooled in their second language, Spanish. The goals of two-way programs are to develop bilingual skills, academic excellence, and positive cross-cultural and personal competency attitudes for both populations (Lindholm-Leary, 2001). Spanish is the most common target language of instruction in two-way programs given the predominance of native Spanish speakers among language minority populations; however, two-way programs exist in Arabic, Cantonese, French, Japanese, Korean, Navajo, Portuguese, and Russian (Christian, Montone, Lindholm, & Carranza, 1997).

The second model to emerge, "structured immersion," also purports to have roots in Canadian-style immersion. Features of the immersion model—an approach to teaching the foreign language to language majority speakers—have been appropriated in the instruction of language minority students. In structured immersion classes, teachers use English exclusively as the medium of instruction and employ special techniques for making content instruction accessible to English language learners (often called "SDAIE"—specially designed academic instruction in English). Structured immersion programs have been implemented at the elementary level in many U.S. school districts and have become the predominant model in California since the passage of Proposition 227, a ballot initiative passed by the voters in June 1998, which generally restricts English language learners to no more than one year of structured immersion before being transferred to mainstream classes.[5]

The bulk of the programs described above are geared toward English language learners in elementary schools. At the middle and secondary school levels, fewer programmatic options exist. "Sheltered" courses are one approach offered to English language learners to give them access to the core curriculum. Sheltered courses are content classes (e.g., math, history, science), typically taught by content teachers who have received training in principles of second language acquisition and sheltered instructional strategies (Echevarria & Graves, 2003).

---

[5] For background information and studies of the impact of Proposition 227, see Crawford (2000), Dicker (2000), and the web site of the University of California Linguistic Minority Research Institute at *www.lmri.ucsb.edu.*

A survey by Minicucci and Olsen (1992) of programs for secondary ELLs, found that regardless of the instructional approach (e.g., primary language instruction or sheltered English), fewer than one-fourth of the schools they surveyed offered full content programs for students learning English. More than one-third of the intermediate schools and half of the high schools had major gaps in their offerings or provided no content classes at all. Furthermore, they found that patterns of course offerings appeared to be related to the nature of district and school site leadership, staff availability and willingness to take training, and the decentralized nature of decisions at these levels. Harklau's (1994) study of mainstream and ESL high school classes in a Northern California school district offers a similarly troubling picture. In this district, mainstream teachers and school administrators lacked awareness of and sensitivity to the needs of English language learners, thus creating an educational environment that did little to facilitate their transition to the mainstream or nurture their success upon the transition. The results of these studies portray a worrisome picture of the realities beyond elementary school for language minority students whose future education career opportunities are dependent on access to quality content-area and English instruction. Walqui (2000) underscores this point, noting that the number of immigrant teenagers in American schools is ". . . numerically significant and increasing, yet we know little about them and their needs. This lack of knowledge leaves school systems facing myriad situations they are unprepared to meet" (p. 1).

Research Results

In general, the accumulation of research in bilingual education indicates that bilingual education, when properly implemented over time and reliably assessed, is beneficial to students learning English as a second language. These positive results, however, have been overshadowed in recent years by the controversies that have raged in both academic circles and the popular press.[6] This section briefly reviews early research regarding the effectiveness of bilingual education and then moves on to a description of studies that elucidate the key features of successful instructional programs for language minority students.

---

[6] For interesting discussions of the politics of bilingual education, see Crawford (1989), articles by Secada and Mulhauser in Cazden and Snow (1990), and Cummins (2000).

The highly publicized Baker and de Kanter (1983) review of the results of 28 bilingual education programs concluded that there was no consistent evidence to support the effectiveness of transitional bilingual education (TBE). It interesting to note that Baker and de Kanter had initially reviewed more than 300 studies, but rejected all but 28 as methodologically unsound (e.g., the studies failed to randomly assign subjects or reported grade-equivalent scores instead of raw scores on standardized tests) (Crawford, 1989). In their conclusions, Baker and de Kanter noted that "An occasional, inexplicable success is not reason enough to make TBE the law of the land...The time spent in using the home language in the classroom my be harmful because it reduces [the time for] English practice" (in Crawford, 1989, p. 92).

A counterpunch to the Baker and de Kanter report was provided by Willig (1985) who used a sophisticated statistical procedure called "meta-analysis" to reanalyze the Baker and de Kanter results. The results of Willig's analysis, in contrast, revealed small to moderate differences favoring bilingual education. A number of other studies have shown the effectiveness of programs with a primary language component for language minority students. In a longitudinal evaluation of an Australian bilingual program, Gale, McClay, Christie, and Harris (1981) found that aboriginal students taught in their primary language and in English performed significantly better on ten different oral and written measures of English after seven years of schooling than aboriginal students who had only received instruction in English. Saville-Troike (1984) investigated the acquisition of oral and written English and academic performance in the subject areas of 19 children, ages 7-12. She found that the two major factors that correlated significantly with the students' academic achievement in English were development of English vocabulary and opportunity for on-going cognitive development in their primary language.

Six California programs with successful bilingual programs were reviewed in Krashen and Biber (1988). Results of standardized testing demonstrated that language minority students who received primary language instruction did as well as or better than comparison children in both English and academic achievement, supporting the authors' claim that time spent developing background knowledge and literacy in the primary language enhanced the abilities and competencies ultimately underlying school success.

A comprehensive eight-year study commissioned by the U.S. Department of Education to SRA Technologies sought to avoid the major methodological weaknesses which had been exposed in the Baker and de Kanter and Willig reviews. In this study, comparison groups were carefully matched and the instructional treatments of the three programs were carefully considered (Ramirez, Yuen & Ramey, 1991; Ramirez, 1992). The objective was to compare three alternative programs at the elementary school level:

1. *Early exit TBE*: In this type of program, initial instruction was provided in the children's primary language, typically to intro- duce initial reading skills, for approximately 30-60 minutes per day. All other instruction was in English. Instruction in the pri- mary language was phased out over the next two years so that by grade two, virtually all instruction was in English and students were expected to be exited from the program and mainstreamed into English-only classrooms by the end of first or second grade.

2. *Late exit bilingual education programs*: Students in this program received a minimum of 40 percent of their total instruction in Spanish (Spanish language arts, reading, and content areas such as mathematics and social studies). Students remained in the program through the sixth grade.

3. *Structured immersion*: All instruction in the program was in English. Teachers had specialized training in working with English language learners and strong receptive skills in the stu- dents' primary language, Spanish, although the use of Spanish was restricted to clarification. Students were mainstreamed within two or three years.

In their final report, the authors concluded that the complexity of the study precluded a direct comparison of the effectiveness of the three programs; however, comparisons of the early-exit and structured immersion were possible and a thorough analysis of the three late-exit programs was reported. Results were as follows:

- After four years in the respective programs, English lan- guage learners in early exit and structured immersion pro- grams demonstrated comparable skills in mathematics, language, and reading when tested in English.

- Differences were found among the three late-exit sites in achievement levels for mathematics, English language, and English reading at the end of the sixth grade. Students in the two sites with the most consistent level of primary language use (in the other site students were exited earlier than 6th grade) exhibited the highest scores in English language and English reading. Interestingly, these two sites differed in the relative amount of instruction provided in English and Spanish from first through six grades. Students from the program with the greatest use of Spanish achieved the same results in English language and reading by the end of sixth grade as the students from the program with the most use of English.

- When compared to the norming population, students who were provided with a substantial and consistent primary language program learned mathematics, English language, and English reading skills as fast as or faster than the monolingual comparisons.

In sum, the SRA study concluded that providing English language learners with substantial amounts of instruction in their primary language did not impede their acquisition of English language skills—in other words, it was as effective as being provided with large amounts of English. Moreover, students were able to master content area subjects and, consequently, make normal progress through the standard school curriculum when instructed in their primary language.

Cazden (1992), in her review of the SRA study, highlighted several important implications of this research. First, she noted: "The most obvious implication is that the amount of time spent using a second language in school can no longer be considered the most important influence on learning it. Such a correlation has been an important assumption in all arguments against bilingual education" (p. 6). The results of this study, she noted, provide strong support for the threshold level posited by Cummins.

Cazden also identified two other factors which are of critical importance in the school success of language minority students. First, it was found that the parents of the late-exit students were the most involved of the three programs (and, interestingly, had the lowest income levels). "More late-exit parents tend[ed] to monitor their child's homework and slightly more tend[ed] to help the child complete homework" (Ramirez, Yuen & Ramey, 1991, p. 361). Clearly, the extensive use of the primary language in the late-exit program had the concomitant effect of creating access to the school for the parents and encouraging increased attention at home to their children's schoolwork. Secondly, the late-exit teachers and principals had more graduate education and more specialized training for working with language minority students than the teachers in the other two program types. Furthermore, the late-exit teachers were more proficient in Spanish than the other teachers and were as proficient as the others in English.

Evaluations of the relatively new two-way immersion model described earlier offer great promise for the efficacy of this type of bilingual education. Results to date indicate that students who participate in elementary two-way programs, both language majority and language minority, develop high levels of first and second language proficiency and, by the upper grades, perform at least at grade level on achievement tests of reading, language, and the content areas (Lindholm-Leary, 2001). Further, positive student, teacher, and parent attitudes undergird the educational climate in which language development and academic achievement takes place for both native English speakers and English language learners.

Collier and Thomas' (Collier, 1987, 1989; Collier & Thomas, 1989; Thomas & Collier, 1997, 2002) extensive research has made important contributions to our understanding of the age factor in schooling language minority students and to the critical issue of how long English language learners take to master English. In general, their research has revealed that the amount of formal schooling in the native language was the strongest predictor of the pace in which English language learners would catch up academically in English. This factor was a stronger predictor than socioeconomic status or the extent to which the students' parents spoke English (Cummins, 2000). Their findings also suggest that it takes five to seven years for second language learners who have received some schooling in their first language to compete with native English speakers; students who have had little or no instruction in the first language may take as long as seven to ten years to achieve academically on par with their native English-speaking peers.

Findings from Collier and Thomas' work also support the claim that older language minority students who arrive in this country at ages 12-15 experience the greatest difficulty with acquisition of academic literacy in English when schooled only in English. Such students in grades 7-12 cannot afford even one or two years' loss of cognitive and academic development in the subject areas while they are attempting to master English. These results, thus, strongly support the advisability of teaching content subjects in the primary language to secondary English language learners while they are learning English.

Hakuta, Butler, and Witt (2000) reprised the length of time issue asking the question: How long does it take English learners to attain proficiency? Reporting on data from four different school districts, two in

California and two in Canada, they concluded that oral proficiency takes three to five years to develop and academic English proficiency can take four to seven years. Furthermore, their results suggest that it may not be possible within regular school hours to offer the kind of instruction that will enable English learners to catch up with native English speakers and that special after-school and summer programs may be necessary.

In sum, the research on length of time needed to acquire high levels of academic proficiency in English is very clear. Regardless of bilingual program type, English language learners need time, many years in fact, to acquire the oral language and academic literacy skills requisite to mastering increasingly demanding content as they move through elementary and secondary school. These findings should offer sobering news to educators in light of the movement to deemphasize bilingual programs with native language components in many parts of the U.S. and to replace them with strict limits on the time in which English language learners may receive some form of special assistance in English such as those mandated in California by Proposition 227. [7]

Finally, in a review of research on the instruction of limited English proficient students commissioned by the California legislature, Gandara (1999) concluded that ". . . while no single program is best for all children under all circumstances, a well-implemented bilingual program can provide outcomes 'at least' as positive as a well-implemented English only program, and has the added advantage of potentially providing students with a second language—a considerable asset" (p. iii). Despite such generally positive findings, bilingual education continues to be perceived negatively by the general public and some segments of the educational community. As such, Faltis and Hudelson (1998), appeal to teachers directly, ". . . we ask you to continue learning about

---

[7] Several studies of the effects of the Proposition 227 are underway. For example, the American Institutes for Research and WestEd are conducting a five-year evaluation of the implementation of Proposition 227. Their second-year report (2002) notes, among other key findings, barriers to implementation such as insufficient guidance for implementing regulations in the law, confusion over what the law requires and allows, and lack of clear operational definitions for the various instructional approaches for English learners. In addition, the report notes that other complex contextual factors may influence the implementation and impact of Proposition 227 (such as class size reduction, testing and accountability programs, reading improvement initiatives, and California's English Language Development standards).

the social, moral, and legal rationales for bilingual education . . . so that you not only keep building your philosophical stance in a proactive manner, but possess the knowledge to present sound counterarguments to the disinformed as well" (p. 16).

Classroom-Based Research: What Does It Reveal about Effective Instruction?

Research in bilingual education has expanded from program comparisons of the type just described toward attempts to document instructional practices which are effective with linguistically and culturally diverse students. McGroarty (2000) characterized this shift in the following way: ". . . it makes little sense to discuss educational models without reference to the social, political, and economic contexts in which they are implemented. . . . Contemporary discussions of bilingual education emphasize the match between the characteristics of an educational program, the sociocultural context of the students it serves, and the resources (both tangible and intangible) available to support educational efforts" (p. 351). Wong Fillmore (1992), "a self-avowed" advocate of bilingual education, adds another perspective: "Bilingual education done well gives excellent results; bilingual education done badly gives poor results, just as one would expect" (p. 367). Hence, the question remains "What are the characteristics of bilingual education done well? or phrased another way "What constitutes effective instruction for English language learners?" Some of the findings of the research dealing with effective features will be highlighted in the next section.

Effective Features, Quality Indicators

In one of the first attempts to describe the characteristics of effective instruction, Tikunoff and Vasquez-Faria (1982) identified five instructional features which, in their research, were significantly related to effective instruction for English language learners: (1) active teaching; (2) using both the native language and the second language for instruction; (3) integrating English language development with academic skills; (4) using cultural referents, and (5) communicating a sense of self-efficacy and high student expectations.

In a comprehensive study of "special alternative instructional projects" (SAIPs) in which instruction was provided primarily in English as an alternative to bilingual instruction, Tikunoff et al. (1991) found that the exemplary programs, in spite of their emphasis on English instruction, still offered students opportunities to use their native languages. Specifically, Lucas and Katz (1991, 1994) described a variety of ways in which students and teachers used the primary language and how the school context provided support for the use of the primary language. Specific uses across the nine exemplary SAIP sites (labeled A-I) are summarized in Table 1 below. From these findings, it is clear that even in programs in which English is the main language of instruction, exemplary programs find many ways to facilitate the use and development of the students' primary languages both at school and at home.

Table 1
Use of the Primary Language by Students and Teachers Across the Nine Exemplary Special Alternative Instructional Programs

Sites	A	B*	C	D	E*	F	G	H	I
Students' use of L_1									
To assist one another	x	x	x	x		x	x	x	x
To tutor other students							x		
To ask/answer questions	x	x	x	x		x		x	
To use bilingual dictionaries		x	x	x		x		x	
To write in L_1	x	x		x	x	x		x	
To interact socially	x	x	x	x	x	x	x	x	x
Teachers' use of L_1									
To check comprehension	x	x				x		x	
To translate a lesson		x				x		x	
To provide instruction	x	x							
To interact socially	x	x	x			x	x	x	
L_1 support in the larger school context									
Content instruction in L_1	x	x		x		x			x
Instruction in L_1 culture, history, and/or language arts	x	x		x		x	x		x
Library books in L_1	x	x			x			x	x
Communication to parents in L_1	x	x	x		x	x			
Parents encouraged to read to students in L_1	x	x			x				

NOTE: x denotes the use of L_1 for the specified purpose.
* Sites B and E include students at the secondary level

Historically, research and policy in bilingual education have tended to focus on elementary school programs where enrollments of English language learners have been greater. Two studies provided much needed research in the post-elementary setting. Lucas, Henze, and Donato (1990) extended the research on effective schooling which had focused on urban elementary schools in low income neighborhoods to the secondary level in schools with large populations of Latino language minority students. Data were collected at five school sites in California and one in Arizona. Criteria for site selection included both qualitative and quantitative factors. Nominations for successful secondary schools were solicited from a variety of people familiar with schools with large numbers of language minority students, including educators at state, county, and district levels. Once the recommendations were received, the principals of the schools were contacted to determine whether their schools had received any formal recognition from local, state, or federal agencies for their programs for language minority students and whether they could provide quantitative evidence of their success (e.g., drop-out rates, standardized tests scores that compared favorably to other minority schools).

From the data collected, which included audiotapes and notes from interviews with school site personnel and students, student questionnaires, classroom observations, records and documents from each school containing such items as policy statements and program descriptions, eight key features emerged which Lucas, Henze, and Donato concluded were the most important in promoting the success of language minority students at the six school sites:

1. Value is placed on the students' languages and cultures;

2. High expectations of language minority students are made concrete;

3. School leaders make the education of language minority students a priority;

4. Staff development is explicitly designed to help teachers and staff serve language minority students more effectively;

5. A variety of course and programs for language minority students is offered;

6. A counseling program gives special attention to language minority students;

7. Parents of language minority students are encouraged to become involved in their children's education; and

8. School staff members share a strong commitment to empower language minority students. (pp. 324-325)

Given the focus in this chapter on the use of the primary language, the first key feature identified by Lucas, Henze and Donato seems worthy of elaboration. In the exemplary school sites, it was found that value was placed on the students' languages and cultures in a number of important ways. First, the ability to speak another language in addition to English was treated as an advantage rather than a liability. A number of teachers and counselors at the schools had learned Spanish in order to function more effectively in their jobs—an effort well-noted by a student who commented "when teachers are bilingual, it makes our learning easier. They treat us equally" (p. 323). A second way in which the schools demonstrated how they valued students' languages and cultures was found in the school curricula. Although these high schools made English literacy a primary goal, they also encouraged students to continue to develop their Spanish skills by offering Spanish courses for native speakers. Advanced Placement classes in which students could earn college credit and content courses taught in Spanish were offered so that students could advance through the curriculum while developing their English skills. Moreover, students were allowed to speak their native language when English language development was not the focus of instruction. Thus, throughout the campuses visited by the team of researchers, students were heard speaking Spanish freely with each other and with Spanish-speaking staff members.

In addition to showing respect for the students' native languages, it was clear that the students' cultures were valued as well. This respect was apparent in obvious ways such as the celebration of customs and holidays, but also in more meaningful ways throughout the year. Teachers made a point of learning about the students' past experiences; some, for instance, had visited Mexican schools to better understand the students' previous educational experiences. At the same time, faculty and staff did not treat students "simply as members of an undifferentiated ethnic group" (p. 325). They recognized students' individual interests and problems and avoided stereotypes and generalization by acknowledging that students from Mexico, Nicaragua, El Salvador, Cuba and other Spanish-speaking countries have different histories and customs and speak different varieties of Spanish. Mexican immigrants, Mexican-

Americans, and Chicanos were also viewed as having their own distinct characteristics, socioeconomic backgrounds, and histories of educational attainment. Effort was made in hiring practices not only to employ high quality instructional staff, but also to find teachers and counselors reflecting the student composition to serve as role models and advocates for the students. As one student remarked, "Mr. A encourages students to break stereotypes by being good in chemistry, physical science, and physics" (p. 327).

In a study seeking to investigate the attitudes of language minority junior high students about what constitutes effective instruction, Snow, Hyland, Kamhi-Stein, and Yu (1996) interviewed 66 students from six junior high schools in a large urban school district in Southern California. The findings from the oral interviews revealed that the students rated highly such activities as journal writing, cooperative learning, peer editing, group work, and study skills. When asked to provide their own "ingredients" for the ideal classroom, they called for increased student participation, more hands-on projects, and opportunities for discussion of issues that concern them. They also emphasized the importance of parental support in the success of the language minority student. One student commented, in Spanish:

> Los padres lo deben ayudar mucho, que le aconsejen mucho, que le aconsejen que debe hacer, asi gana buenos grados.

> [The student's] parents should help him a lot; they should advise him; they should advise him what to do, so that he gets good grades. (p. 18)

A Rationale for Interaction

The emerging picture of effective instruction for English language learners is an interactive, student-centered classroom. Yet, the Ramirez et al. (1991) study discussed in an earlier section of this chapter found that teachers in all three types of programs they examined offered language minority students a passive language learning environment in which opportunities for students to produce language (either the primary language or English) and to develop complex language and thinking skills were limited.

Research in both first and second language acquisition provides a rationale for the interactive classroom. The social interactionist perspective is reflected in the view of human development that draws predominantly from the work of the Russian psychologist Vygotsky and others such as Jerome Bruner who belong to a school of social science referred to as "Neo-Vygotskianism." A key feature of this school of human development is that higher-order functions develop out of social interaction. Vygotsky (1978) talked about the "Zone of Proximal Development" which he defined as "the distance between the actual developmental level as determined by individual problem solving and the level of potential development as determined through problem solving under adult guidance or in collaboration with more capable peers" (p. 86).

Tharp and Gallimore (1988) applied the notion of the Zone of Proximal Development (ZPD) to the classroom: "Teaching consists in assisting performance through the ZPD. Teaching can be said to occur when assistance is offered at points in the ZPD at which performance requires assistance" (p. 31). Wood, Bruner, and Ross (1976) coined the metaphor "scaffolding" to describe the ideal role of the teacher in assisting the learner through the ZPD. The teacher's responsibility in the social interactionist view is to structure and model appropriate solutions to problems by building a scaffold from the learner's current state of competence which extends his/her skills or knowledge to a higher level of competence.

The major implication of social interactionist theory for language learning is that language is learned by taking part in social engagement with others. According to Wells (1981), children learn their first language through interaction with caregivers "which gives due weight to the contribution of both parties, and emphasizes mutuality and reciprocity in the meanings that are constructed and negotiated through talk" (p. 115). "Negotiation of meaning" is a complex, collaborative process which occurs regularly in the strategies used by parents in talking to their young children. The term connotes the reciprocity entailed in the process of human communication. Negotiation of any kind involves a give and take, a back and forth until the parties reach agreement. These processes have been applied to teaching in the form of "instructional conversations" in which teachers encourage the expression of students' own ideas, build upon information students provide and experiences they have had, and guide them to increasingly sophisticated levels of understanding (Goldenberg, 1991).

The social interactionist perspective has led quite naturally to Vygotskian perspectives on second language research (Lantolf & Appel, 1994), and is reflected in studies of language use in elementary and secondary school classrooms which investigate how certain types of classroom organizations and activities give English language learners opportunities to use language for a variety of purposes that contribute to their learning (Gersten & Hudelson, 2000). Wong-Fillmore (1985), for instance, was interested in how teachers' language use affects language learning. Specifically, she asked the question "When does teacher talk work as input?" In a large-scale study of over 40 elementary classrooms which had sizable numbers of English language learners, Wong-Fillmore examined the characteristics of the language used in lessons that seemed to work well for language learners. Several of her findings are relevant for our purposes here. First, she found that clear separation of languages was essential. In other words, translation or concurrent instruction in both languages did not promote success in language learning. Separation of languages forces students to utilize all the cues available in instruction to negotiate the message; they cannot wait for the message to be delivered in their first language. Thus, instruction for language minority students should be delivered in the primary language or the second language, not used interchangeably in concurrent translation.[8]

Another finding of the study was that in successful classrooms emphasis was on communication. Wong-Fillmore noted that the language used in the effective classrooms was "in the service" of communicating subject matter to students. Successful teachers negotiated meaning with their students. Teacher talk that worked as input was rich in its variety; it built in redundancy through the use of routines and patterns and provided students with multiple cues to meaning. It helped learners expand and refine their linguistic repertoire by gaining greater command over the forms, functions, and uses of language.

Hawkins (1988) looked for instances of scaffolding or assisted performance in the elementary school setting. After extensive observation, she found that scaffolding only occurred in classroom situations which were highly interactive *and* cognitively demanding. Thus, true teaching in the Tharp and Gallimore sense may only occur when students are

---

[8] Perez and Torres-Guzman (1992) note, however, that while bilingual educators are, in general, in agreement about the separation of languages for instruction, the value of switching back and forth for some teaching purposes has been demonstrated. They cite examples from the literature in which the use of the two languages or "code switching" has been effective in the teaching of poetry and in peer teaching situations; they also discuss the New Concurrent Approach in which planned code-switching was found to be as effective as, and in some subjects, more effective than, the language separation approach which is generally advocated.

given the opportunity to negotiate meaning in interactive, cognitively demanding situations.

Thus far in our discussion of the interactive classroom, we have been concerned with the importance of interaction between the teacher and the learner. It is also important to consider the potential benefits of interaction between learners in the negotiation of meaning process. Studies have shown that in a typical class, teachers talk for at least half, and often for as much as two-thirds of any class period. Harklau's (1994) ethnographic study of mainstream and ESL high school classes revealed even grimmer results. She found only *eight* instances in which ESL students talked in mainstream classes over the course of twelve days of school. To correct this kind of imbalance, Long and Porter (1985) were among the first to document that well-planned group work has the possibility of improving the quantity and quality of ESL student talk and helping to individualize instruction. Careful selection of groups and assignments can take into consideration the great variety of personalities, attitudes, motivations, interests, cognitive and learning styles, and linguistic and cultural backgrounds in a typical classroom. Group work also promotes a positive affective climate. For many students, being called upon in front of the whole class is very stressful. Small groups provide a much less threatening environment, often freeing students up to take more risks. It may also motivate learners because it is more tailored to individual differences and provides a change of pace from the typical teacher-controlled format.

Work in cooperative learning grew out of concern that competitive classrooms do not promote access to learning for all students equally. To counteract the traditional classroom organizational structure, Kagan (1986) reconfigured the classroom, dividing the class "into small teams whose members are all positively interdependent" (p. 241). In order to accomplish any assigned task, all members of the team have a designated role or responsibility. Groups are assigned a group grade, creating the interdependence on members which makes cooperative learning different from the more general group work activities described above. Research on the value of cooperative learning shows positive results on academic achievement, race relations, and the development of mutual concerns among students in a wide variety of settings, subject areas, and grade levels. The approach also appears to be particularly effective with low achieving students. In the context of second language acquisition, cooperative groups and activities provide opportunities for English language learners to develop and apply a range of language functions and communication skills (Coelho, 1994).

The Development of Academic Literacy:
The Language of School

A number of scholars have attempted to describe the types of language used in school. Snow (1987) characterized the language of the home as "contextualized." It tends to deal with shared background knowledge about the family, the house, pets, or common experiences such as holidays, vacations, or important events. In addition, the language used in the home often has a "here and now" focus. Talk centers around concrete objects within the present time frame. In contrast, the language of school is "decontextualized"—it does not assume shared background knowledge among participants. Furthermore, the language of school becomes more decontextualized as students progress through school. By the upper elementary school grades, information is mainly disseminated through textbooks and lectures, rather than through experiential activities more typical of the early school years. To be successful in school, language minority students must learn the kinds of language skills required to perform academic tasks which rely mainly on decontextualized information.

Furthermore, teachers need to know about language as they teach students from diverse language backgrounds. According to Wong Fillmore and Snow (2002), teachers must know how English language proficiency develops in native speakers and learners of English as a second language. They also need to understand features of oral and written language in their roles as agents of socialization in order to help English language learners conform to the social and academic expectations of American schools and function effectively in another language and culture.

Heath's (1986) influential work on language socialization has investigated the kinds of language used in both home and school settings. From her observations, she concluded that implicit in the American school curriculum are six very specific kinds of language demands. First, students need to use language to label and describe the objects, events, and information that "non-intimates" present them. This language function in school typically takes place in form of "display" or "factual" questions where the teacher already knows the answer—"How many states are there in the U.S.?" A second common language function is the use of language to recount past events or information in predictable order and format. Heath refers to this function as "event casts" and gives the following example to illustrate: "Teacher to class: What happened the other day when someone didn't follow the rules for putting books away?" A third type of language used is that needed to follow directions from oral and written sources. This function includes many of the management routines found in school—lining up for recess, changing groups, preparing to go home. A fourth demand is the use of language to sustain and maintain the social interactions of the group. In school, this often means subordinating individual or personal goals to maintain group relations. Thus, students are taught to share, to wait their turn, etc. The use of language to obtain information from non-intimates is the fifth demand. Children need to know how to request and clarify information. Once they are given information, they are expected to generalize from one situation to other similar situations. For instance, the procedures for cleaning up might be the same regardless of the kind of project that students are working on at any given time. Finally, the sixth demand is the ability to use language to account for one's unique experiences, to link these experiences to generally known ideas or events, and to create new information or integrate ideas in innovative ways.

In their study of a cross-age tutoring project involving at risk fifth graders at a California school with a large language minority student population, Heath and Mangiola (1991) investigated the development of literate behavior. Twice a week the fifth graders read to their first grade tutees. The tutors took field notes about the tutoring sessions, reported to the first grade teachers on their tutee's progress, and viewed and analyzed video tapes of the tutoring sessions. They also met with the researchers to talk about the tutoring sessions and to discuss what they themselves did as readers and writers. The goal of the discussions was to help the tutors see themselves developing expertise about the processes of reading, writing, and talking about what can be learned from personal experience, books, and the oral retellings of others.

Importantly, the tutors and tutees were allowed to read and interact in either English or Spanish. It was felt that whether the students read in one language or the other, they would ask the same kinds of questions and make the same progress in their reading and writing—since literate behaviors are fundamental skills that are transferable to other areas of academic performance. Results of the analysis revealed that the students who began the program speaking and reading exclusively in Spanish began to read and discuss books with their tutees in English. Another impressive result of the project was that students had numerous authentic occasions for extensive, highly motivated, and varied student writing (e.g., field notes, letters to tutees and teachers, book synopses) of the kind that engaged students in real communication with an audience—a stark comparison to the more typical "dead-end" writing

assignment directed at the teacher. From this study, Heath and Mangiola defined literate behavior as learning to:

- interpret texts

- say what they "mean"

- tie them into personal experience

- explain and argue with passages of text

- make predictions based on the text

- hypothesize outcomes of related situations

- compare and evaluate

- talk about doing all of the above (p. 41)

Rosebery, Warren, and Conant (1992) report on a study of the effects
of a collaborative inquiry approach to science with language minority
students. Two groups of students, most of whom had never studied science before and some who had had very little schooling were exposed
to "doing science" in ways practicing scientists do. The goal was to
teach the students to use language, to think, and to act as members of
the scientific community. One of the groups was composed of seventh
and eighth grade Haitian Creole speakers who received science instruction in their primary language. The second group that took part in the
study was composed of high school students from a variety of language
and cultural backgrounds who attended a basic skills program for academically weak students. Results were reported for the Haitian Creole
students from both the seventh and eighth grade and from the high
school groups.

Before the onset of the inquiry science program, interviews with the students showed no evidence that they understood what it meant to reason
scientifically. The researchers concluded that the students did not differen-
tiate the discourse context for science—in other words, their responses
demonstrated that: (1) literal comprehension was valued over inferential
reasoning, and (2) questions were asked by "knowing" adults to ascertain
whether students knew the right answer. By June, after exposure to the
inquiry approach, however, the students began to show signs of reasoning

in terms of a larger explanatory framework. They used the content knowledge about water pollution and aquatic ecosystems, which they had learned, to generate explanations and hypotheses. More importantly, from the students' use of language—they presented multiple hypotheses and used conditional statements—they demonstrated awareness of the tentative character of hypothesis formation. This use of language was in contrast to their initial concern with finding the right answer before the program. The June interviews suggested that hypothesis making now functioned as part of a larger inquiry process linking conjecture and experimentation. The students had begun to learn how to appropriate scientific discourse for their own uses in the science classroom.

Solomon and Rhodes (1996) conducted a survey of elementary, middle and high school ESL teachers, graduate students training to become ESL professionals, ESL teacher trainers, and administrators to find how they defined academic language. The majority of the respondents focused on vocabulary as the key feature of academic language, giving examples of terms such as "triangle," "habitat," and "protein" from math, social studies, and science; others contrasted academic language with social language, noting that "pick" would be used more typically in conversation, but "select" would appear in written form. Respondents also defined academic language in terms of typical classroom activities; learners have to use academic language to write in journals, follow directions, present findings to classmates, participate in discussions in science labs, and state opinions.

More recently, Bailey and Butler (2001) sought to describe academic language proficiency in even more specific terms for the purposes of designing assessments of English language development. They define academic language as "language that stands in contrast to the everyday informal speech that students use outside of the classroom environment" (p. 7). According to Bailey and Butler, academic language can be characterized at the lexical (vocabulary), syntactic (grammar), and discourse (larger units of text in written or spoken form) levels; it also includes the academic language functions of the classroom. Examples of such language functions can be found in Short (1997) who analyzed middle school social studies classes. She found that both teachers and students use academic language to: define terms, retell a series of related events, compare historical outcomes, and request information. Teachers, however, were more likely than students to ask questions, rephrase student responses, conduct reviews of information, and give directions. In observations of fourth and fifth grade science classrooms, Bailey, Butler, La Framenta, and Ong (2001) found that teachers primarily used four language functions: assessment, comparison, description, and explanation. Student talk in these science classes consisted of three of the same academic language functions—comparison, description, and explanation—and two others, commenting and questioning.

Findings from research on academic language development have important implications for helping teachers integrate content-area and ESL standards into instruction. The *ESL Standards for Pre-K-12 Students* (TESOL, 1997) specify the language competencies—what students should know and be able to do as a result of instruction—needed by English language learners in elementary and secondary schools in order: ". . . to become fully proficient in English, to have unrestricted access to grade-appropriate instruction in challenging academic subjects, and ultimately to lead rich and productive lives (TESOL, 1997, pp. 1-2). TESOL's standards have been adopted by such states as New Jersey; other states such as California have developed their own standards for English language development (see *www.cde.ca.gov/cdepress/Eng-Lang-Dev-Stnd.pdf*).

Research on academic language also has critical implications for developing reliable and valid assessments of academic language proficiency for English language learners of the kind required by recent federal legislation (*No Child Left Behind Act of 2001*, 2001) which mandates that districts provide annual assessments of English language proficiency, including oral language, comprehension, reading, and writing. Enhanced understanding of the actual academic language characteristics of each of the skill areas will enable test developers to design assessments which truly measure the kinds of language that English language learners need to succeed academically. Underpinning the development of academic language is the integration of language and content instruction. In Snow's (in press) model, academic literacy results when English language learners expand their linguistic knowledge (lexicon, syntax, discourse/text structure, academic language functions); background knowledge (of content, culture, expectations of school); cognitive knowledge (form and patterns, e.g., temporal relationships and categories); and knowledge of the specific discourse community (e.g., science vocabulary, typical history genres). In order for English language learners in both elementary and secondary schools to develop academic literacy, teachers must deliver instruction focused on integrating academic language skills with content-area learning.

Conclusion

This chapter has covered research in several key areas that inform practice for teachers of English language learners. It might best be summarized in the nine critical features of enriched education for K-12 instruction outlined by Cloud, Genesee, and Hamayan (2000):

- Parent involvement is integral to program success.

- Effective programs have standards.

- Strong leadership is critical for effective programs.

- Effective enriched education programs are developmental.

- Effective instruction is student-centered.

- Language instruction is integrated with challenging academic instruction.

- Teachers in effective enriched education programs are reflective.

- Effective enriched education are integrated with other school programs and schools.

- Effective enriched education programs aim for additive bilingualism.

- Similarly, Walqui (2000), with a particular focus on secondary immigrant students, has identified ten priorities to consider when designing instruction:

- The culture of the classroom fosters the development of a community of learners, and all students are part of that community.

- Good language teaching involves conceptual and academic development

- Students' experiential background is used as a point of departure and an anchor in the exploration of new ideas.

- Teaching and learning focus on substantive ideas that are organized cyclically.

- New ideas and tasks are conceptualized.

- Academic strategies, sociocultural expectations, and academic norms are taught explicitly.

- Tasks are relevant, meaningful, engaging, and varied.

- Complex and flexible forms of collaboration maximize learners' opportunities to interact while making sense of language and content.

- Students are given multiple opportunities to extend their understandings and apply their knowledge.

- Authentic assessment is an integral part of teaching and learning.

Clearly, the job of the teacher of linguistically and culturally diverse students is a challenging one. In fact, Clark (1990) identified 74 attitudes, knowledge types, and skills that teachers must possess to be effective in multicultural settings! Factors such as the shortage of bilingual teachers, the lack of models for providing primary language instruction for linguistic and cultural populations, limited availability of suitable materials for the less commonly primary taught languages and the lack of time to develop appropriate materials and curricula, the dearth of appropriate instruments for assessing primary language, and the press of time that the school system places on teachers to transition students to mainstream classes are among the many challenges facing today's teacher of English language learners. Moreover, considerable effort has been directed toward elementary school bilingual programs and toward Spanish-speaking school populations given their critical mass in many regions of the country, but much remains to be learned about effective instruction at the intermediate and secondary levels and about the many other linguistic and cultural groups that constitute our language minority population.

The results of the research described in this chapter have powerful implications for the role of the primary language in the development of the literate behaviors prerequisite to academic success. Perhaps the most significant finding is that the strongest predictor of student achievement in English is the amount of formal schooling students receive in their primary language. The research reviewed in this chapter on effective instructional practices also tells us that the bridge to literacy is not crossed simply by using the primary language for instruction, but rather by primary language instruction in combination with interactive, cooperative, student-centered teaching that equips students with the academic literacy practices needed for success in the mainstream. In other words, primary language instruction must draw on effective techniques and strategies used in native, second, and foreign language teaching. Furthermore, the research on academic language proficiency implies a reconceptualization of the kind of instruction which promotes academic literacy. It requires systematic planning of language, content knowledge, and skills in an interactive environment where students have multiple opportunities to produce English and develop higher order thinking skills. Language minority students must be exposed to challenging subject matter instruction in English that includes authentic literature and interdisciplinary topics, or what Yawkey and Prewitt-Diaz (1990) call "massed" experiences with the same concepts from various themes and subject areas. This challenging instruction has students keep journals, learn writing as a process, take part in hands-on activities and experiments, produce plays, use graphic organizers, read both for pleasure and to study, learn to interpret time lines, charts, diagrams, and maps, guess the meaning of unfamiliar vocabulary from context, learn to use computers—to name just a few activities which will prepare English language learners for academic success.[9]

We also know from the research that monolingual teachers who do not speak their students' languages can still support primary languages in many valuable ways, both attitudinally and instructionally. Assigning students who speak the same language to work in pairs or small groups

---

[9] For many more suggestions for challenging, interactive teaching strategies, see Richard-Amato and Snow (1992), *The Multicultural Classroom: Readings for Content-Area Teachers*; Richard-Amato and Snow (in press), *The Multicultural Classroom: Helping English Language Learners Succeed*; Freeman and Freeman (1998), *ESL/EFL Teaching: Principles for Success*; and Carrasquillo and Rodriguez (2002), *Language Minority Students in the Mainstream Classroom*.

to assist one another, allowing students to use bilingual dictionaries, and using students as linguistic resources are some of the multitude of ways in which monolingual teachers can support the use of the primary language and demonstrate value of students' language and culture.

Finally, we know from the research that parents play a pivotal role in the academic success of their children. Virtually every study reviewed in this chapter identified home-school collaboration as an essential component of effective programs for English language learners. The parents of language minority students must be encouraged to provide rich oral and literate environments at home in the native language. Teachers must help them to realize how vital their linguistic input is and to understand the rationale behind the use of the primary language. And, if the parents do not speak English well, teachers should discourage them from interacting in English at home in the mistaken notion that it will benefit their children. Teachers can forge the link between the home and school in a variety of ways.[10] They can encourage parents and/or older siblings to read books aloud in the home language and tell stories, folk tales, riddles, and sayings from the home culture. Cultural knowledge, traditional celebrations, music, dance, poetry and artifacts such as photos, records, and letters in the primary language or culture can also be shared with the children and incorporated into class activities. Teachers can encourage participation in a home-school library program where children bring primary language stories, magazines, and books from home for use in class and, in turn, check out primary language materials from the school library for use at home. Providing parents with specific strategies for helping their children with homework and class projects is a critical way to strengthen home-school collaboration. Lastly, teachers can work with their school or district administrators to establish orientation workshops for parents of English language learners and to design parent literacy programs. Assisting parents to learn to read and write in the home language or English is an essential bridge to literacy for both them and their children.

Opportunity awaits us. By developing the primary language skills of our language minority students, we are creating a foundation of literate behaviors which will ultimately prepare them for the rigors of the mainstream classroom and for successful entree into the English-speaking

---

[10] These useful suggestions are taken from Legarreta-Marcaida (1981), p. 107. See also Becker (2001) for helpful suggestions for ways in which teachers can facilitate more parent involvement.

academic and work environment. Furthermore, we are preserving the vital natural resources our students possess upon arrival at school. Heath and Mangiola (1991) remind us "...that the students we are becoming accustomed to labeling 'at risk' are actually—like all our students—children of promise" (p. 11). Primary language instruction, a bridge to English language literacy, offers a compelling route for assisting our language minority students to reach this potential.

REFERENCES

American Association of Teachers of Spanish and Portuguese. (2000). *Professional development series handbook for teachers K-16,* Volume 1, *Spanish for native speakers.* Fort Worth, TX: Harcourt College Publishers.

American Institutes for Research and WestEd. (2002). *Effects of the implementation of Proposition 227 on the education of English learners, K-12: Year 2 report.* Retrieved February 10, 2003, from *http://www.lmri.ucsb.edu.*

Bailey, A. L., & Butler, F. A. (2001). An evidentiary framework for operationalizing academic language for broad application to K-12 education: A design document. University of California, Los Angeles: National Center for Research on Evaluation, Standards, and Student Testing (CRESST).

Bailey, A. L., Butler, F. A., LaFramenta, C., & Ong, C. (2001). Towards the characterization of academic language. Final deliverable to OERI/OBEMLA, Contract No. R305b60002. University of California, Los Angeles: National Center for Research on Evaluation, Standards, and Student Testing (CRESST).

Baker, K., & de Kanter, A. (1983). Federal policy and the effectiveness of bilingual education. In K. Baker & A. de Kanter (Eds.), *Bilingual education: A reappraisal of federal policy* (pp. 33-86). Lexington, MA: Lexington Books.

Bialystok, E. (1987). Words as things: Development of word concept by bilingual children. *Studies in Second Language Learning, 9,* 133-140.

Becker, H. (2001). *Teaching ESL K-12: Views from the classroom.* Boston, MA: Heinle & Heinle.

Brecht, R.D., & Ingold, C. W. (2002, May). Tapping a national resource: Heritage languages in the United States. *ERIC Digest.* Washington DC: ERIC Clearinghouse on Languages and Linguistics. Retrieved February 10, 2003, from *http://www.cal.org/ericcll/digest/brecht01.html*

Carrasquillo, A. L., & Rodriguez, V. (2002). *Language minority students in the mainstream classroom* (2nd ed.). Clevedon: Multilingual Matters.

Cazden, C. B. (1992). *Language minority education in the United States: Implications of the Ramirez report.* Educational Practice Report 1. Santa Cruz, CA: The National Center for Research on Cultural Diversity and Second Language Learning.

Cazden, C. B., & Snow, C. E. (Eds.). (1990). *English plus: Issues in bilingual education.* The Annals of the American Academy of Political and Social Science, 508.

Christian, D., & Montone, C. L., Lindholm, K. J., & Carranza, I. (1997). *Profiles in two-way immersion education.* McHenry, IL and Washington, DC: Center for Applied Linguistics and Delta Systems.

Clark, E. R. (1990). The state of the art in research on teacher training models with special reference to bilingual education teachers. In Office of Bilingual Education & Minority Languages Affairs, *Proceedings of the first research symposium on limited English proficient students' issues* (pp. 361-391). Washington, DC: U.S. Department of Education.

Cloud, N., Genesee, F., & Hamayan, E. (2000). *Dual language instruction: A handbook for enriched education.* Boston, MA: Heinle & Heinle.

Coelho, E. (1994). *Learning together in the multicultural classroom.* Markham, Ontario: Pippin Publishing Ltd.

Collier, V. P. (1989). How long? A synthesis of research on academic achievement in a second language. *TESOL Quarterly, 23,* 509-531.

Collier, V. P. (1987). Age and rate of acquisition of second language for academic purposes. *TESOL Quarterly, 21,* 617-641.

Collier, V. P., & Thomas, W. P. (1989). How quickly can immigrants become proficient in school English? *Journal of Educational Issues of Language Minority Students, 5,* 26-38.

Crawford, J. (2000). *At war with diversity: US language policy in an age of anxiety.* Clevedon: Multilingual Matters.

Crawford, J. (Ed.). (1992). *Language loyalties: A source book on the official English controversy.* Chicago, IL: University of Chicago Press.

Crawford, J. (1989). *Bilingual education: History, politics, theory and practice.* New Jersey: Crane.

Cummins, J. (2000). *Language, power and pedagogy: Bilingual children in the crossfire.* Clevedon: Multilingual Matters.

Darcy, N. T. (1953). A review of the literature on the effects of bilingualism upon the measurement of intelligence. *Journal of Genetic Psychology,* LXXXII, 21-57.

Dicker, S. J. (2000). Official English and bilingual education: The controversy over language pluralism in U.S. society. In J. K. Hall & W. G. Eggington (Eds.), *The sociopolitics of English language teaching* (pp. 45-66). Clevedon: Multilingual Matters.

Echevarria, J., & Graves, A. (2003). *Sheltered content instruction: Teaching English-language learners with diverse abilities* (2nd ed.). Boston, MA: Allyn & Bacon.

Faltis, C. J., & Hudelson, S. J. (1998). *Bilingual education in elementary and secondary school communities: Toward understanding and caring.* Boston, MA: Allyn and Bacon.

Fishman, J. A. (2001). 300-plus years of heritage language education in the United States. In J. K. Peyton, D. A. Ranard, & S. McGinnis (Eds.), *Heritage languages in America: Preserving a national resource* (pp. 81-97). McHenry, IL and Washington, DC: Center for Applied Linguistics and Delta Systems.

Freeman, Y. S., & Freeman, D. E. (1998). *ESL/EFL teaching: Principles for success.* Portsmouth, NH: Heinemann.

Gale, K., McClay, D., Christie, M., & Harris, S. (1981). Academic achievement in the Milingimbi bilingual education program. *TESOL Quarterly, 15,* 297-314.

Gandara, P. (1999). *Review of research on the instruction of limited English proficient students: A report to the California Legislature.* The University of California Linguistic Minority Research Institute, Education Policy Center. Retrieved February 1, 2003, from *http://www.lmri.ucsb.edu*

Garcia, E. (1991). *Education of linguistically and culturally diverse students: Effective instructional practices.* Educational Practice Report 1. Santa Cruz, CA: The National Center for Research on Cultural Diversity and Second Language Learning.

Genesee, F. (1987). *Learning through two languages: Studies of immersion and bilingual education.* Rowley, MA: Newbury House.

Gersten, B. F., & Hudelson, S. (2000). Changing populations, changing needs in teacher preparation. In M. A. Snow (Ed.), *Implementing the ESL standards for P-K-12 students through teacher education* (pp. 75-102). Alexandria, VA: Teachers of English to Speakers of Other Languages.

Goldenberg, C. (1991). *Instructional conversations and their classroom application.* Educational Practice Report 2. Santa Cruz, CA: The National Center for Research on Cultural Diversity and Second Language Learning.

Hakuta, K. (1986). *Mirror of language: The debate on bilingualism.* New York: Basic Books.

Hakuta, K., Butler, Y. G., & Witt, D. (2000). *How long does it take English learners to attain proficiency?* The University of California Linguistic Minority Research Institute Policy Report 2000-1. Retrieved February 1, 2003, from *http://www.lmri.ucsb.edu*

Harklau, L. (1994). ESL versus mainstream classes: Contrasting L2 Learning environments. *TESOL Quarterly, 28*(2), 241-272.

Harklau, L., Losey, K. M., Siegal, M. (1999). *Generation 1.5 meets college composition: Issues in the teaching of writing to U.S.-educated learners of ESL.* Mahwah, NJ: Lawrence Erlbaum.

Hawkins, B. (1988). *Scaffolded classroom interaction and its relation to second language acquisition.* Unpublished doctoral dissertation, University of California, Los Angeles.

Heath, S. B. (1986). Socio-cultural contexts of language development. In *Beyond language: Social and cultural factors in schooling language minority students* (pp. 143-186). Los Angeles: Evaluation, Dissemination and Assessment Center, California State University.

Heath, S. B., & Mangiola, L. (1991). *Children of promise: Literate activity in linguistically and culturally diverse classrooms.* Washington, DC: National Education Association.

Johnson, R. K., & Swain, M. (1997). *Immersion education: International perspectives.* Cambridge: Cambridge University Press.

Kagan, S. (1986). Cooperative learning and sociocultural factors in schooling. In *Beyond language: Social and cultural factors in schooling language minority students* (pp. 231-298). Los Angeles: Evaluation, Dissemination and Assessment Center, California State University.

Krashen, S., & Biber, D. (1988). *On course: Bilingual education's success in California.* Sacramento, CA: California Association for Bilingual Education.

Kuhlman, N., & Murray, D. E. (2000). Changing populations, changing needs in teacher preparation. In M. A. Snow (Ed.), *Implementing the ESL standards for P-K-12 students through teacher education* (pp. 33-47). Alexandria, VA: Teachers of English to Speakers of Other Languages.

Lambert, W. E. (1980). The social psychology of language: A perspective for the 1980s. In H. Giles, W. P. Robinson, & P. M. Smith (Eds.), *Language: Social psychological perspectives* (pp. 415-424). Oxford: Pergamon Press.

Lantolf, J. P., & Appel, G. (1994). *Vygotskian approaches to second language research.* Norwood, NJ: Ablex.

Legarreta-Marcaida, D. (1981). Effective use of the primary language in the classroom. In California State Department of Education, *Schooling and language minority students: A theoretical framework* (pp. 83-116). Los Angeles: Evaluation Dissemination and Assessment Center, California State University.

Lessow-Hurley, J. (1990). *The foundations of dual language instruction.* New York: Longman.

Lindholm-Leary, K. J. (2001). *Dual language education.* Clevedon: Multilingual Matters.

Long, M., & Porter, P. (1985). Group work, interlanguage talk, and second language acquisition. *TESOL Quarterly, 19*, 207-228.

Lucas, T., & Katz, A. (1994). Reframing the debate: The roles of native languages in English-only programs for language minority students. *TESOL Quarterly, 28*(3), 537-561.

Lucas, T., & Katz, A. (1991). *A contradiction or sound pedagogy? The roles of language minority students' native languages in exemplary English-based programs*. Paper presented at the annual meeting of the American Educational Research Association, Chicago.

Lucas, T., Henze, R., & Donato, R. (1990). Promoting the success of Latino language-minority students: An exploratory study of six high schools. *Harvard Educational Review*, 60, 315-340.

Macnamara, J. T. (1966). *Bilingualism and primary education: A study of Irish experience*. Edinburgh: Edinburgh University Press.

Marcos, K. (1999, October). Are we wasting our nation's language resources? Heritage languages in America. *Language link: An online newsletter from the ERIC Clearinghouse on Languages and Linguistics*. Retrieved from *www.cal.org/ericcll/langlink/1099.html#featurearticle*

McGroarty, M. (2000). Bilingual approaches to language learning. In M. Celce-Murcia (Ed.), *Teaching English as a second or foreign language* (3rd ed.) (pp. 345-356). Boston, MA: Heinle & Heinle.

Minicucci, C., & Olsen, L. (1992). Programs for secondary limited English proficient students: A California study. *Focus*, 5. Washington DC: National Clearinghouse for Bilingual Education.

No Child Left Behind Act of 2001. (P.L. 107-110). United States Statutes at Large. (*www.NoChildLeftBehind.gov*)

Peal, E., & Lambert, W. E. (1962). The relation of bilingualism to intelligence. *Psychological Monographs*, 76, Whole No. 546.

Perez, B., & Torres-Guzman, M. E. (1992). *Learning in two worlds: An integrated Spanish/English biliteracy approach*. New York: Longman.

Peyton, J. K., Ranard, D. A, & McGinnis, S. (Eds). (2001). *Heritage languages in America: Preserving a national resource*. McHenry, IL and Washington, DC: Center for Applied Linguistics and Delta Systems.

Ramirez, J. D. (1992). Executive summary. *Bilingual Research Journal*, 16, 1-62.

Ramirez, J. D., Yuen, S. D., & Ramey, D. R. (1991). *Longitudinal study of structured English immersion strategy, early-exit and late-exit transitional bilingual programs for language-minority children*. Final report to the U.S. Department of Education. Executive Summary and Vols. I and II. San Mateo, CA: Aguirre International.

Richard-Amato, P. A., & Snow, M. A. (Eds.). (in press). *The multicultural classroom: Helping English language learners succeed*. New York: Longman.

Richard-Amato, P. A., & Snow, M. A. (Eds.). (1992). *The multicultural classroom: Readings for content-area teachers*. New York: Longman.

Rosebery, A. S., Warren, V., & Conant, F. (1992). *Appropriating scientific discourse: Findings from language minority classrooms*. Research Report 3. Santa Cruz,

CA: The National Center for Research on Cultural Diversity and Second Language Learning.

Rumbaut, R. G., & Ima, K. (1988). *The adaptation of Southeast Asian refugee youth: A comparative study.* Final report to the Office of Resettlement. (ERIC Document Reproduction Service No. ED299372).

Saville-Troike, M. (1984). What really matters in second language learning for academic achievement? *TESOL Quarterly*, 18, 199-219.

Short, D. J. (1997). Reading and 'riting and . . . social studies: Research on integrated language and content in secondary classrooms. In M. A. Snow & D. M. Brinton (Eds.), *The content-based classroom: Perspectives on integrated language and content* (pp. 213-232). White Plains, NY: Longman.

Simon, P. (1980). *The tongue-tied American: Confronting the foreign language crisis.* New York: Continuum.

Snow, C. E. (1990). Rationales for native language instruction: Evidence from research. In A. M. Padilla, H. H. Fairchild & C.M. Valdez (Eds.), *Bilingual education: Issues and strategies* (pp. 60-74). Newbury Park, CA: Sage Publications.

Snow, C. E. (1987). *Second language learners' formal definitions: An oral language correlate of school literacy.* Technical report No. 5, University of California, Los Angeles: Center for Language Education and Research.

Snow, M. A. (in press). A model of academic literacy for integrated language and content instruction. In E. Hinkel (Ed.), *Handbook on research in second language teaching and learning.* Mahwah, NJ: Lawrence Erlbaum.

Snow, M. A., Hyland, J., Kamhi-Stein, L., & Yu, J. H. (1996). U.S. language minority students: Voices from the junior high classroom. In K. M. Bailey & D. Nunan (Eds.), *Voices from the language classroom: Qualitative research in second language education* (pp. 304-317). Cambridge: Cambridge University Press.

Solomon, J., & Rhodes, N. (1996). Assessing academic language: Results of a survey. *TESOL Journal*, X, 5-8.

Teachers of English to Speakers of Other Languages (TESOL). (1997). *ESL standards for P-K-12 students.* Alexandria, VA: Author.

Tharp, R. G., & Gallimore, R. (1988). *Rousing minds to life: Teaching, learning, and schooling in social context.* New York: Cambridge University Press.

Thomas, W. P., & Collier, V. P. (2002). *A national study of school effectiveness for language minority students' long-term academic achievement.* University of California, Santa Cruz: Center for Research on Education, Diversity & Excellence.

Thomas, W.P., & Collier, V. P. (1997). *School effectiveness for language minority students.* Washington DC: National Clearinghouse for Bilingual Education.

Thompson, G. G. (1952). *Child psychology.* Boston: Houghton Mifflin.

Thompson, L., Christian, D., Stansfield, C. W., & Rhodes, N. (1990). Foreign language instruction in the United States. In A. M. Padilla, H. H. Fairchild, & C. M.

Valdez (Eds.), *Foreign language education: Issues and strategies* (pp. 22-35). Newbury Park, CA: Sage Publications.

Tickunoff, W. J., Ward, B. A., van Broekhuizen, D., Romero, M., Castaneda, L. V., Lucas, T., & Katz, A. (1991). *Final report: A descriptive study of significant features of exemplary special alternative instructional programs.* Los Alamitos, CA: Southwest Regional Laboratory.

Tickunoff, W. J., & Vasquez-Faria, J. A. (1982). Successful instruction for bilingual schooling. *Peabody Journal of Education, 52.*

Tucker, G. R. (2003). A global perspective on bilingualism and bilingual education. In C. B. Paulson & G. R. Tucker (Eds.), *Sociolinguistics: The essential readings* (pp. 464–471). Malden, MA: Blackwell Publishing.

Tucker, G. R. (1990). Second-language education: Issues and perspectives. In A. M. Padilla, H. H. Fairchild, & C. M. Valdez (Eds.), *Foreign language education: Issues and strategies* (pp. 13-21). Newbury Park, CA: Sage Publications.

Tucker, G. R. (1984). Toward the development of a language-competent American society. *International Journal of the Sociology of Language, 45,* 153-160.

UNESCO. The use of vernacular languages in education. Monographs on fundamental education No. 8. Paris: UNESCO.

Valdez, G. (2001). Heritage language students: Profiles and possibilities. In J. K. Peyton, D. A. Ranard, & S. McGinnis (Eds), *Heritage languages in America: Preserving a national resource* (pp. 37-77). McHenry, IL and Washington, DC: Center for Applied Linguistics and Delta Systems.

Vygotsky, L.S. (1978). *Mind in society: The development of higher psychological processes.* Cambridge, MA: Harvard University Press.

Walqui, A. (2000). *Access and engagement: Program design and instructional approaches for immigrant students in secondary school.* McHenry, IL and Washington DC: Center for Applied Linguistics and Delta Systems.

Webb, J. B., & Miller, B. L. (Eds.). (2000). *Teaching heritage language learners: Voices from the classroom.* Yonkers, NY: American Council on the Teaching of Foreign Languages.

Wells, G. (1981). *Learning through interaction.* Cambridge: Cambridge University Press.

Williams, J. D., & Snipper, G. C. (1990). *Literacy and bilingualism.* New York: Longman.

Willig, A. C. (1985). A meta-analysis of selected studies on the effectiveness of bilingual education. *Review of Educational Research, 55,* 269-317.

Wong Fillmore, L. (1992). Against our best interest: The attempt to sabotage bilingual education. In J. Crawford (Ed.), *Language loyalties: A source book on the official English controversy* (pp. 367-376). Chicago: University of Chicago Press.

Wong-Fillmore, L. (1985). When does teacher talk work as input? In S. Gass & C. Madden (Eds.), *Input in second language acquisition* (pp. 17-50). New York: Newbury House.

Wong Fillmore, L., & Snow, C. E. (2002). What teachers need to know about language. In C. T. Adger, C. E. Snow, & D. Christian (Eds.), *What teachers need to know about language* (pp. 7-53). McHenry, IL and Washington, DC: Center for Applied Linguistics and Delta Systems.

Wood, D. J., Bruner, J. S., & Ross, G. (1976). The role of tutoring in problem solving. *Journal of Child Psychology and Psychiatry*, 17, 89-100.

Yawkey, T. D., & Prewitt-Diaz, J. O. (1990). Early childhood: Theories, research and implications for bilingual education. In Office of Bilingual Education & Minority Languages Affairs, *Proceedings of the first research symposium on limited English proficient students' issues* (pp. 161-192). Washington, DC: U.S. Department of Education.

Reading Instruction for Language Minority Students

Eleanor Wall Thonis

Introduction

A dozen years have passed since the publication of *Schooling and Language Minority Students: A Theoretical Framework*. The purpose in 1981 was to examine some of the issues related to the improvement of reading instruction for an ever-increasing number of such students. It was agreed that minority language groups, without question, face many challenges when they enroll in schools of the United States. They may possess few skills in English, the language of the instructional program. They may also have a limited awareness or a television-distorted understanding of American cultural expectations. They may encounter a totally different school environment among peers who do not speak their language. The 1981 collection of papers focused on topics of first language acquisition, second language learning, natural approaches, effective classroom strategies, and reading program alternatives. The views of the contributors, as expressed then, were drawn from the research and practices of the sixties and seventies. This revision of the chapter on reading restates some of the earlier constructs, affirms many of the previous intuitions, updates several of the findings from relevant research, and poses a few of the continuing questions in the quest for improving reading instruction.

This chapter is organized into seven sections as follows: the relevant constructs, the developmental nature of reading, the student background factors, the methods, the materials, the transferability of skills, and the best of biliteracy.

Relevant Constructs

Given the enormous complications implicit in designing reading instruction for language minority students, it seems prudent to suggest that there is no *single* solution applicable to all students who are not native

English speakers. Generally, if students cannot speak a language and use its vocabulary, syntax, and functional grammar at the approximate level of a six-and-one-half-year-old child, learning to read that language will be difficult. If they are not encouraged to develop at least *one* language fully across all four modalities of listening, speaking, reading, and writing, then a functional illiteracy may be the unfortunate result. If the natural course of language acquisition and language development has not been encouraged as students interact with an environment and use language as an organizer, then ability to mediate meaning at higher levels of cognition may be thwarted. Maturation, language, age and other variables must be considered. In addition, there are social, political, and economic factors that may support or militate against the best conditions for learning to read. These concerns have been the subject of research and argument among educators everywhere.

In American schools, the past debate has centered around English-speaking children who are struggling with the capricious nature of the English writing system. Children who speak English advance quite logically to the written language for which they have oral forms. For more than a century, despite voluminous literature in the field of reading instruction, the controversy continues over methods and materials best suited for ensuring literacy in English. For educators interested in the teaching of reading to language minority children, however, there is not such a long history of combat nor as impressive a number of combatants. Recognition of the unique literacy needs of language minority students in classrooms where English is the language of instruction is relatively recent. The research has been controversial and the recommendations, contradictory. Data from investigations of native language literacy as the introductory program have been overruled by data on the success of immersion in second language literacy plans (Bowen, 1977; Tucker, 1977). Findings suggesting early introduction to second language writing systems have been canceled by conclusions on the effectiveness of later introduction. Achievement levels in school subjects have been variously determined as better or worse when offered in native or second language. See Cummins's discussion of the length of time required for language minority students to develop proficiency in English in this volume.)

Well-developed speech, functional literacy, and adequate thinking ability are essential for success in school. Teachers at all levels agree that learning can best take place when students speak well, read easily, and think effectively. When all the students in a class are native English speakers, teachers are challenged to provide for *personalized* growth of listening and speaking abilities, for *individualized* literacy skills, and for the *unique* thinking strategies demonstrated by different students with diverse competencies in the *one* language. When students not native to English are in classrooms designed for English speakers, teachers are even more sorely pressed to adapt the educational offerings for students. Among the questions tormenting teachers are: Should the native language be used for instruction? Should reading and writing be introduced in the native language? How does language processing influence thinking? Partial answers to such questions may be found in an appraisal of the underlying assumptions that form the basis of available programs. Teachers should consider the various theoretical positions with a view to the influences each would exert in preserving the vital bond between speech and print and in promoting a unity between language (both oral and written) and thinking. If it can be argued that these three elements are essential requirements for optimum school achievement, then it follows that classroom practices must nurture the speech-print-thought triangle in consistent and appropriate ways. All normal human beings use language in their daily lives. This ability serves individuals in personal and social situations requiring communication.

Communicative Competence. There are several definitions of communicative competence: the ability to interact with other speakers (Savignon, 1991), the appropriate use of language in social contexts, and the sensitivity to sociocultural differences in the ways that students learn. (See Crawford's review of communicative approaches in this volume.)

The Functions of Teachers. Among the several attributes described by Berliner (1985) as the "executive functions of teacher" is the responsibility for creating a pleasant environment that emphasizes mutual respect, shared responsibility, politeness, and the valuing of social groups. Often, these aspects of teaching are thought to refer only to the control of deviant behavior and to the maintenance of a workplace where students attend to the business of learning. Yet, the value of a pleasant, respectful workplace for both students and adults is self-evident.

Learning Styles of Students. Archambeault (1992) has suggested that students' study styles may be identified in two areas: the students' preferences for strategies, and the environmental conditions in which students learn. She points out that the preferences for specific strategies may have already developed on the basis of the successes or failures of previously applied strategies. However, the learning environments may still contribute to effective or distracting habits, such as self-monitoring and self-awareness needed for metacognitive techniques.

Reflection in Learning. Reflection is the art of "turning inward" to consider thoughtfully ideas and responses beyond information that is provided through the senses. In classroom practice, there may be little time allowed for students to reflect silently so that communicative competence may be appreciated as *interpersonal* as well as *intrapersonal* characteristics of intelligent answers. Unfortunately, such limited opportunities for reflective thought may promote poor learning strategies and careless work habits (Tarvin and Al-Arishi, 1991).

The Developmental Nature of Reading

A very sensible definition of reading is given by Johnson and Myklebust (1967) who state that reading is a response to a visual symbol superimposed on auditory language. Beginning readers bring their experiences as encoded and stored to the page of print. They practice making accurate and speedy associations between auditory and visual language symbols. They grow to be efficient, rapid readers until they are scarely aware of the speech-print relationship. Capable students who are free from any serious learning problems read well, expand their real and imaginary worlds, and become literate. Accomplished readers have engaged in a process taking them through a sequence of activities as follows: (1) see print, (2) transform print into recognizable sounds and arrangements of sounds, (3) relate what has been recognized to experience, (4) construct meaning from prior knowledge and print, and (5) store print and the associations (meaning) for further use. This process moves the reader from the known to the unknown, from a reality represented by sounds to a new reality represented by symbols. Successful reading depends upon the number and quality of experiences stored; the general level of oral language development; the keenness of sensory-motor skills; the suitability of the instructional program for the reader; and the personal levels of interest, motivation, intelligence, and health. For all persons reading any language, reading is a process of seeing print, hearing speech, and associating whatever it is that has been seen and heard with stored and remembered experiences, called *referents.* When the reader sees the word *acrolith,* for example, this visual stimulus must be changed into an auditory one. The reader may decide, according to the word recognition strategies he or she uses, to say the word. If the reader doesn't know very much about Greek statues, the meaning of what has been seen and said will be unclear or completely lacking. Reading has not been accomplished until the meaning is constructed or discovered. Sometimes a reader can use context clues, picture clues, or other techniques that will help gather the meaning from material that may be unfamiliar. If reference to *acrolith* is within the subject matter content of Greek art, then the reader may be able to *reduce the uncertainties* in Smith's terms (1971) and gain an understanding of what has been read. The nature of the process itself calls to mind the "Vernacular Advantage Theory" (Modiano, 1968; Engle, 1975; Ramirez, 1991).

Oral language grows out of specific contacts with a particular environment. These experiences are mediated by the conventions of a specific speech community. Spoken language, as acquired, forms the basis for the specific conventions of the writing system of that same community. The mutuality, the interdependence between spoken and written language, can be perceived by the reader. There is little need to be reminded that many readers have difficulty learning to read their own language. Reading is more than a perceptual and a sensory-motor process; it is also a cognitive process. The successful reader must bring a background of concepts and ideas to a page of print. The amount and kind of comprehension the reader takes from that page is in direct proportion to what is brought. The reader must supply or infer the context. Unlike personal exchange in informal situations where meaning can be obtained from the contextual flavor of the situation, the exchange between reader and author may have a context that is known only to the writer. As Cummins (1980) has suggested, while language development of students may be adequate for situations in which the context is supplied informally, such language development may be quite inadequate for successful functioning in the decontextualized demands of formal schooling, particularly in the written language of textbooks. This statement could apply to both language majority and language minority students alike. The important difference for language minority students is one of distance from the context. They may have had far less exposure to the concepts represented by the vocabulary and may have not had the time to become familiar with the vocabulary and/or the grammatical and syntactical clues needed to predict meanings.

Human speech is graphically represented in a variety of forms that may be alphabetic, syllabic, logographic, or otherwise symbolic of the spoken word. Speech existed long before its graphic representation. Both oral and written forms of language are interdependent and share a mutual relationship. Well-developed speech provides the foundation for skill development in reading and writing. When students learn to read and write, they must organize the visual system of language in such a way as to make it meaningful according to the auditory system. They must make sense of writing by making a connection with the spoken language as represented. Words and their arrangements that students have learned to describe and explain their experiences become available to them in a visual form. The act of reading is a receptive one in which students see print, hear speech, and connect them to referents remembered and stored from their personal experiences (Thonis, 1976). Until the essential attachment to a meaningful referent has been accomplished, it cannot be said that students are reading.

In the usual course of human development, normal children learn to understand and to speak the language of the speech community into which they have been born. If the language has a written form, it is generally expected that the children will also learn to read and write that same language. In most parts of the world, this learning of the written forms of language is ordinarily provided during the years of middle childhood. Literacy is a task of the school-age years and is accomplished in a school setting. Thus, the students learn to listen, speak, read, and write the language that makes sense to them in the total environment in which they are living and growing. Reality has been interpreted and labeled by speech; speech is preserved through its representation in writing; and discrepancies that may exist between what is heard or said and what is read or written can be clarified and supplemented by the connections between reality, its oral label, and its written form. All writing systems are imperfect, but their imperfections can be managed and meaning can still come through when the students fill in any gaps in comprehension from their experiences and from their reservoir of oral language.

Students who speak Cantonese, Korean, Punjabi, Spanish, or one of the hundreds of languages other than English and who are learning to read and write in English, often have difficulty in supplying the needed information to obtain meaning. They may have a wealth of data stored, but their memories and concepts are not retrievable in response to English stimuli. The essential connections among speech, print, and referent cannot be formed. Smith (1971) has referred to reading comprehension as an act of "reducing the uncertainties" found in written language. When language minority students are attempting to deal with the uncertainties, they are (or may be) already burdened by the additional unknowns of the new visual forms, the unfamiliar structures, the strange vocabulary items, and the different view of reality. When these students see English print, hear their native speech, and seek meaningful referents drawn from their cultural heritage, they may fail to make connections. At best, their reading skill is stopped at the decoding level or, at worst, the written material may not make any sense to them at all. School districts with large numbers of language minority students only need to examine their own annual testing programs to discover the failure rates of these students.

There has been interest and excitement generated over the programs of reading instruction among select groups who have been introduced to reading by way of the second rather than the first language (Bowen, 1977; Tucker, 1977; Cohen, 1974). The "immersion" programs may take a variety of organizational models. The investigators take issue with the assumption that the speech-print connection is of primary importance and suggest that social-cultural factors may contribute more positively to the literacy skills of language minority students. English-speaking children placed in the Spanish language arts curriculum or French-speaking children assigned to English classes are two examples of immersion programs. The theorists have been careful to distinguish between immersion programs and submersion ones. Though they both represent a plan of instruction in which the child's home language is not used primarily, the important difference in programs of submersion may be found in the status of the school language, the continued valuing and use of the home language outside of school, the point at which all students begin in the school's language, and the attitudes of the school-community toward learning the language (Cohen and Swain, 1976). It has been suggested that language minority students immersed in a second language are given rewards and approval for each small increment of learning via that second language. This distinction becomes an important one for language minority students who are mixed in reading classes with English speakers. For these students, their submersion practically guarantees reading difficulties and limited achievement.

The Lambert and Tucker research (1972) suggested that English-speaking children immersed in French reading programs in Canada continued to achieve adequately in English reading without receiving instruction in it. Cohen (1975) found that English-speaking students who learned to read Spanish first, achieved grade level competence in English. These experiments and others of a similar type are generally cited as support for placing students from language minorities in English reading programs immediately. Immersed or submersed, the language minority students must keep afloat, learn to swim, or eventually sink. The data from studies on immersion and submersion point up the social and cultural determiners of successful school achievement, the potential for language skill transfer, and effective dimensions of learning. Setting aside for the moment the social and cultural factors, it appears reasonable to suggest that the advantage of dealing with one's experiences, speech, and written language all within the same common framework of the vernacular is undeniable. If the home language is absolutely unacceptable for political or social reasons or if the language has positively no economic value, then the speech-print connections must still be made in the second language. The language minority students from this group should have opportunities for extended readiness to read with rich and varied activities designed to promote oral language sufficient to support the print of English.

Student Background Factors

The language minority student is first a student and must be seen as a maturing, developing person. Students in elementary and secondary schools are normally en route to the expected developmental milestones in physical, social, emotional, and intellectual maturity according to the universal rules of human growth. Sometimes it is necessary to remind teachers and administrators of this ordinary fact when language minority students are under discussion. The descriptor *language minority* appears to take precedent over the word *student,* as educational plans are considered for them. Language minority students share the same needs as students of any language. Every serious professional in education knows what these common needs are. When it comes to identifying language and literacy needs, however, there is likely to be little agreement as to what those needs may be. One of the serious drawbacks of planning for minority language students stems from a lack of information about the language background. Often, all of the students are grouped together under one description: bilingual. The nature of the individual student's bilingualism is rarely identified with care and precision. In fact, the label *bilingual* often conceals more about the student than it reveals. Students may be at a serious disadvantage because once labeled bilingual, they may then be assumed to fit some predetermined category. Thus, their basic needs may be ignored and their language needs may be undifferentiated. The descriptive designation *bilingual* has been applied to students who come from another country, to students with certain physical characteristics, to students with ethnic surnames, and to students whose parents speak accented English. The criteria for using the term are often vague or misunderstood. To be bilingual suggests that students are capable of using two languages. Further, it is assumed that both languages can be used with relatively equal facility. To describe precisely what is meant by the term *bilingual student,* it is necessary to determine how the students can function in both oral and written language. There are sounds, structures, vocabulary, and meaning systems for both dimensions. When students are competent listeners, speakers, readers, and writers in one language, they control eight dimensions as native speakers. When the students add the sounds, structure, vocabulary, and meaning systems of the second language, eight more are added. Thus, bilingual persons are capable of managing sixteen separate and mutually supportive facets of both languages (proficient bilingualism). These students are rare, especially in United States' classrooms where monolingual, monoliterate education has inhibited or eradicated dual language opportunities.

If reading programs are to suit the varying degrees of language proficiency that language minority students bring to school, they must be designed on the basis of better information about language minority students and their functioning levels in the several dimensions. Language minority students may listen and understand but not speak, or speak but not read or write, or write and read but not speak. The combinations of possible competencies among the receptive and expressive phases of both oral and written language are many. The decision to assign a student to a reading class in the first language, to immerse the student in a second language reading group, to submerse the student in a particular reading program, or to offer two reading programs simultaneously could be improved by careful, thoughtful assessment of language strengths in all language functions.

The schooling opportunities that language minority students may have enjoyed in another setting may influence their abilities to cope with programs of reading instruction. Young students may not have had formal lessons in reading. They may still be at the prereading level of development and may only need to continue along the usual course of reading readiness. A few older students may also be found to be preliterate because they may have come from small towns and villages where they could not have attended school. Both of these groups of students share similar needs in getting ready to read. They need to coordinate eye and hand, refine motor responses, become aware of directionality and spatial factors of the written language, and sharpen their perceptual skills. These prerequisites for skillful reading apply across languages. There are specific background skills needed for different languages that must be addressed specific ways. At the prereading level, it is essential to consider the general factors that promote strong background abilities for literacy and the specific skills that must be nurtured within the context of a specific language. For example, the accuracy and speed with which students note differences in forms of written language is a general ability that promotes attention to fine visual details. This awareness can be applied in a global way to any writing system. But the distinction of detail between *b* and *d* or *w* and *m* would only be specific to forms of the Roman alphabet and would not necessarily apply to all alphabets.

Language minority students who have already learned to read their own language often amaze the reading teacher in a second language class. Adequate or better skills in the first language and good study habits may contribute to helping such students ease into the demands of the new writing system. If students are developmentally mature enough to have reached levels of thinking logically and abstractly, then they appear to be much better able to fit well into the new reading program. Such students call to mind the several constructs proposed to explain the apparent success of older students. Lambert (1975) writes of the *additive* effects of learning a second language while retaining the first. Majority language students who are immersed in a second language program have the opportunity to acquire the second language at no cost to the first. Older students already fluent and literate in one language may also enjoy this additive quality. On the other hand, it would appear that students with poorly developed language and literacy skills in the first language who are forced to take on another system prematurely or at the expense of the first may suffer *subtractive* effects. Cummins (1979) has considered these positive and negative influences in his *Threshold Hypothesis,* which posit that the level of language competence of language minority students may influence intellectual growth. Cummins (1980) also states that a *Developmental Interdependence Hypothesis,* which assumes that second language competence is partially a function of first language competence at the time of exposure to the second language, may account for the modest results of native language and literacy programs in the elementary grades. One obvious effect of such programs would be the time and opportunity provided to acquire concepts and to develop the vocabulary that explains them. Also, practice with more complex syntactical patterns and instruction in word formation and informal grammar improves the understanding of how a language system works and what generalizations about written forms can apply.

Many of the language minority students can be described as functionally illiterate. These are students who appear to have poorly developed language and literacy skills in two languages. They may not ever have learned to read and to write in their native language and may have had little success in learning to read the second one. These students are at a great disadvantage in the classroom because after the first or second grade, most of the school work is carried on in reading and in writing. Lambert (1975) would see these students as suffering from the subtractive effects of their language experiences. In Cummins's terms (1979), they would still be functioning below the first threshold. Language minority students who are failing to learn to read in school can easily be recognized in this group of underachievers. It would appear that the vital role of first language development in nurturing intellectual growth has been ignored, and most of these students have been struggling to organize school content in the second language. Both first and second language organizing fails because neither is fully developed. An unfortunate consequence is the loss of self-esteem and the deep sense of failure that may prevent students from becoming successful readers even when supportive programs are offered. Then students are likely to perceive their school problems as their own fault rather than the possible fault of an inappropriate program of reading instruction.

The Methods

Reading methods for language minority students are often debated from the viewpoint of whether the code or the meaning approach is the better. The synthetic method emphasizes the letters, sounds, syllables, and smaller segments of the written language. The analytic method in which whole words or utterances are presented stresses meaning at every level. How the parts of the writing system go together is not considered of great importance. Making sense of the written material and comprehending the ideas and events are the important goals of the reading instruction. For languages with many irregularities in the speech-print correspondence, like French or English, the analytic approach has worked well for some students. Eclectic methods offer the opportunities both to learn the code and to obtain meaning. Regardless of the method, to read is to comprehend and to comprehend is to think.

In the broadest sense, all methods may be grouped into three major categories: (1) synthetic approaches, (2) analytic approaches, or (3) approaches that combine both the synthetic and analytic. Synthetic methods stress part-whole relationships and give emphasis to building meaningful words or sentences as letters, sounds, and/or syllables are mastered. There is a heavy responsibility to learn how to "crack the code." Analytic methods focus on whole words and meaningful sentences which are examined further for their elements. A synthetic-analytic method may combine features that offer both the *code* and the *meaning* emphasis.

Synthetic Approaches

Several of the traditional reading methods used in learning to read those languages based upon an alphabetic writing principle are synthetic. For example, the onomatopoeic method in Spanish is one in which the students learn to make a single sound association for each visual symbol in order to remember the speech-print relationship that is represented. Each time the students see a symbol, they are to associate the letter with a familiar sound from the environment. For example, when learning the *u*, children are told to recall the sound of a train whistle; or when learning the *t*, they are reminded of the ticking of a clock. As they build a repertoire of such associations, they gradually accumulate enough of them to read at least at the level of decoding. The onomatopoeic method is frequently a delight to young learners. It *is* fun and it can be paced according to the rate at which students are making, storing, and retrieving connections between sounds and symbols. However, it can be a very artificial approach, one resulting in lessons that are very contrived and that contain stilted, unnatural language. It places such a strong emphasis on the recall of discrete elements that the *code* may emerge to detract from the *meaning*.

Another synthetic method is the alphabetic method. The pupil learns all the *names* of the letters of the alphabet. Unlike the onomatopoeic method, no attention is given to the sounds represented by the letters. The learner uses his/her knowledge of letter names to unlock words by spelling them, letter by letter. The method is easy to initiate and convenient for teachers, but it can be cumbersome and limiting. The students are blending *letters*, not *sounds*, and they may become confused when they are unable to unlock words that have been obscured by their spellings. Because the *whole* of anything is more than the sum of its parts, attention to small elements of written language may tend to create readers who fail to grasp the larger, more meaningful units.

The phonic method has many enthusiastic supporters. A phonic method is one in which the sound system of the language is primary. Students must hear speech sounds (the phonemes) and make accurate and rapid associations with the written symbols (the graphemes) representing them. Once they have the speech-print connections mastered, they are expected then to decode; that is, they can transform the written symbols back into the spoken ones. The phonic method has been very popular in languages where there is a good *fit* between speech and print, and when the written language is a fairly consistent, predictable representation of speech. The sound-symbol associations can be learned with relative ease by most students. There are in many languages what the linguists call a *poor fit* between speech and print. The same letter may represent different sounds, different letters may represent the same sound, or letters change their sounds in different word environments. There may be a very elaborate diphthong system or a system of diacritical marks to be learned in some languages. Speech-symbol relationships may be presented by means of picture-symbols, which require the learners to make an association with a picture, usually one representing an object in their world. The pictured object's name begins with the sound to be represented by the letter. The sound-symbol relationships may also be taught directly by presenting the letter name and the sound represented by the letter together with illustrations of the sounds in words familiar to the children. In Spanish, *el método fónico*, in its several variations, lends itself to a reasonable sequence with short units of speech-print understandings to be acquired and practiced as the program progresses. It can become boring and seem unrelated to the *total* act of reading unless the teacher adds the element of interest with tongue twisters *(trabalenguas)*, rhymes *(rimas)*, poems *(poesia)*, and other language activities. Further, the method does focus on parts of words and may result in students learning to decode at the expense of gaining meaning. It is wise to remember that phonic skills in many languages may be great for unlocking unfamiliar words but, by themselves, contribute little to the comprehension of those words.

The syllabic method is another very traditional and time-honored method that depends heavily on the child's auditory memory. Part-whole approaches in small units of speech-print relationships can be offered to students as they are able to internalize and use them. Syllables may be organized and sequenced carefully to permit students to begin using them immediately in words and in sentences that provide meaning. The opportunity to apply the skills directly to the act of reading allows learners to feel that they are not merely acquiring some isolated information like letter names and letter sounds, which may often appear only peripherally related to *real reading*. Of this method it must be said, however, that it falls heir to the same criticism as other approaches that emphasize small units of speech sounds and their written representations in symbols.

Analytic Approaches

Among the analytic ways of teaching reading, the language experience approach has been used with some degree of success. The students are encouraged to respond to events in their experience by recalling what they have thought about and can put into words. The teacher or teacher aide then writes what has been said, reads it back, asks for several repetitions of it until the students, too, can read what has been written. Since the material comes from a meaningful experience in the students' own world, there is no question of comprehension. The students see the relationships among thinking, speaking, reading, and writing. They next learn the writing system and can create their own accounts of personal experiences. The teacher is responsible for maintaining a rich and interesting classroom environment that will elicit language and generate experiences about which talking, writing, and reading can be accomplished. For students from any language, the language experience approach can be a delight. They may draw upon culturally relevant and familiar topics that are near and dear to them. They are assimilating written language in whole phrases or sentences that make instant sense because they are their very own thoughts. The teacher enjoys the students' interest and motivation. However, this approach demands much of both teacher and learners. The teacher must manage an enormous amount of material, different for each child, since each student's language and experiences are unique. There is the ongoing requirement to change and to create new stimuli for more complex language and its written representation. In order to keep track of student progress, there is the considerable burden of recordkeeping so that the teacher will be able to follow individual development in the various reading skills. There is little or no control of vocabulary so that practice needed for mastery may not occur and words learned today may be forgotten tomorrow. The success or failure of such a reading approach depends in large measure upon many other classroom variables, one of which is how the teacher uses stories the students have produced.

The global method is one in which whole words and entire sentences are produced visually and the students are told what they are. They then memorize the words without ever taking them apart to look at their small elements. It is a *look-say* approach that stresses meanings and ignores the writing system as a code. Expressions such as *Today is Monday;* or customary classroom amenities such as *Good morning* are taught in their entirety. Theorists who support this method argue that dividing the words into syllables and learning the letters and sounds may create absurdities and destroy meaning, the heart of the reading process. The global method has its merits. It offers reading activities that students can readily understand *if the written material is prepared by the teacher at a level commensurate with students' experience.* It places a great burden on memory, however, and has been said to offer few or no opportunities to acquire basic awareness of how the writing system works. Expansion of the reading vocabulary and development of specific reading skills may not take place unless the teacher goes further with supplementary activities.

The generative word method operates much as the global method. Whole words and complete sentences are presented, illustrated, and pronounced by the students. After they have memorized the material and can read it, they *then* are taught how to analyze sentences and words into their component elements. Thus, they go from a meaningful emphasis to the code and analyze how the code has been put together to create the meanings for them. They may discover syllables, sounds, letters, punctuation marks, and capitalization. The students have finished the analysis, and they have a good grasp of both the *code* and the *meaning*. It has been said that one danger is the pitfall of passivity in the students. The teacher must do most of the analyzing; and once the students *know* what the written language represents, there is not much motivation for them to dig back into the *parts* that have created a meaningful *whole* for them already.

Eclecticism

The eclectic method is one that combines successful elements of both synthetic and analytic approaches in an attempt to offer students an effective reading program. It may include the presentation of whole sentences, identification of speech-print relationships by phonics, *look-say* practice with flash cards, use of the learner's own language, use of pictures for clues, and a variety of other features drawn from several methods.

It is prudent for teachers to consider *first* the student who is to be served by the reading approach and to recognize that no *one* method has a monopoly on success in the classroom. There are students with great visual memories, students with well-developed oral language, and students with good tactile-kinesthetic skills. There are *also* students who are weak in one or more of these areas. Add to this the fact that some students have long attention spans and some do not; some can persist in the completion of a task and some cannot; some are able to take direction and follow instructions and some are not. Yet all students have *something* the teacher may draw upon to ensure that they find a measure of success in learning to read.

Which of the methods are applicable to the teaching of both English and native language reading? Any method wisely used by a careful, knowledgeable teacher can be applied *if* it is suitable for the background and unique needs of students (Thonis, 1976, 1983). If students' auditory integrities are weak, a method that demands hearing and discriminating among fine speech differences (as required by the phonic method) would be a poor choice. If students have phenomenal visual strengths, a method that taps this ability to remember visually presented materials and arrange them in proper sequence (as the global method demands) may be an excellent alternative. Students with impressive command of oral language and rich stores of experiences may find an introduction to print that uses their language and experience an exciting encounter. The teacher is the one who must select the best methods to make the most of the reading opportunities. For language minority students, the language experience approach could be very effective in the teaching of *both* English and native language reading. A phonics method, one demanding the pupil to hear sounds and speech patterns, could be productive for native language reading and a disaster for English reading. Students could find it difficult if not impossible to hear accurately and to discriminate among the sounds of English. A method using whole words and sentences taken solely from an English-speaking cultural setting may be totally devoid of sensibility or interest for language minority students. Thus, the choice of methods certainly could be different for the *two* reading classes. It would be a grave error to assume that the *same* methods would necessarily apply to the teaching of both. It is essential to determine the method on the basis of first- and second-language readiness to read *each specific language* and the levels of language development in both native language and in English.

Lesson Design

Identifying a blueprint for lesson design, Merino (1991) outlines six principles as follows:

- Use of contextualized language (Krashen, 1982)
- Active student participation in high interest areas (Swain, 1983)
- Problem-solving activities, through joint negotiation (Long, 1990)
- Hierarchical presentation of concepts (Krashen, 1982)
- Recycling of concepts (Krashen, 1982)
- Cooperative grouping of limited and fluent English-speaking students (Kagan, 1986)

In summarizing the blueprint, Merino drew upon Krashen's construct of comprehensible input; the socio-affective filter; hierarchical presentation of concepts; and the recycling of concepts. They also use Kagan's cooperative groupings of limited and fluent students; Long's theory of negotiation of interaction; and Swain's theory of comprehensible output. Merino concludes by writing: "Simply put, we must have reasons for what we do."

Hiebert (1991) writes that some strategies have not been fully explored. For example, an examination of word-level strategies has become an unpopular topic because it is considered to be closely associated with traditional teaching skills. Hiebert also asks, "Can word-level strategies be revisited within the context of authentic reading and writing tasks?" These strategies may need different emphases for students who are discovering books and print for the first time in contrast to students who have enjoyed such experiences at home. Hiebert worked with small groups of students who, after shared reading, practiced writing on chalkboards or magnetic boards. Later, they had an opportunity to use these same words in their writing. Their shared reading had the advantage of allowing the students to see the text and read it along with the teacher and peers. It was important for the teacher to use the specific words as the highlight of the lessons. Hiebert points out that more study about the effectiveness of word-level practice in this manner should be carried out.

Social Context

The social context in which language is acquired has been addressed by several researchers. From these investigations such variables as cooperative learning, metalanguage communicative competence, groupings practices, and writing as a social act have been examined (Johnson, 1991; Savignon, 1991; Murphy, 1991; Bruder and Henderson, 1986; Hiebert, 1991; Hernandez-Chavez, 1984; Dolson, 1985; see also Snow's comments on the nature of the interactive classroom and the benefits that accrue to learners as they negotiate meanings in this volume).

Cooperative Learning

Encouraging students to work in small groups has been hailed as a great improvement over solitary, individual learners who struggle and compete in a classroom. Learning to work together collaboratively while pooling talents, knowledge, and skills has drastically altered the environment of many classrooms. Increased student achievement depends upon these variables: (1) individual responsibility and (2) the nature of the group goal. (See also Snow's description of the effectiveness of small group instruction in promoting classroom interaction among students in this volume.)

The natural processes of perceiving, thinking, and learning are receiving greater attention from the area of cognitive psychology and its related fields. Bransford and Vye (1989) and Beck (1989) ask the questions: (1) What do competent readers and writers know and do? (2) What is the initial (pre-instructional) state of the learner and how does this initial state match the goals of instruction? and (3) How do students *progress* from where they were initially and how do they develop more competence? Researchers remind the practitioners in classrooms that learners do not begin instruction as blank slates and may bring misconceptions to instruction. If the learner is full of misinformation, then a primary goal of the activities must be to clear up these misconceptions. Students then will be equipped to move on from factual knowledge to procedural knowledge. This viewpoint leads to the emphasis on "learning by doing," not merely providing additional practice in workbook-type exercises. One of the significant elements is "coached practice" in a social setting that emphasizes cooperative learning.

Palinscar and Brown (1989) recommend reciprocal teaching, an oral language activity, as a variant of cooperative learning. They note that reciprocal teaching in small groups of primary children has been an effective means of improving listening comprehension. Bermudez and Prater (1989) make a strong case for direct instruction to improve comprehension and retention. They think teachers cannot assume that ESL students will have the ability to solve and organize their ideas purely on the basis of opportunities to brainstorm, cluster, or summarize. They suggest that ESL students especially need to think, read, and write in "an integrated manner as they are acquiring communicative skills in English." They also believe that writing opportunities will enhance the students' abilities in higher-order thinking skills.

The Classroom Environment

Glatthorn (1989) asks the question: What kind of classroom environment will be most conducive to the development of writing and thinking skills? His view of the research summarizes these *traditional* teacher behaviors:

- Sets and enforces limits for behavior
- Sets reasonably high expectations for students

- Provides a clear structure for organizing verbal learning
- Provides guided and independent practice
- Monitors behavior and keeps students on task
- Provides feedback

These descriptions cover a task-oriented, highly *structured* environment. The fact that these teacher behaviors are described as *traditional* does not necessarily mean that they have no place in the contemporary classroom. Like many practices labeled as traditional, they have value in a classroom environment where there is a balance of structure and freedom.

Integration of Skills

Adams (1990) in her summary of *Thinking and Learning About Print* asks the question: "With so much underlying agreement, why is there so much outward dispute?" Her conclusions are described in five categories as follows:

- Predictors of reading acquisition
- Before formal instruction begins
- Beginning to read
- Phonics instruction
- Beyond the basics

Considerations of each of these five areas include reminders that instruction is effective or ineffective only to the extent to which these pieces are "fitted together" to complement and to support the needs of the students. In each of them, there are strong statements relative to the importance of listening, speaking, reading, writing, and thinking in activities that encourage the integration of language and literacy skills in meaningful context. Adams makes a strong case for the maxim that the *whole* is certainly more than the *sum* of its parts.

Whole Language

Whole language principles in teaching reading and writing suggest the following (Goodman, 1987; Rigg, 1991):

- Knowledge is socially constructed.
- Language creates and communicates meaning.

- Functions of language must be authentic and make sense.
- Materials must be real.
- Writing must have a real and relevant purpose.
- Language is both social and individual.
- Literacy is a *part* of, not separate from, language.

These principles as implemented in a classroom mean that language instruction is student-centered; activities must have real, not contrived purposes; students may select from among activities offered; students and teachers both must enjoy the respect of their peers. (See Crawford's connection among sheltered English, whole language, and communicative approaches in this volume.)

Grammar

The formal teaching of grammar has been criticized by many theorists. Grammar has only a small influence on the acquisition of communicative competence according to Krashen (1985). There are some teachers and students, too, who may find explicit grammar task assignments boring. It appears that second language learners do not always have the *metalanguage* to talk about grammar as a subject. The present research does not fully address the effective formats for presenting grammar tasks. Formats that could enliven the social interaction have not been given much attention. Grammar "purists" are at times offended when told to ignore errors as a natural occurrence in the course of language growth (Fotos and Ellis, 1991).

Goldenberg (1990) suggests caution in selecting one method over another. He sees value in early opportunities for beginning readers to learn about letter-sound associations and the formation of syllables. He found that in his Spanish reading program, such practices were very successful. Goldenberg and the two very competent teachers with whom he worked found that it was more difficult to implement the listening experiences, dictation of stories, and other "top-down" approaches. Although this project of teaching Spanish-speaking children to read specifically examined the code emphasis versus the meaning emphasis in learning to read Spanish, the questions generated by the researchers are the same ones asked by those who explore early reading English. Goldenberg (1991) asks similar questions in his exploration of the balance of skills and meaning in the beginning literacy programs of New Zealand.

The Materials

When majority language students are learning to read, one of the joyous opportunities they have is their practice outside the classroom. They can take their readers and school library books home or go to the community libraries with their parents or family members. They are surrounded by signs, advertisements, newspaper, menus, and numerous written reminders that reading and writing are valued. Out-of-school practice reinforces the skills being developed in their daily lessons and results in improved learning. For language minority students, however, the practice depends on several conditions. Some language minority children learning to read the vernacular have parents who do not read. There are few library books in the home language on the shelves in the school and community libraries to challenge and delight them. The majority language surrounds them when they leave the classroom. Newspapers, magazines, restaurant lists, notices, and other written materials are offered in the language of the majority. Or, if language minority students are attempting to read in the second language, they may find it very difficult to handle the concept loading and speech-print connections of the media beyond the classroom. If they wish to share their second language literacy skills with their family, it may turn out that parents do not read the language. These are social and cultural factors discussed by Bowen (1977) and Tucker (1977) who feel that social and cultural considerations are more important than linguistic ones in deciding which literacy program is best for language minorities. The school is an institution created by society and is expected to reflect the values of that society. The expectations of the school and community certainly must be considered and weighed carefully.

An important issue is the selection of reading materials for language minority students. Both the suitability of the materials and their availability must be considered. If language minority students are being taught to read in their native language, it may be very disappointing for the students to find few or no books to read. When majority language students learn to read, they are likely to find the delight and wonder of stories, records, tapes, and other media for practice and for pleasure. Minority language students ordinarily do not find such treasures in school and community libraries of the United States. Like most skills, the skills of literacy are of little value if they are not used. If these students are to enjoy their hard-won skills, the school must consider seriously the addition of native language books and other materials to supplement the classroom instruction and to extend opportunities for growth in reading and thinking skills.

An appraisal of the suitability of materials is often a difficult task because there are so many elements involved in their selection. Minimally, teachers should take into account the appearance, the illustrations, the authenticity of language, the representative nature of the content, the relevance to the curriculum, and the cost. Materials should be attractive; the print should be an appropriate size; the quality of paper and binding should be adequate for the kind of use anticipated; the structures, vocabulary, sentence length, and concept loading should be suitable; and the political or religious content should be acceptable to the community. It is especially important that the materials not be hastily patched together translations of English. The cultural content should be interesting and relevant to the language minority students. The international literature of childhood and adolescence is stocked with charming stories that enchant students everywhere. Many classics from English have been lovingly translated into other languages with great care and with attention to idiomatic expressions, figurative language, vocabulary, and cultural detail. The concepts and values drawn from other cultural settings should be free from stereotyping. The views of various ways of living should be presented objectively. Reading materials should emphasize the commonalities among various groups as well as their differences. Reading materials carefully chosen on the basis of the language needs and developmental levels of minority students contribute greatly to learning success.

The Parents

It is noteworthy that successful reading programs, regardless of approach or language sequence, generally include strong support for reading at home. The literature describes the importance of the value given to reading. The reading interests of parents, the availability of reading materials, and many other family variables all may contribute or detract from students' learning to read. The traditional recommendations offered have been to invite parents to volunteer in classrooms; serve on school committees; read to their children at home; take them on visits to museums and places of historic interest; and other such suggestions requiring time, transportation, materials, money, and a knowledge of community resources that many minority language families lack. School personnel also have been fairly consistent in their recommendations that language minority families use the majority language in the home.

Parents who do attempt to follow this suggestion are likely to be providing poor language models and restricted language practice in the majority language while at the same time denying their children the richness and variety of their native language competence. It would appear that educators need to be more aware of the practical realities of language minority families and more knowledgeable about the impact of language on literacy before making suggestions that may not be in their students' best interests.

It is highly consistent with the research to encourage parents to continue using the native language at home. They should be urged to speak with and listen to their children. Both listening and speaking vocabularies can be increased and the background of concepts extended. Language development is part of total development. Children's home experiences can offer vital opportunities for learning about the family's history and heritage. The songs, dances, proverbs, poetry, recipes, games, and the hundreds of other remembrances from the childhoods of parents and grandparents offer not only a sense of self, but also a wealth of language skills. Legarreta-Marcaida (1981) has an exciting and practical list of suggested activities that enhance the parents' contribution to their children's reading potential.

In encouraging parents to continue using the home language, educators must take time to explain clearly their reasons for this recommendation. Often, parents do not appreciate the educational value of the home language in an English-speaking society. They need to be reassured that English language competence is a major instructional goal. They also need to be told that native language proficiency contributes to these second language skills. The school has a significant responsibility to foster understanding of the rationale that supports the sequence of language and literacy instruction. (See also Snow's practical suggestions for effective home-school collaboration in this volume.)

The Teacher

The teacher is the most important element in an instructional plan for minority students who are learning in a classroom designed for the language majority students. A competent and caring teacher can make the method and materials work. The teacher ideally should know and appreciate the language and culture of the students. The teacher should be skillful in assessing language, development, and achievement levels. The teacher needs to be flexible and creative in making adjustments to the plan of reading instruction to accommodate a variety of levels in language achievement. The teacher needs to be well-organized and well-informed about the availability of materials, personnel, and other resources to supplement classroom opportunities. The teacher should be strong in the conviction that language minority students are capable of learning to read and write at the same level of excellence as their majority language peers. The teacher needs to continue to search for improved methods of assessment and instruction as new research points the direction toward better reading programs for language minority students. The teacher must be willing to take the time necessary to bring these students along.

All instruction for all children should be intended to increase self-confidence and self-esteem. The school is only one source of nurturance of ego strengths; but it is a very powerful one for developing, maturing students. When the reading program alternatives are considered in relation to this sense of self-worth, it may be useful to consider first the status of the minority language in the school and outside of it. When the value of the minority language is rejected by the community, this message may diminish students' sense of self. There are certainly some social conditions over which the school has little or no control, and the societal rejection of a minority group and their language may be one of them. Within the school itself, however, everyone who works with language minority students should be made aware of the importance of the mother tongue in the enhancement of intellectual growth; the relevance of the speech-print connection in the improvement of literacy skills; and the role of first language development in the extension of second language competency. School-community contacts should be used to explain and describe the needs of language minority students from the framework of human development and learning theories. A climate of acceptance at school may serve the students well in supporting their self-esteem and in increasing their confidence in their abilities to succeed in language and literacy activities.

Keeping Records

What is the role of a management system in a bilingual reading program? It is always desirable to have *some* means of charting students' progress in reading. If they are learning to read in one language, *it is important;* if they are learning to read in *two* languages, *it is absolutely essential.* Yet, the teacher must guard against the management system taking over the program. The management system is a bookkeeping system only; it is not the reading program. To be useful, the system should be short and simple. It should be easy to use and convenient for the teacher who will use it. The system should contain some built-in flexibility to accommodate differential levels of students and the transiency rates in areas where students experience a high rate of school transfer. A management system should be neither too costly, in terms of a school's budget, nor too exacting in terms of the teachers' time, tears, and frustration. The system should be selected on the basis of its consistency with the established program within the district. If some provision for the students' checking of their own progress can be built into the system, it provides greater freedom from the paper chase that so often burdens teachers and teacher aides. Wise, experienced teachers have always had a management system of some kind. The system should work for the reading program and be supportive of it. Teachers and administrators must be cautious that the management system does not work against the program and does not become an end in itself.

Assessment of Student Progress

Evaluation has shifted from formal skills-based norm-referenced instruments to informal teacher and student assessments. Among the measures are teacher observations, conferences with students, prepared checklists, student-selected portfolios of work, and responses to questionnaires. The debate persists over the best way to evaluate student progress in general. When assessment of language minority students is considered, the argument increases in protestations and in volume. As schools change curriculum and instruction, they must also modify their evaluation methods. What is the importance of assessment? Assessment can be very important and can contribute greatly to the success of a program of reading two languages. The major problem lies in finding the most appropriate ways to assess the gains students are making and to redirect one's efforts if gains are not in evidence. Assessment may involve the administration of standardized tests, the observation of students, the application of informal measures, and other assessment techniques. It is wise to remember that assessment is an appraisal of the program; *it is not the program.* Therefore, assessment should be economical of both teacher and pupil time. The *use* of information obtained through assessment is of much greater value. As teachers appraise the progress of students, they may change objectives, edit materials, or alter timelines to improve students' chances for success. Assessment should be the servant, not the master, of the reading program.

Transferability of Skills

Transfer occurs when learning in one situation influences the potential for performance in a new situation. If it were not possible to draw upon previous experiences and information, human beings would be limited in the amount or kind of knowledge acquired in a lifetime. Transfer of learning is a significant element in the context of planning reading programs for non-native English speakers. Once students leave the primary grades, they are expected to read and write in almost every school subject. Therefore, the potential for transferability of skills from one system of written language to another should be seriously examined. Transfer takes place when there are elements in the new task similar to those in the task or skill previously acquired. For languages that share the same alphabet and have common features in the visual symbols, there are immediate transfer possibilities. For Asian languages with logographic writing systems, for other non-alphabet systems, or for different alphabetic writing such as the Armenian alphabet, transfer is not based on the similarity of elements but on the more general understanding that the visual symbols represent the auditory ones. This transfer is based on the application of principles and generalizations. The sensory-motor requirements of reading and writing involve the transfer of other skills. Students who have learned how to use pencils, pens, rulers, protractors, and other classroom tools do not have to develop fine muscle control or eye-hand coordination a second time. The tracking of the eye and hand in the direction required by the conventions of the writing system may vary (Chinese is read from top to bottom, Hebrew from right to left, Spanish from left to right, and Japanese from top to bottom and then from right to left), but the awareness that there is a directionality and that it is an arbitrary feature of the specific writing system is transferable. There are good reasons to believe that attitudes and habits transfer. Positive feelings about reading in one language are likely to carry over to another. The habits of attention, concentration, persistence, and task completion can transfer well to learning the new language.

Transfer of reading abilities from the first language to the second language can be identified in both general and specific terms for pre-reading, decoding, and comprehension skills. During the preparation for reading, students have been encouraged to develop good listening habits. Having learned how to listen for a sequence of events, immediate recall of facts, rhyming elements, discovery of relationships, and for other receptive language tasks, the students carry over their response set to the demands of the new, unfamiliar language. Visual-perceptual training transfers as well. When students have become skillful in observing the visual details of one form of written language, this observation of the visual symbol system's significant features is readily available for transfer to another form. If the writing system is one that uses diacritically marked forms, the attention to detail which is necessary to see differences in specific words as in *río, rio* or *papá, papa* (words whose meanings are significantly altered by the small detail of an accent mark or its placement), will transfer. Figure must be distinguished from ground in any language, and the background of page must be separated from the material written upon it. This visual-perceptual skill developed in one language transfers easily to another.

The visual-motor skills needed to track the eyes and hand in a specific direction to follow the sequence of written patterns, the coordination of eye and hand in writing and spelling those patterns, and the development of strength and motor control are abilities that need to be learned and practiced. The application of motor skills to any reading and writing system may be transferred without change or put to use in new language learning with modifications to accommodate the differences that may exist between the first and second language writing conventions. For languages that use a left-to-right direction such as English, Vietnamese, Spanish, and Portuguese, no change in eye or hand movement is needed. Farsi, Hebrew, or other languages that read from right to left, however, require the student to change direction. Yet the eye and the hand must still move smoothly together. Though preparation for reading and writing is *specific* to the language in the matter of oral vocabulary development, ear training for language sounds, and knowledge of word order, all the sensory-motor skills and visual perceptual abilities will transfer exactly as they have been learned or with modification that can be readily encouraged.

The act of making a connection between the sounds of a language (speech) and the graphic representation of that language (print, logograph, and ideograph) has been referred to as *decoding*. Developmental programs designed to introduce reading, writing, and spelling may stress the acquisition of techniques and strategies that assist students in making the speech-print associations needed to recognize the code. Using sound-symbol relationships, applying knowledge of word structures, and finding grammatical clues are examples of such skills that are encouraged in initial instruction. These are tools intended to help students recognize in written form what is known by the student in oral context. Thus, students begin to see what they have heard. The extent to which decoding skills transfer from one language to another depends upon the two writing systems. Those using a Roman alphabet may have greater potential for transfer according to the doctrine of identical elements. Languages written according to alphabetic principles may have common features that will transfer. Written languages vary; and transfer potential will also vary on the basis of the likenesses *and* the differences to be found among their alphabets, their syllabaries, and/or other arbitrary conventions of their written systems. Awareness of the rule-governed manner by which reading skills are learned, remembered, and practiced will transfer by generalization. There is little or no effective reading at the decoding level. Until students have made the meaning connection, they are not reading. Essentially, comprehension of written material requires the exercise of intellectual skills. Students must draw upon specific backgrounds of experience and concepts. They must use memory, reasoning, and creativity as they interpret and judge what has been read. Each comprehension task calls upon students to think. At the early levels, simple, literal comprehension is required; but as the reading material becomes more complex, the reader is expected to exercise interpretive and inferential abilities of a higher order. Reading comprehension demands thinking in *any* language. If students learn in the primary language to recognize a main idea, find supportive details, order a sequence of events, identify major characters, determine the existence of bias, or analyze emotional tone, then these *thinking* skills are abilities that do not ever have to be learned again. There is complete transfer of cognitive function to the new language. For the prereading, decoding, and comprehension levels, the power and potential of transferability cannot be underestimated.

It is reasonable to infer that the basis for language transfer in reading is found in the Cummins (1980) construct of cognitive academic language proficiency which undergirds the potential for literacy in general and contributes to the ultimate flowering of literacy skills specific to the instructional program. However, it is vital to recognize that only *strong* skills transfer and that the sequence of reading in any language may be arranged to make the most of the transfer possibilities between languages. This precept of transfer should give teachers in simultaneous reading programs in two languages or those in programs of premature introduction to the second language literacy pause for thought. Violations of learning principles could easily be responsible for the reading failure presently found among the minority language students.

Potential for L1 Reading Skill Transfer to L2

The Transfer Period. When is the best period during which the student is led from first to second language literacy in English? Reading teachers should develop their own criteria for placing their language minority students in the reading classes in English. Among these criteria are such considerations as the students' successful accomplishments in the native language reading class, their proficiency in oral English, their specific ear-training for the English sound system, and their expressed interest in discovering the content to be unlocked in English print. The most important consideration in these criteria is time. Students must be given sufficient time to establish strong literacy skills in their first language.

Once the decision is made that the students have met the standards set and that they could benefit from instruction in reading English, there are some additional factors to consider. The first concern is with the reading skill, whether the students will be able to transfer immediately from native language reading to English reading. The greatest transfer benefit, however, is the confidence of an already literate learner who has successfully managed the rigors of print and will face the second writing system with self-assurance. The second consideration is the recognition of potential phonological, lexical, or structural sources of interference from the writing system that need to be anticipated and minimized. The English reading teacher must watch for any problems and attempt to prevent them or to use them for learning. A third concern is to provide knowledge and opportunities to practice new skills specific to English reading. Word order patterns, punctuation rules, multi-semantic vocabulary items, and other features unique to written English must be learned in addition to those elements that have transfer possibilities. Thus, transition to English demands *at least* the following: (1) definitive criteria for assessing students' readiness to engage in reading English; (2) recognition of areas that do not have to be taught again; (3) clear understanding of skills that may transfer immediately; (4) keen sensitivity to interference problems and the expertise to deal effectively to minimize them; and (5) considerable competence in the contrastive sounds and structural systems of both the native language and English.

Good choices for the transfer stage might be the language experience approach supported by a cautious program of phonic skills based on sounds students can *hear* and *say*. Another method might be a *linguistic* program, which presents short written patterns on the basis of a regular sound-symbol correspondence *(man - Dan - ran - fan, etc.)* and supports this somewhat sterile, artificial written language by rich oral English in poems, storytelling, choral speaking, and dramatizations. Still another might be a carefully paced basal reader approach augmented by pictures, news events, and descriptions of life in the language minority community as written in English. In this manner, the content of the basal stories could be enlivened by content of cultural relevance to learners. The use of a variety of authentic stories in literacy and trade books presented through a whole language approach also could be appropriate, enjoyable, and effective. There are many combinations of methods that could well support the second language literacy plan in English. Teachers should be encouraged to sift among the many methods for the winning combination for their own students.

The Best of Biliteracy

Cummins (1980) has stated that cognitive academic language potential is strongly related to reading and writing skills. This potential permits readers to process written language and manipulate the content in reasoning and in dealing with abstractions. It is this ability that promotes effective reading comprehension skills. The question of the most appropriate reading program alternatives for the minority language student can then be considered from the multiple viewpoint of: (1) which language promotes cognitive development; (2) which writing system makes the best connection with language and cognition; (3) which reading program will be supported by social, political, and cultural factors; and (4) which alternative is best suited to the minority student's stage of development. There are doubtless other variables to consider in reviewing the many complexities of literacy and biliteracy in a country where the expected outcomes of the program in the past have been the creation of monolingual and monoliterate students. This goal has been in place for a long period of educational history in the United States.

The case for native language reading instruction for language minority students is strong. The rationale can be defended on logical grounds and empirical evidence. The perceptual, sensory-motor, and cognitive processes learned and practiced in any language have tremendous potential for transfer if developmental and learning principles are not violated. Once language minority students have learned to read well and have understood the strategies for obtaining meaning from print, these abilities provide a solid foundation for literacy skills in the second language. The essential characteristic of first language skills available for supporting the addition of the second language is *strength*. Only *strong* learnings transfer. Hasty, premature introduction to the second writing system may result in two weak sets of skills, neither of which serves well enough to be the carrier of content in school subjects.

Language minority students need access to content areas by way of the language and literacy which makes sense to them. Mathematics, social science, physical science, and other school subjects can be acquired and clarified in the stronger language and, once fully understood, can be labeled in the second language. Reading instruction is not an end in itself. The reason that the years of middle childhood are usually emphasized as the period for acquiring reading and writing skills may be found in the timetable of human development. These are the years for acquiring the basic instruments for lifelong learning. The growing complexities of subject matter after the fifth grade matches the students' increased abilities to manage abstractions and formal logic. Reasoning abilities, well-supported by language and literacy, allow students to expand their understanding of the world and the people in it. If students are not given the opportunity to learn and fully develop their native language, the subject areas must be taught at a slower pace and with as much nonverbal representation as possible. Sheltered English is one modification that has been effective. Even with this effort, language minority students may not be able to keep up with their language majority classmates. High achievement is possible when students are given textbooks for content areas in their stronger language and at the suitable level for their age and grade placement. If the students cannot read second language texts, alternative methods of presenting concepts must be identified.

There is no argument among language researchers, developmental psychologists, and reading theorists that written language is strongly related to some aspects of oral language. There is also agreement that language and literacy skills are mutually supportive and essential to cognitive growth. In the best possible conditions for learning, students would all read first the language which has made their world a meaningful place. They could come from the language of their families to the language of instruction with confidence and ease. With the addition of literacy, students could advance through the curriculum to the extent that good instruction and intellectual potential would permit. Language majority students do this and some are very successful; others are not. Yet, the difficulties when they do arise are not compounded by language differences as they are for minority students. With the growing numbers of these students in classrooms of the United States, there is a serious need to re-examine reading instruction alternatives for them. It is only reasonable to expect that not all communities can offer the advantages of vernacular reading for all language minority students. It is also very reasonable to expect consideration of initial and continuing native language reading instruction in communities where large numbers of the same language groups are found.

Regarding the differences existing between immersion and submersion programs, it may be useful to attempt to change some of the negative influences through a better exchange of information. The language majority group often fails to understand that the end in view is also excellence in English. There must be a continued effort to clarify the speech-print connection in literacy and to emphasize the important role that language and literacy skills play in the development of intelligence. A central purpose of the school is to teach students to think. Thinking includes, among other entities, problem solving, evaluating, creating, and reasoning. Well-developed speech and strong reading skills are instruments that nurture thinking. For language minority students, there is the rich potential for speaking, reading, writing, and thinking in two languages.

Transferability of first language skills, both oral and written, is important and possible. The potential for transfer of sensory-motor skills, identical elements, principles, patterns, and attitude must be recognized and promoted depending upon the languages involved. There should be a sequence of language and literacy skills that searches out transfer possibilities and watches carefully for potential interference. Exit criteria are *not* applied, as the central issue to consider is the *addition* of more formal second language instruction and the introduction of the written English forms. There must be the expectation that when English language skills are sufficiently strong they, too, will carry content in the subject areas. Self-esteem is promoted not only through the accomplishment of English but also by the advancement of native language abilities. The school personnel, rather than recommending use of English in the home, continues to encourage use of the native language in family activities, which enlarges the students' view of their environment and improves their background of information. The program is based on the *common underlying proficiency model,* which recognizes the value of stimulating general language growth by way of the native language channel. (See Cummins, in this volume, for a discussion of the two models—separate and common underlying proficiencies.) The common underlying proficiency model also makes sense in terms of stressing the use of the stronger language for instructional purposes. There is the logical assumption that first language strength contributes to second language acquisition and that second language achievement is not diminished by the development of the first language. Rather, excellence in the native language improves the chances of better second language functioning. It is reasonable to expect that students who talk well, read easily, think effectively in their own first language, and have developmentally reached the stage of abstract thinking will *also* talk well, read easily, and think effectively in the second language.

Glossary

Communicative Competence - The ability to interact with other speakers in social contexts with the appropriate use of language that is sensitive to cultural difference.

Learning Styles - The students' characteristic preferences for strategies and conditions through which students can best learn.

Functions of Teachers - The ways in which teachers create and control the values and responses of students in a learning environment.

Reflection - The thoughtful consideration of ideas in both interpersonal and intrapersonal responses.

Synthetic method - A method that emphasizes the parts of words and builds meaning through the learning of small elements of language.

Analytic method - A method that focuses on meaning through the learning of whole words and larger units of thought.

Eclectic method - A method that selects from both synthetic and analytic approaches to combine the optimum benefits for students.

Lesson Design - A plan for incorporating the relevant learning principles to support classroom practices.

Social Context - The setting in which language is acquired and expressed, including classroom groupings, cooperative learning activities, and shared learnings.

Cooperative Learning - The collaboration of students who work for a group purpose while pooling knowledge, talents, and skills.

Reciprocal Teaching - An oral language activity as a cooperative endeavor intended to improve listening, comprehension, and retention of material.

Integration of Skills - The skills of thinking, listening, speaking, reading, and writing are practiced together in classroom instruction.

Transferability of Learning - The transfer that occurs when knowledge and skills acquired in one learning situation can be applied to the demands of a new or unfamiliar one.

Table

Skill Areas	Language Specific Transfer	Language General Transfer
I. Sensory Motor Transfer		
A. Visual Skills		
1. Eye-hand coordination		X
2. Fine muscle control		X
3. Visual attention to detail		X
4. Figure-ground awareness		X
5. Visual perception	X	X
6. Visual discrimination	X	X
7. Visual memory	X	X
8. Visual sequencing		X
B. Auditory skills		
1. Figure-ground awareness		X
2. Auditory perception	X	X
3. Auditory memory	X	X
4. Auditory discrimination	X	X
5. Auditory sequencing		X
C. Spatial skills		
1. Directional organization		X
2. Top-to-bottom orientation	X	X
3. Lateral orientation	X	X
4. Spatial integration		X
II. Transfer of Identical Elements		
A. The Common Features in Writing Systems		
1. Logographs, ideographs	X	
2. Alphabets	X	
3. Sound-symbol association	X	
4. Capitalization	X	X
5. Punctuation	X	X
6. Lines or other spatial constraints of the writing		X

Skill Areas	Language Specific Transfer	Language General Transfer
III. Transfer by Principles and Generalizations		
A. Reading as a Process		
1. Understanding speech-print relationships		X
2. Speech-print connections	X	X
3. Concepts of words, syllables, sentences, paragraphs		X
4. Comprehension (thinking skills)		
a. Main idea		X
b. Sequence of ideas		X
c. Supportive details		X
d. Inferencing		X
e. Predicting outcomes		X
f. Drawing conclusions		X
g. Recognizing emotions		X
h. Seeing cause and effect		X
i. Distinguishing fact from fiction		X
5. Rule-governed aspects of reading	X	X
6. Study skills		X
IV. Transfer of Habits and Attitudes		
A. Non-cognitive Transfer		
1. Attention		X
2. Listening skills		X
3. Concentration		X
4. Persistence		X
5. Task completion		X
B. Self-esteem Transfer		
1. Being literate		X
2. Feeling capable		X
3. Possessing specific competencies		X
4. Achieving		X
5. Believing in one's ability to learn		X

REFERENCES

Adams, M. (1990). *Beginning to read: Thinking and learning about print.* Urbana-Champaign, Illinois: Center for the Study of Reading.

Archambeault, B. (1992). Personalizing study skills in secondary students. *Journal of Reading, 35*(6), 468-472.

Beck, I. (1989). Improving practice through understanding reading. In *Toward a thinking curriculum: Current cognitive research.* Alexandria, VA: Association for Supervision and Curriculum Development.

Berliner, D. (1985). The executive functions of teaching. In J. Osbourne, P. T. Wilson, & R. C. Anderson (Eds.), *Reading education: Foundations for a literate America.* Lexington, MA: D. C. Heath.

Bermudez, A., & Prater, D. (1989). Evaluating the effectiveness of writing on the comprehension and retention of content reading. *NABE Annual Conference Journal,* 151-156.

Bowen, J. D. (1977). Linguistic perspectives on bilingual education. In B. Spolsky and R. Cooper (Eds.), *Frontiers of bilingual education.* Rowley, MA: Newbury House.

Bransford, J., & Vye, N. (1989). A perspective on cognitive research and its implications for instruction. In *Toward the thinking curriculum: Current cognitive research.* Alexandria, VA: Association for Supervision and Curriculum Development.

Bruder, M., & Henderson, R. (1986). *Beginning reading in English as a second language.* Washington, DC: Center for Applied Linguistics.

Cohen, A. (1974, March). The Culver City Spanish immersion program: The first two years. *The Modern Language Journal, 58*(3), 95-103.

Cohen, A. (1975). *A sociolinguistic approach to bilingual education: Experiments in the Southwest.* Rowley, MA: Newbury House.

Cohen, A., & Swain, M. (1976, March). Bilingual education: The "immersion" model in the North American context. *TESOL Quarterly, 10*(1), 45-53.

Cummins, J. (1979, September). Linguistic interdependence and the educational development of bilingual children. *Bilingual Education Paper Series.* Los Angeles, CA: National Dissemination and Assessment Center, California State University, Los Angeles.

Cummins, J. (1980, March). *The construct of language proficiency in bilingual education.* Paper presented at the Georgetown Roundtable of Language and Linguistics, Georgetown University.

Dolson, D. (1985). Bilingualism and scholastic performance: The literature revisited. *The NABE Journal, 10*(1), 1-35.

Engle, P. L. (1975). *The use of vernacular languages in education: Language medium in early school years for minority groups.* Papers in Linguistics Bilingual Education Series, 3. Arlington, VA: Center for Applied Linguistics.

Glatthorn, A. (1989). Thinking, writing, and reading: Making connections. In D. Lapp, J. Flood, and N. Farnam (Eds.), *Content area reading and learning* (pp. 283-296). Englewood Cliffs, NJ: Prentice-Hall.

Goldenberg, C. (1990). Research directions: Beginning literacy instruction for Spanish-speaking children. *Language Arts, 67,* 590-596.

Goldenberg, C. (1991). *Instructional conversations and their classroom application.* (Practice Report: II.) Santa Cruz, CA: The National Center for Research on Cultural Diversity and Second Language Learning.

Goodman, K. (1987). *What's whole in whole language?* Portsmouth, NH: Heinemann.

Fotos, S., & Ellis, R. (1991, Winter). Communicating about Grammar: A task-based approach. *TESOL Quarterly 25*(4).

Hernandez-Chavez, E. (1984). The inadequacy of English immersion education as an educational approach for language minority students in the United States. In *Studies on immersion.* Sacramento, CA: California State Department of Education.

Hiebert, E. (1991, March). The development of word-based strategies in authentic literacy task. *Language Arts, 68.*

Johnson, D. (1991). Some observations on progress in research in second language learning and teaching. In M. McGroaty and C. Faltis (Eds.), *Language in school and society: Politics and pedagogy.* Berlin: Mouton de Gruyter.

Johnson, D., & Myklebust, H. (1967). *Learning disabilities: Educational principles and practices.* New York: Grune and Stratton.

Kagan, S. (1986). Cooperative learning and sociocultural factors in schooling. In *Beyond language: Social and cultural factors in schooling language minority students.* Los Angeles: Evaluation, Dissemination and Assessment Center, California State University.

Krashen, S. (1982). *Principles and practice in second language acquisition.* New York: Pergamon Press.

Krashen, S. (1985). *Input in second language acquisition.* Oxford: Pergamon Press.

Lambert, W. E. (1975). Culture and language as factors in learning and education. In A. Wolfgang (Ed.), *Education of immigrant students.* Ontario, Canada: Ontario Institute of Studies in Education.

Lambert, W. E., & Tucker, C. R. (1972). *Bilingual education of children: The St. Lambert experiment.* Rowley, MA: Newbury House.

Legarreta-Marcaida, D. (1981). Effective use of the primary language in the classroom. *Schooling and language minority students: A theoretical framework.* (1st ed.) (pp. 83-116). Los Angeles: Evaluation, Dissemination and Assessment Center, California State University.

Long, M. (1990). The least a second language acquisition theory needs to explain. *TESOL Quarterly, 24,* 649-666.

Merino, C. (1991). Discourse processes in the second language classroom. In M. McGroaty and C. Faltis (Eds.), *Languages in school and society: Politics and pedagogy* Berlin: Mouton de Gruyter.

Modiano, N. (1968, Spring). National mother tongue in beginning reading: A comparative study. *Research in the Teaching of English, 11*(1), 32-43.

Murphy, J. (1991). Oral communication in TESOL: Integrating speaking, listening and pronunciation. *TESOL Quarterly, 25,* 51-74.

Palinscar, A., & Brown, A. (1989). Instruction for self-regulated reading. In *Toward the thinking curriculum: Current cognitive research.* Alexandria, VA: Association for Supervision and Curriculum Development.

Ramirez, A. (1991). Discourse processes in the second language classroom. In M. McGroaty and C. Faltis (Eds.), *Languages in school and society: Politics and pedagogy.* Berlin: Mouton de Gruyter.

Rigg, P. (1991, Autumn). Whole language in TESOL. *TESOL Quarterly, 25*(3), 521-542.

Savignon, S. (1991). Communicative language teaching: State of the art. *TESOL Quarterly, 25,* 261-277.

Smith, F. (1971). *Understanding reading: A psycholinguistic analysis of reading and learning to read.* New York: Holt, Rinehart, and Winston.

Swain, M. (1983). *Communicative competence: Some roles of comprehensible input and comprehensible output, in its development.* Paper presented at the 10th University of Michigan Conference on Applied Linguistics, Ann Arbor, MI.

Tarvin, W., & Al-Arishi, A. (1991, Spring). Rethinking communicative language teaching: Reflection and the EFL classroom. *TESOL Quarterly, 25,* 1.

Thonis, E. (1976). *Literacy for America's Spanish speaking children.* Newark, DE: International Reading Association.

Thonis, E. (1983). *The English-Spanish connection.* Compton, CA: Santillana.

Tucker, G. R. (1977). The linguistic perspective. In *Bilingual education current perspectives.* Arlington, VA: Center for Applied Linguistics.

Research Applications for Bilingual Education: Designing and Monitoring Program Delivery

David P. Dolson

In the first edition of *Schooling and Language Minority Students: A Theoretical Framework* (1981), the appendix contained a copy of the then current version of the *Bilingual Education Program Quality Review Instrument, Kindergarten Through Grade Six (Bilingual PQRI)*. At the time, the *Bilingual PQRI* was used by the Bilingual Education Office of the California Department of Education to promote research-based standards for the design and implementation of bilingual education programs.

Gradually, school district personnel began to use the Bilingual PQRI as a resource document to design new programs and to review those currently in place. Since the items contained in the *Bilingual PQRI* were based on a synthesis of the most recent research and evaluation studies, the instrument was considered a useful way to compare the elements of a program against a set of standards which represented the best information available at the time.

Because of a continued need to assist school districts in the application of research knowledge, we have revised and updated the items in the *Bilingual PQRI* and recast the document into a more flexible and easier-to-use checklist format. The items of quality contained in the *Bilingual Program Delivery Checklist* are based primarily on the research reported in this volume and are consistent with other well-controlled research and evaluation studies on bilingual education published elsewhere.

The *Bilingual Program Delivery Checklist* is designed specifically for the review of full bilingual education programs, that is, programs organized to provide language minority students with instruction in and through English and the native language according to the educational needs of individual participants. At a minimum, full bilingual programs include instruction that (1) develops native-like proficiency in English and the minority language, (2) provides access to and sustains normal attainment in all courses required for grade level promotion and graduation, and (3) promotes the development of a positive self-concept and crosscultural knowledge and skills. Although the checklist is most closely aligned with the full bilingual education program model, most of the indicators of quality, with some minor adaptations, apply to other program approaches such as two-way bilingual, early-exit bilingual, and even structured immersion/sheltered instructional programs.

In the early planning stages, schools that enroll significant numbers of language minority students typically conduct a needs assessment of their student population and community. They also survey their teachers and other educational staff members. Based on the results of the needs assessment and deliberations concerning the goals and objectives of the proposed program, the school eventually selects a general direction or a program model for educating language minority students at the site. The items of quality found in the *Bilingual Program Delivery Checklist* collectively provide a framework for developing an instructional delivery system centered on effective program practices.

Even at this beginning stage, there are severe challenges to the maintenance of high levels of program quality. Invariably, schools are forced to design their bilingual programs in ways that accommodate local realities, especially in terms of competing priorities and the availability of the human and material resources needed for implementation.

Once implementation begins, there is a need for on-going monitoring to determine the degree to which the instructional treatment is actually being delivered as planned. Proper monitoring is also an appropriate safeguard against insidious encroachments of mediocrity which over time erode the overall quality of the program. The items contained in the *Bilingual Program Delivery Checklist* can be used to guide initial and enroute adjustments to both the program design and implementation practices. The items can also serve as a reminder to mend flaws in program delivery which develop over time as demands are made upon staff members to come up with interim but often "second-best" solutions to pressing problems.

The *Bilingual Program Delivery Checklist* is divided into three sections. The first section contains the items of program quality organized by the major components of a bilingual education program:

I.   Spanish Language Development
II.   English Language Development

III.   Access to the Core Curriculum
IV.   Crosscultural Development
V.   Staffing and Professional Development
VI.   Home/School Communication and Collaboration

The degree and quality of implementation of each item is to be rated on a simple four-point scale as indicated below:

3 = Superior
2 = Satisfactory
1 = Unsatisfactory
0 = Not Implemented
X = Not Observed

The "Not Observed" (X) rating is used only in instances where program reviewers do not obtain sufficient information on which to base a rating. The comments section is to be used by the program reviewers to clarify their findings.

Program reviewers should use a variety of strategies to collect data. The most obvious methods of investigation include: (1) review of program documents, reports, and student records; (2) interviews with teachers, paraprofessionals, administrators, parents, community, and students; and (3) observations of classroom and other instructional and instructional support activities.

The second section of the document consists of a list of several operational definitions provided to ensure a common understanding of key terminology used in the document. Whenever operational definitions are used in the text of the checklist, they appear in bold to alert the reader that a term with a specialized meaning has been encountered. Any item containing one or more operational definitions should conform to the specifications of the particular definitions in order for the item to be rated at "satisfactory" or "superior" levels.

The third and final section contains the bibliographic references. Only those references associated with the operational definitions are listed here. The actual references for the items of quality are drawn from the various articles contained in this volume and their corresponding bibliographies.

Bilingual Education Program Delivery Checklist for Full Bilingual Education Program, Spanish/English, Kindergarten through Grade Six

This sample version of the *Bilingual Education Program Delivery Checklist* has been developed specifically for school sites enrolling Spanish-speaking students in a full, late-exit bilingual education program covering kindergarten through grade six.

To use this checklist to review programs serving students from other language groups, enrolled at grades 7-12, or being instructed in another program model (such as early-exit or sheltered/structured immersion), a number of relatively minor modifications would be needed. For example, each item should be reviewed for applicability to the alternative setting. In some cases revisions in terminology might be necessary. New and additional items should be added to fully address import programmatic features that are not adequately emphasized in this version. The process of revising the checklist will not only result in a customized and therefore more useful review instrument, but also will serve as an excellent learning experience for the staff members involved in the program review, allowing them to gain further insights into the design and delivery of the program.

Items of Program Quality

I. Spanish Language Development

The program provides the instruction and instructional support services necessary to develop native-like proficiency in Spanish.

1. An assessment system is in place which provides information on the initial and current levels of Spanish language proficiency for individual students.

    ☐ Superior   ☐ Satisfactory   ☐ Unsatisfactory

                      ☐ Not Implemented   ☐ Not Observed

    Comments: _____

    _____

    _____

    _____

2. Teachers can show a schedule or lesson plan indicating that students receive planned instruction in Spanish language arts.

    ☐ Superior   ☐ Satisfactory   ☐ Unsatisfactory

                      ☐ Not Implemented   ☐ Not Observed

    Comments: _____

    _____

    _____

    _____

3. The teaching staff is knowledgeable of the main features of the methodology selected for Spanish language literacy instruction.

    ☐ Superior   ☐ Satisfactory   ☐ Unsatisfactory

                   ☐ Not Implemented   ☐ Not Observed

    Comments: _____

    _____

    _____

    _____

4. Critical thinking skills are interwoven in the teaching of reading and writing through the use of strategies such as **Critical Literacy** and **Process Writing.**

    ☐ Superior   ☐ Satisfactory   ☐ Unsatisfactory

                   ☐ Not Implemented   ☐ Not Observed

    Comments: _____

    _____

    _____

    _____

5. Students have access to a variety of reading materials in the Spanish language that are appropriate for their age and grade levels.

    ☐ Superior   ☐ Satisfactory   ☐ Unsatisfactory

                   ☐ Not Implemented   ☐ Not Observed

Comments: _____

_____

_____

_____

6. Children's literature books in Spanish represent proportionately the heritage background of the Latino students in the program as well as other Spanish-speaking groups from other parts of the world and other regions of the United States.

☐ Superior   ☐ Satisfactory   ☐ Unsatisfactory

☐ Not Implemented   ☐ Not Observed

Comments: _____

_____

_____

_____

II. English Language Development

The program provides the instruction and instructional support services necessary to develop native-like proficiency in the English language.

1. An assessment system is in place which provides information on the initial and current levels of English language abilities of individual students.

☐ Superior   ☐ Satisfactory   ☐ Unsatisfactory

☐ Not Implemented   ☐ Not Observed

Comments: _____

_____

_____

_____

2. Students are provided adequate exposure to acquire the English language through **planned instruction** using the following strategies:

   a. communicative-based second language instruction;

   b. content-based second language instruction;

   c. opportunities to practice the second language at school;

   d. opportunities to practice the second language outside of school.

☐ Superior   ☐ Satisfactory   ☐ Unsatisfactory

☐ Not Implemented   ☐ Not Observed

Comments: _____

_____

_____

_____

3.   Students are provided with **planned instruction** in the English language in order to learn those aspects of the language most efficiently learned through direct instruction.

☐ Superior   ☐ Satisfactory   ☐ Unsatisfactory

☐ Not Implemented   ☐ Not Observed

Comments: _____

_____

_____

_____

4.   Teachers providing English language development are knowledgeable of the main features of the second language teaching methodologies selected for use in the program.

☐ Superior   ☐ Satisfactory   ☐ Unsatisfactory

☐ Not Implemented   ☐ Not Observed

Comments: _____

_____

_____

_____

III. Access to the Core Curriculum

The program ensures access to the core curriculum for every student by providing instruction in all courses required for grade level promotion and graduation in both Spanish and English, depending on the individual needs of students.

1. **Planned instruction** is provided through the Spanish language in the following subject areas:

   Social Science   Natural Science   Other:

   Mathematics   Health/P.E.   Other:

   ☐ Superior   ☐ Satisfactory   ☐ Unsatisfactory

                         ☐ Not Implemented   ☐ Not Observed

   Comments: _____

   _____

   _____

   _____

2. In most cases, Spanish medium instruction in the following subject areas is conducted almost entirely in Spanish:

   Social Science   Natural Science   Other:

   Mathematics   Health/P.E.   Other:

   ☐ Superior   ☐ Satisfactory   ☐ Unsatisfactory

                         ☐ Not Implemented   ☐ Not Observed

   Comments: _____

   _____

   _____

   _____

3. There are sufficient basic and supplementary materials in the Spanish language to support **planned instruction** in each of the following subject areas:

Social Science	Natural Science	Other:
Mathematics	Health/P.E.	Other:

☐ Superior   ☐ Satisfactory   ☐ Unsatisfactory

☐ Not Implemented   ☐ Not Observed

Comments: _____

_____

_____

_____

4. Spanish medium instruction is of sufficient scope and quality to sustain academic achievement. At least 50 percent of the students enrolled in Spanish medium instruction for a period of at least four years or more are at or above grade level in each of the following subject areas when assessed through Spanish:

Social Science	Natural Science	Other:
Mathematics	Health/P.E.	Other:

☐ Superior   ☐ Satisfactory   ☐ Unsatisfactory

☐ Not Implemented   ☐ Not Observed

Comments: _____

_____

_____

_____

5. As Spanish-speaking students acquire advanced levels of English proficiency, the amount and level of difficulty of English medium instruction increases accordingly. Designated students are enrolled in the following subject area courses in English using **specially designed academic instruction** or mainstream approaches, depending on the individual proficiency levels of the students:

| Social Science | Natural Science | Other: |
| Mathematics | Health/P.E. | Other: |

☐ Superior ☐ Satisfactory ☐ Unsatisfactory

☐ Not Implemented ☐ Not Observed

Comments: _____

_____

_____

_____

6. English medium instruction is of sufficient scope and quality to sustain academic achievement. At least 50 percent of the students enrolled for a period of one year or more in English mainstream instruction are scoring at or above grade level in each of the following subject areas when assessed through English:

| Social Science | Natural Science | Other: |
| Mathematics | Health/P.E. | Other: |

☐ Superior ☐ Satisfactory ☐ Unsatisfactory

☐ Not Implemented ☐ Not Observed

Comments: _____

_____

_____

_____

IV. Crosscultural Development

Children learn to respect and value their heritage language and culture as well as the heritage languages and cultures of others.

1. The school has adopted and staff is manifesting a multicultural perspective with corresponding learning activities in all aspects of the curriculum.

    ☐ Superior   ☐ Satisfactory   ☐ Unsatisfactory

                    ☐ Not Implemented   ☐ Not Observed

    Comments: _____

    _____

    _____

    _____

2. Cross-ethnic experiences and friendships are fostered through the use of integrative strategies such as **cooperative learning.**

    ☐ Superior   ☐ Satisfactory   ☐ Unsatisfactory

                    ☐ Not Implemented   ☐ Not Observed

Comments: _____

_____

_____

_____

3. There are a number of on-going activities at the school aimed at
    providing students with accurate information about their own heri-
    tage group as well as about the other cultural groups represented in
    the school, including:

    a. library materials written by representatives of the
        respective groups;

    b. presence of staff members who are role models;

    c. visitations to community centers and other points of
        interest;

    d. involvement of community members in regular and spe-
        cial school activities.

    ☐ Superior   ☐ Satisfactory   ☐ Unsatisfactory

                        ☐ Not Implemented   ☐ Not Observed

Comments: _____

_____

_____

_____

4. As a result of inservice training programs such as **Teacher Expectations and Student Achievement** (TESA, and its gender equity counterpart GESA), staff members at the school have high achievement expectations for all students.

    ☐ Superior   ☐ Satisfactory   ☐ Unsatisfactory

               ☐ Not Implemented   ☐ Not Observed

    Comments: _____

    _____

    _____

    _____

5. The school is involved in a cultural and language exchange project with a sister school in a Spanish-speaking country similar to the **Orillas Computer Network Program.**

    ☐ Superior   ☐ Satisfactory   ☐ Unsatisfactory

               ☐ Not Implemented   ☐ Not Observed

    Comments: _____

    _____

    _____

    _____

6. Through the use of a multicultural interventions such as **Antibias Curriculum**, students and staff develop a sense of empowerment and skills to act alone or in concert with others against social injustices generated by racism and prejudice.

    ☐ Superior   ☐ Satisfactory   ☐ Unsatisfactory

                        ☐ Not Implemented   ☐ Not Observed

    Comments: _____

    _____

    _____

    _____

V. Staffing and Professional Development

Instruction in the program is provided by qualified teachers, who along with other colleagues at the school, are provided with opportunities for collaboration and inservice training.

1. There are a sufficient number of qualified teachers to provide instruction in and through Spanish.

    ☐ Superior   ☐ Satisfactory   ☐ Unsatisfactory

                        ☐ Not Implemented   ☐ Not Observed

    Comments: _____

    _____

    _____

    _____

2. There are a sufficient number of qualified teachers to provide English language development and **specially designed academic instruction** in English.

    ☐ Superior   ☐ Satisfactory   ☐ Unsatisfactory

                        ☐ Not Implemented   ☐ Not Observed

    Comments: _____

    _____

    _____

    _____

3. Teachers and other staff members hold regularly scheduled meetings to share information, review program implementation practices, and plan activities.

    ☐ Superior   ☐ Satisfactory   ☐ Unsatisfactory

                        ☐ Not Implemented   ☐ Not Observed

    Comments: _____

    _____

    _____

    _____

4. The training needs of each teacher and other staff members are assessed at least annually.

    ☐ Superior   ☐ Satisfactory   ☐ Unsatisfactory

                        ☐ Not Implemented   ☐ Not Observed

Comments: _____

_____

_____

_____

5. The program provides regularly scheduled training sessions that are based on the individual needs of teachers and other staff members.

☐ Superior   ☐ Satisfactory   ☐ Unsatisfactory

☐ Not Implemented   ☐ Not Observed

Comments: _____

_____

_____

_____

VI. Home/School Communication and Collaboration

Parents and community members are aware of the purposes and major features of the bilingual education program. They are knowledgeable of various ways that they can assist their own children with the academic and social demands of school.

1. The school provides parents and community members with a **bilingual education program orientation guide**, available in both English and Spanish versions.

☐ Superior   ☐ Satisfactory   ☐ Unsatisfactory

☐ Not Implemented   ☐ Not Observed

Comments: _____

_____

_____

_____

2. Staff members employ a variety of strategies to disseminate and explain the contents of the **bilingual education program orientation guide**, including at least three of the following:

   a. Sent home with students or mailed;

   b. Presented as topic at parent meeting;

   c. Explained at parent/teacher conference;

   d. Explained during home visits;

   e. Other:

   ☐ Superior   ☐ Satisfactory   ☐ Unsatisfactory

   ☐ Not Implemented   ☐ Not Observed

Comments: _____

_____

_____

_____

3. The school encourages and assists parents to become involved in the education of their children by sponsoring activities such as:

    a. Dissemination of a parent/student activity guide;

    b. Home/school learning projects such as the **Pajaro Valley Family Literacy Experience**;

    c. Child development training.

☐ Superior   ☐ Satisfactory   ☐ Unsatisfactory

                  ☐ Not Implemented   ☐ Not Observed

Comments: _____

_____

_____

_____

Operational Definitions

1. **Antibias Curriculum** is an integrated multicultural approach developed by early childhood educators to enable young children of various racial, ethnic and class backgrounds, and physical abilities to develop positive concepts of self and of others in a diverse world (Derman-Sparks, 1989).

2. **Bilingual Education Program Orientation Guide** is a written document that describes the intent and content of the bilingual education program. Information included in the guide addresses the following topics:

    a. individualized instruction based on language and academic needs;

    b. desired individual pupil and program outcomes;

    c. student identification, assessment, and placement procedures;

    d. nature of the curriculum;

    e. staff characteristics and staffing arrangements;

    f. parent and community involvement and educational opportunities.

3. **Cooperative Learning** is the structuring of classrooms so that students from diverse backgrounds study and work together in small groups in ways that (1) stimulate academic achievement, especially for language minority students, (2) create positive intergroup relations, and (3) socialize students toward prosocial values and behaviors (Kagan, 1986).

4. **Critical Literacy** is an approach to reading instruction based on Freire's (1973) pedagogical approach which organizes lessons into four phases: (1) descriptive reading, (2) interpretive reading, (3) critical analysis, and (4) creative response, that is, relating the

reading to one's own context and selecting possible resolutions or appropriate courses of action. This process integrates the development of critical thinking skills with fundamental literacy instruction (Ada, 1986).

5. **Orillas Computer Network Program** is a project that promotes Spanish literacy development through a computer information exchange between sister schools. For example, schools in Connecticut, California, and Mexico formed a network to share student writings on issues of mutual interest (Sayers and Brown, 1987).

6. **Pajaro Valley Family Literacy Experience** is a home/school literacy program conducted in Spanish. Parents and their children select books and works together using the **Critical Literacy** approach described in operational definition No. 4. School personnel conduct orientation sessions in which parents learn how to discuss the books with their children. Follow up sessions are held to cover other subjects such as questioning strategies and writing projects (Ada, 1988).

7. **Planned Instruction** means at least three organized lessons totaling at least 120 minutes per week.

8. **Process Writing** is an approach where students are allowed to acquire writing skills by engaging in writing activities that are creative and intrinsically interesting. Beginning writers, when they realize that they have something to say, become confident that they can communicate through the written form of the language. Traditional approaches to writing instruction which stress correctness of surface forms of language are deemphasized initially (Graves, 1983).

9. **Specially Designed Academic Instruction** is an instructional approach which uses English as a medium of instruction for subject matter classes such as mathematics, science, and social science. This type of instruction is sometimes used with Spanish-speaking students at intermediate or advanced levels of English proficiency when these students are initially introduced to English medium sub-

ject matter instruction. Various techniques are employed to make the English academic input comprehensible to the Spanish speakers:

a.   a focus on content rather than surface language;

b.   use of concrete contextualized referents (realia);

c.   no restrictions on Spanish use by pupils;

d.   grouping students by English proficiency levels;

e.   no overt correction of language form errors;

f.   frequent comprehension checks;

g.   overriding concern to always negotiate meaning.

10. **Teacher Expectations and Student Achievement** (TESA) is a professional development program in which teachers learn to identify specific teaching behaviors, which when used in an equitable manner with so-called "underachievers" (i.e., language minority students), stimulate scholastic performance. Examples of teacher behaviors include listening attentively to students; providing students opportunities to respond; giving individual attention to students; personalizing the students' participation in the class; and using expressions of courtesy (Kerman et al., 1980).

REFERENCES

Ada, A. F. (1986). Creative education for bilingual teachers. *Harvard Educational Review, 56*, 386-394.

Ada, A. F. (1988). The Pajaro Valley experience, working with Spanish-speaking parents to develop children's reading and writing skills in the home through the use of children's literature. In T. Skutnabb-Kangas and J. Cummins (Eds.), *Minority education: From shame to struggle.* Clevedon, England: Multilingual Matters.

Derman-Sparks, L. (1989). *Antibias curriculum: Tools for empowering young children.* Washington, DC: National Association for the Education of Young People.

Freire, P. (1973). *Education for critical consciousness.* New York: Seabury.

Graves, D. (1983). *Writing: Children and teachers at work.* Exeter, NH: Heinemann.

Kagan, S. (1986). Cooperative learning and sociocultural factors in schools. In *Beyond language: Social and cultural factors in schooling language minority students.* Los Angeles: Evaluation, Dissemination and Assessment Center, California State University, Los Angeles.

Kerman S. et al. (1980). *Teacher expectations and student achievement.* Downey, CA: Office of the Los Angeles County Superintendent of Schools.

Sayers, D., & Brown, K. (1987). Bilingual education and telecommunications: A perfect fit. *The Computing Teacher, 17,* 23-24.